Philip Paul is a former Fleet Street journalist and chief information officer in the public service sector. He is an investigative author who has made an extensive study of crime and criminals.

This book is the result of a three-year survey of the contribution that is made by forensic scientists towards the solution of criminal mysteries and the administration of justice in the capital. Aided by access to official archives, Philip Paul also carried out numerous interviews with scientists, police officers and others.

MURDER UNDER THE MICROSCOPE is addressed to the intelligent, reasoning and responsible reader who does not necessarily possess scientific knowledge. A damning indictment of criminal savagery, it is also a heartening appraisal of the dedication and capabilities of forensic scientists who, in co-operation with detectives, assist in the fight against lawlessness.

MURDER
Under the Microscope

The Story of Scotland Yard's
Forensic Science Laboratory

Philip Paul

With a foreword by
Lord Walton

Futura

A Futura Book

First published in Great Britain in 1990 by
Macdonald & Co (Publishers) Ltd
London & Sydney
Reprinted 1990
This edition published by Futura Publications in 1990

ISBN 0 7088 4767 6

Reproduced, printed and bound in Great Britain by
BPCC Hazell Books
Aylesbury, Bucks, England
Member of BPCC Ltd.

Futura Publications
A Division of
Macdonald & Co (Publishers) Ltd
Orbit House
1 New Fetter Lane
London EC4A 1AR
A member of Maxwell Macmillan Pergamon Publishing Corporation

Tremble thou wretch,
that hast within thee undivulged crimes
Unwhipp'd of justice.

WILLIAM SHAKESPEARE
King Lear

DEDICATION

To the police officers and forensic
scientists without whom
life could revert to barbarity.

CONTENTS

PART FOUR THE FUTURE

Acknowledgements

I AM GRATEFUL TO MANY people for assistance, of various kinds, extended to me during the writing of this book. Without their help the task would have been infinitely more difficult. Sadly, it is impossible to name them all individually.

Special thanks are due to members of the staff at the Metropolitan Police Forensic Science Laboratory and their police colleagues. In appreciation of their co-operation a share of the royalties is being credited to the Metropolitan Police. At the time of writing their representatives are deliberating on the question of the use to which the money should be put.

I express particular gratitude to:

Deputy Assistant Commissioners Richard Wells QPM and Brian Worth OBE; Commanders George Churchill-Coleman and Raymond Adams BEM; Dr Raymond Williams CBE, the 'longest in office' former director of the laboratory; Dr Brian Sheard, the present director; the deputy directors, Michael Loveland, Peter Martin, Godfrey Lee and Dr William Wilson; Detective Chief Inspector James Wadd and Detective Sergeant Simon Newlands, for information and support.

Dr Roger Berrett, formerly staff officer to the director and now a member of the Fire Investigation Unit at the laboratory, whose pilotage and introductions were vital during the processes of information-gathering.

The late John Jackson, of the laboratory's scientific staff, for the collection of notes (albeit some in his own system of indecipherable shorthand!) and publications which he assembled, shortly before his untimely death, in preparation for the production of a history of the laboratory.

The late Dr Hamish Walls, a former director of the laboratory; Miss Margaret Pereira CBE, a former member of the laboratory's scientific staff who became controller of the Home Office Forensic Science Service; Mrs Dawn Banks, a former personal assistant to directors of the MPFSL; and David Ellen, 'oldest scientific

11

inhabitant' of the laboratory, for their candid recollections of years gone by.

Dr John Brennan, Dr Clive Candy, Kenneth Creer, John Giles, Miss Pamela Hamer, Robin Keeley, David Pryor, Dr David Rendle, David Rudram and Brian Wheals, all scientists at the laboratory, for information about equipment, techniques and current activities.

Dr John Havard and John McCafferty, for permission to reproduce extracts from their books *The Detection of Secret Homicide* and *Mac, I've Got a Murder*, respectively.

Mrs Constance Walls, for permission to reproduce extracts from *Forensic Science* and *Expert Witness*, two of the books written by her husband, the late Dr Hamish Walls.

Professor Martin Bobrow, Prince Philip Professor of Paediatric Research at Guy's and St Thomas' Hospitals, for guidance in respect of DNA profiles in instances of identical twins and other multiple births.

Bill Waddell, curator of the 'Black Museum' at New Scotland Yard, for invaluable help, drawing upon his three-dimensional archives and four-dimensional memory.

The late Detective Superintendent James Hood, head of the police liaison staff at the laboratory, his colleague, Detective Inspector Norman Quick, and the detective sergeants of his team for welcoming me so kindly into their midst and for many acts of helpfulness in terms of direction-pointing and the ferreting-out of information.

Robin Goodfellow, director of public affairs to the Metropolitan Police; Bob Cox, of the press bureau; Hilary Addicott, formerly of the public affairs department and now with the BBC, and Ray Elmes, formerly of the public affairs department and now press and publicity officer to the Met's north and east areas, for kind co-operation.

Professor James Cameron, of the London Hospital, for information about his pig-burning experiment during inquiries into the 'contract killings' perpetrated by Henry Jeremiah MacKenny and his associates.

Desmond Lewis, former secretary and registrar of the Pharmaceutical Society of Great Britain, for valuable background information regarding the youthful poisoner Graham Young.

Martin Wyld, chief restorer at the National Gallery, for information about the repair of the Leonardo da Vinci cartoon.

John Burrow OBE LLB, Chief Constable of Essex, and Chief Superintendent Thomas Rogers, of the Essex Police, for permission to reproduce photographs depicting the attempted 'autocide' of David Philip Jobling.

The following members of the laboratory's scientific staff for information in respect of their work on specific investigations:

Brian Arnold *The 'contract killings' by Henry MacKenny and associates and the shooting of the Leonardo da Vinci cartoon.*

David Castle *The murders of Peter Arne and Stephen Gaspard and the road death of Victor Gladen.*

Andrew Clatworthy *The murder of Michael Barber.*

Dr Brian Connett *Death of drugs smuggler Ian Fuller.*

Kenneth Creer *The murder of Marie Payne.*

Mrs Anne Davies *The murders committed by Dennis Nilsen and the murders of Alison Day, Maartje Tamboezer, Anne Lock, Eileen Emms, Janet Cockett, Valentine Gleim, Zbigniew Stabrawa, William Carmen, William Downes, and Florence Tisdall.*

Dr Christopher Davies *The murder of David Hamilton.*

Adrian Emes *The murders of Robert Vaughan and Michelle Sadler.*

Nigel Fuller *The poisoner Graham Young.*

Raymond Fysh *Pilocarpine poisonings of geriatric patients.*

Dr Brian Gibbins *The road death of Denise Rumney.*

David Halliday *The fire at King's Cross underground station.*

Robin Keeley *The murder of Georgi Markov.*

Dr Richard Lambourn *The road death of Christopher Stafford.*

Adair Lewis *The burning of 18 Denmark Place.*

Dr John Metcalfe *Illegal drugs factory at Grays, Essex.*

Dr Christopher Price *The murders of Peter Arne and William Choi.*

Dr Ann Priston *The murders of Mohan Gulrajani, Roy Porjes and Doria Schroder.*

David Pryor *The 'contract killings' by Henry MacKenny and associates.*

Dr Geoffrey Roe *The murders of Alison Day, Maartje Tamboezer, and Anne Lock.*

Douglas Stoten *The road deaths of Victor Gladen and Paul David Ray.*

Dr John Taylor *The attempted murder of Dr Madhu Baksh.*

Geoffrey Willott *The murder of William McPhee and attempted murder of Dr Madhu Baksh.*

Dr Elizabeth Wilson *The 'contract killings' by Henry MacKenny and his associates and the murder of Marie Payne.*

The following police officers, for information in respect of their work on specific inquiries:

Sergeant (formerly Constable) Stuart Anderson *The road death of Denise Rumney.*

Detective Chief Superintendent Christopher Bird★ *The murder of William Choi.*

Detective Chief Inspector John Bunn *The murder of Doria Schroder.*

Detective Sergeant Richard Cain *The murders of Robert Vaughan and Michelle Sadler.*

Sergeant Raymond Carver *The road death of Paul David Ray.*

Former Commander Frank Cater* *The 'contract killings' by Henry MacKenny and associates.*

Former Detective Chief Superintendent Geoffrey Chambers *The murders committed by Dennis Nilsen and the burning of 18 Denmark Place.*

Detective Superintendent Robert Chapman* *The murder of David Hamilton.*

Deputy Assistant Commissioner Simon Crawshaw QPM* *The murder of Doria Schroder.*

Detective Chief Inspector John Grieve *The death of drugs smuggler Ian Fuller.*

Detective Sergeant Roy Grover *The murders of Roy Porjes and William Choi.*

Detective Sergeant Derek Hancock *The attempted murder of Dr Madhu Baksh.*

Inspector David Hicks *The attempted 'autocide' of David Philip Jobling.*

Commander Brian Jackson *The murders committed by Kenneth Erskine.*

Former Detective Chief Inspector Peter Jay* *The murders committed by Dennis Nilsen.*

Former Detective Chief Superintendent Michael John *The murder of Stephen Gaspard.*

Detective Sergeant Peter Kent-Woolsey *The murder of Marie Payne.*

Detective Chief Inspector Michael Lawrence* *The 'contract killings' by Henry MacKenny and associates*

Former Detective Chief Superintendent David Little *The murder of Marie Payne.*

Detective Chief Superintendent Vincent McFadden *The murders of Alison Day, Maartje Tamboezer and Anne Lock.*

Former Commander James Nevill* *The murder of Georgi Markov.*

Detective Chief Inspector Hugh Parker *The murder of William Choi.*

Former Detective Chief Superintendent John Pole *The murder of Mohan Gulrajani.*

Detective Sergeant Sandy Sanderson *The murder of Marie Payne.*

Former Deputy Assistant Commissioner James Sewell *The murder of Angela Wooliscroft.*

Detective Chief Superintendent Douglas Shrubsole* *The murders of Robert Vaughan and Michelle Sadler.*

Detective Sergeant Ronald Stocks *The murder of Peter Arne and the murders committed by Dennis Nilsen.*

Detective Sergeant Barry Strong *Illegal drugs factory at Grays, Essex.*

Inspector Derek Talbot* *The road death of Denise Rumney.*

Detective Chief Superintendent Kenneth Thompson *The burning of 18 Denmark Place and the murders committed by Kenneth Erskine.*

* Information provided via New Scotland Yard.

Inspector Norman Till *Pilocarpine poisonings of geriatric patients*.
Detective Sergeant Brian Tilt *The murder of William McPhee*.

Those who serve in the second and third floor places of
refreshment in the laboratory building – venues where, in the course
of convivial conversations, I gained several initial leads to subjects of
interest.

My agent, Amanda Little, of Watson, Little Ltd, for her usual
sterling services.

Alice Wood, of Macdonald & Co (Publishers) Ltd, for her
discernment, patience and understanding.

PHILIP PAUL

FOREWORD

by

LORD WALTON
Warden, Green College, Oxford
Past-President, General Medical Council

FORENSIC PATHOLOGY AND FORENSIC science are topics which some find chillingly forbidding or even gruesome, as the horrifying evidence which is brought to light in the course of criminal investigation all too often lays bare the depths of human depravity or alternatively the devastating effects which mental illness can sometimes have upon behaviour. But there can be very few people, whether medical, scientific or lay, who have not at times looked upon these subjects with a degree of morbid fascination, deriving from the remarkable skills deployed in the course of such investigations. Even as a young teenager not then committed to a career in medicine, I recall that the name of Sir Bernard Spilsbury was one to conjure with, being regularly mentioned in the much less sensational and (I believe) more accurate and reliable reporting which we read in the newspapers of the 1930s.

Even though I have had no personal training in this field since my student days and cannot claim any skill or expertise in the subject, I have found this book by Philip Paul totally fascinating and, indeed, at times riveting. For one without scientific training to be able to write so lucidly, so succinctly and yet so convincingly on complex scientific issues in so meaningful a manner for scientist and layman alike is, I believe, a major achievement. He has sketched the history of the science superbly with due attention to anthropometry ('Bertillonage' after its first proponent in criminal investigation, Bertillon) and to finger printing (paying due tribute to the respective contributions of Herschel, Faulds and Galton). He then goes on to consider in detail firearms, serology and toxicology, with subsequent commentary upon DNA fingerprinting, the latest in a long line of new techniques available to the forensic scientist. There follow first a most readable account of the vicissitudes which delayed unduly the establishment of a forensic science laboratory and next a dispassionate commentary upon its first fifty years, its successes, its failures, its organization and its funding. A series of detailed case histories is then included, illustrating the innumerable ways in which scientific investigation has assisted the police in the investigation of murder. Finally, the author expresses his own trenchant views on the current ills of society and what he perceives as some of their causes and shares with us the outcome of some 'crystal ball gazing' into the future of forensic science.

Beautifully written by an experienced scientific journalist, as compelling and eminently readable as a detective novel by one of the masters (or mistresses) of the genre, such as Dorothy L. Sayers or Agatha Christie, I think that this is a remarkable book, assured of success.

JOHN WALTON
Oxford
May 1989

PROLOGUE

A case in point: The murder of Angela Wooliscroft

FOR 20-YEAR-OLD Angela Mary Wooliscroft the grey morning of Wednesday November 10 1975 dawned much as any other day. Fit, five feet six tall and sturdily built, she was a hockey player of some distinction. Over breakfast at her parents' home in Newlands Way, Chessington, Surrey, she spoke eagerly about the trip to Jersey, to represent a Barclays Bank hockey team, she was scheduled to make the following day.

Mercifully unknown to her, she was never to go on that journey. In fact, less than six hours remained before she was to die in a welter of her own blood, murdered by a merciless thief after she had handed over £2,000 in response to his demand for money.

As was her custom, she drove to her work at Barclays Bank in Upper Ham Road, Richmond, Surrey, in her white Ford Cortina car. It was not a particularly busy morning and Angela, serving as she sat at till number three, had time to chat to a customer she knew, 35-year-old building contractor William Bennett. She had worked at the bank for four years. Things were still quiet at 12.30 when she suddenly saw, through the glass security screen separating cashiers from customers, the twin barrels of a sawn-off shotgun. Pointed at her, the weapon was held by a black-haired, dark-coated man of average build whose dark-skinned face was strangely streaked. 'Give me your money!' he snarled. Fearing the consequences of reaching for the alarm button just beyond her feet, she opened a drawer, took out wads of £5 notes and put them into the tray beneath the screen for the man to pick up. It was her last action on earth. The gun went off with a deafening roar in the confined space, blowing a large hole through the glass and blasting Angela in the face, neck and chest. For a split second she rose to her feet before falling, face downwards, to the floor. Throwing down a woman's yellow plastic raincoat under which he had concealed the gun, the raider grabbed the money and walked from the bank. Outside, he made an unhurried departure in a maroon-coloured Austin car that had been parked nearby.

While 33-year-old bank clerk Mrs Sheila Reid sounded the alarm and did what she could to comfort her groaning colleague, the manager, 56-year-old John Rapp, telephoned for the police and an ambulance. On his arrival at 12.46, 41-year-old ambulanceman Ivor Poet found that Angela was unconscious, bleeding from the mouth and an open wound in the throat, and had no pulse in her carotid artery. At Kingston Hospital at 1.00 pm, 29-year-old Dr Ayad Ghaib Majeed certified that she was dead. At 4.30, in the presence of Detective Chief Superintendent (later Deputy Assistant Commissioner) James Sewell and other police officers, Arthur Keith Mant, Professor of Forensic Medicine at Guy's Hospital, performed an autopsy. His report described gunshot wounds extending from shoulder to shoulder (17 inches) and from lower forehead to lower chest (18½ inches), with superficial injuries caused by finely divided glass. The principal wound, almost an inch in diameter, contained fibre and cardboard cartridge wads. Death had occurred in consequence of haemorrhage from the left common carotid artery. Angela's body revealed no natural disease and she was *virgo intacta*. She was formally identified by her heartbroken father, William Woolscroft, a 58-year-old administrative officer.

Among the statements made to the police, that of Sheila Reid was the most descriptive. She said that she had been bending down towards a cupboard when she heard a loud explosion. Almost simultaneously with the bang she heard Angela speak – 'An utterance more than anything, not enough words to amount to a sentence.' Angela then seemed to stand up before falling, 'making a horrible noise'. Before she crouched down to activate the alarm, which was electronically logged as going off at 12.31, she saw a man, 'dark skinned but not black' aged between 30 and 40, hatless and with dark, tight curly hair, standing back from Angela's till with 'what looked like a machine gun' pointed at the glass. She had stayed below the counter until she heard someone say 'He's gone' then she had crawled to Angela.

The evening radio and television news bulletins and the following day's papers described the killing and the inquiries that had begun under Sewell's leadership. Barclays Bank announced that a reward of £50,000 (then a record sum) would be paid for information leading to the capture of the killer. The television programme *Police Five*, presented by Shaw Taylor, featured the case.

Among the mass of information received by the police was a telephone call from a 41-year-old car cleaner, Tony Paice. He expressed suspicions about a man known as 'Hartie' whom he had met at his place of work, Chivers Garage in Basingstoke, Hampshire. Paice told of 'Hartie' returning to the garage because of trouble with a Vauxhall Victor car he had bought there. He had been loaned a gold-coloured Wolseley while the Vauxhall was being repaired and Paice had seen him transferring things into the boot of the Wolseley, among them what looked like a shotgun wrapped in a cloth. Then the murder had happened. Paice added that he had been told that 'Hartie' had since paid in cash for the purchase of a pale blue Ford Consul and that when he (Paice) had been cleaning the Wolseley 'Hartie' had borrowed, he had found a spent .22 cartridge on the floor of the car. 'Hartie' was added to Sewell's long and growing list of suspects and inquiries. Among the 'leads' he was following was the description of the raider as 'dark skinned', coupled with a report that Angela had been friendly with a Tunisian man. The inquiries, Sewell decided, would have to follow a process of elimination.

Just after 2.00 am on November 23 – 13 days after the murder – Hampshire police constables Ian McIlwraith and Stephen Mycock were cruising in their Rover patrol car on the M3 motorway at Basingstoke when they received a radio call to a break-in at Jackson's Garage, Basingstoke. As they approached the garage, they saw a pale blue Ford Consul, registration number WLM 370M, coming towards them. When he saw them, the driver turned his lights out and

accelerated away. The policemen gave chase, following the
Ford in the wrong direction round a roundabout. Next, the
driver of the Ford was seen to light something from a cigarette
and toss it into the pursuers' path. They avoided it. At last the
Ford went out of control, hit a road sign, and stopped. A man
who ran from the car was recognised as 38-year-old Michael
George Hart, a known criminal with a number of convictions
for fraud, theft, and violence, who had absconded from bail
and was wanted by the British police on a warrant from
Winchester Crown Court and by the French for the stabbing
of a taxi driver and attempted shooting of a policeman near
Roissy airport. Mycock chased him on foot but Hart got away.

The officers then examined the abandoned car. The boot
contained a .22 Hendaye automatic pistol, 72 rounds of .22
ammunition, jewellery, several driving licences bearing
different names, an auburn wig, a quantity of cigarettes, a
cash register and other incriminating items.

At 3.15 am that day, with the permission and in the
presence of his wife, Maureen, the police searched Hart's
home in St Peter's Road, Basingstoke. They found a box of
Eley trapshooting shotgun cartridges and jewellery in the
pocket of a raincoat. Another search later the same day located
more property suspected of having been stolen.

During the night of November 23/24, the Supreme petrol
filling station on Basingstoke by-pass was broken into and
property taken. Hart was seen there but escaped. There was a
bizarre background to this incident. The same premises had
been broken into the previous August and Hart, by trade a
painter and decorator, had been engaged to repair the
damaged doors! During a renewed police search of his home
on November 24 more suspected stolen items were discovered
and a quantity of ashes and burnt tins was found near the back
door.

The police combed Hart's known haunts but he had gone to
ground. Christmas came and went. And then, on January 4,
Hart telephoned the office of Stations Supreme, the retail
company of Texaco Ltd, and arranged to call to collect the
money due for his repair work. An appointment was made and
the police were alerted, but Hart did not turn up. Instead, his

wife telephoned suggesting that she should collect the money on his behalf. This proposal was refused.

More time passed. Then, on January 20, Hart called at the Hounslow office of Stations Supreme and asked for his money. Having been informed about the situation, the manager, William Smith, contrived to delay Hart's departure while the police were summoned. Hart submitted to arrest, by two police constables, without violence. He was found to be in possession of a stolen Fiat car. He was taken to Richmond police station and locked up for the night.

Next day, Friday January 21, he was interviewed in the station's surgeon's room and was returned to his cell at 6.25 pm. At 7.30 he was found unconscious and with his breathing stopped, hanging by the neck from a leather belt attached to the cell door. He was resuscitated by the police and rushed to West Middlesex Hospital, where he recovered sufficiently to be returned to police custody 24 hours later.

There followed five days of interviews by Detective Chief Superintendent Sewell, who was assisted by Detective Inspectors Robert Geggie and Alan Wordsworth, Detective Sergeants Robert Hancock and Graham Forsyth, Police Sergeant Noel Fisher, Detective Constable Kenneth Mason and, later, Woman Detective Constable Brenda Regan. Thousands of words of questions and answers were recorded in writing during the sessions, which were interspersed with numerous cups of tea, meal breaks and 'rest periods', when Hart was left to wrestle with whatever might remain of his conscience. For four more days he resolutely denied having any connection with the murder, although admitting his guilt in respect of many other charges. Then, at 6.20 pm on January 26, in the presence of his wife and brother-in-law, he suddenly admitted shooting the girl but claimed it was an accident. When Mrs Hart exclaimed 'What girl?' Hart seized her hand and answered 'The girl in the bank. I'm sorry about all the publicity, but it was an accident.'

Asked to describe the event, Hart said, 'I went to the bank. I had the gun under my coat. I said "Give me some money." She was ages and ages. I banged on the glass like that and said "Hurry up." The money dropped into the tray. It went off then.' With the aggrieved tone of a man who had been cheated, he added 'There was only nineteen hundred, not the two and a half grand what the papers said.'

Responding to further questions, he said he had buried the sawn-off barrels of the gun and had thrown the rest of the weapon into the river. He promised to show the police the places. Before entering the bank he had put on a black wig and covered his face with makeup bought in Woolworth's – 'I looked like a Pakistani.' He had driven to Kingston-on-Thames in the gold-coloured Wolseley, which he left in a multi-storey car park belonging to Bentalls, a large department store. From the same car park he stole an Austin A40 in which he drove to the bank and back. ('How cool can you get?' Sewell commented later.) While returning to Basingstoke the Wolseley had broken down and he had called the RAC to help. In another grotesque aside, he added 'It cost me £14 to join – that's for me and the wife.'

Giving more details, he said that, in the bank, he had covered the gun with a yellow plastic mackintosh he had found in the A40. He had also worn a pair of tortoiseshell-framed sunglasses that were in the car. After leaving the bank he had broken the glasses up and thrown them out of the vehicle window. In the garden at his home he had burnt the clothes and gloves – 'I always use gloves' – he had been wearing. Admitting that he had cocked the firing hammers of both barrels of the gun before entering the bank, he added 'But I didn't mean to use it. I knew I had hit the girl because she screamed. I just hoped she was wounded. I heard that she was dead on the television that night.'

Securely handcuffed, Hart was taken to the places where he said he had disposed of the weapon. The sawn-off barrels were dug up from a garden and, after valiant efforts in icy conditions, an underwater search unit recovered the gun from the Thames alongside Hampton Court Road.

Continuing police inquiries led to the arrest, by WPC Regan, of a 19-year-old associate of Hart's, Sharon Denise Stacey, described as a secretary, of Wilmot Way, Basingstoke. Her statements, in a series of interviews at Richmond police station, made it clear that she had helped him in a number of robberies, but she denied being with him on the day of the murder. Although she had no licence, she said she loved driving and had often driven Hart, in a variety of cars, to and from various destinations. Describing one of their robberies, in a Christchurch jeweller's shop she said that Hart had surreptitiously scattered and ignited petrol to create a diversion while she snatched a tray of rings.

Suddenly, during questioning, she blurted out an admission that she had driven Hart to Kingston on the day of the murder but had tired of waiting for him and had travelled by train back to Basingstoke, where she had been caught for not paying the fare and had given a false name and address – Judy Bywater of 54 Grove Road, Basingstoke. Next day she retracted these remarks, saying 'It was all lies. I would have told you anything then, I was in a state.'

Patient police work went on. The owner of the stolen Austin A40, Miss Sylvia Marshall, of Mitcham, Surrey, was traced. She told of parking her car on November 10 and later finding that it had been moved. The passenger-side door lock was not functioning, she said. Her sunglasses, an old yellow raincoat and an old umbrella were missing from the car. Hart's next-door neighbour, George Pullinger, an industrial progress chaser, and his wife Muriel, a store detective, told of seeing Hart burning things in his garden and placing ashes in a sack. Charred material collected from the garden was examined at the Metropolitan Police Forensic Science Laboratory and was found to contain remnants of cloth with part of a zip attached and the remains of dark brown human head hair, possibly from a wig.

With the assistance of Professor Mant, Sewell reconstructed the events at the scene of the crime, from which it became clear that Angela could not have been in the leaning position, potentially activating the alarm and putting him in danger of detention, that Hart said she was in when the fatal shot was fired. The shotgun, an 80-year-old reconditioned Reilley, was found to have been stolen together with the .22 pistol discovered in Hart's car and a .32 Webley revolver from a gun dealer's shop in Reading, Berkshire.

Aware that Hart was likely to withdraw his admission of

guilt and concoct a further web of defensive lies, Sewell was acutely conscious of the need to secure concrete forensic evidence. He arranged the swift despatch to the laboratory of the shotgun and sawn-off barrels, the .22 pistol, the discharged .22 cartridge found by Paice, ten live .22 cartridges found in Hart's car, three shotgun cartridges found at Hart's home, the shattered glass screen, pieces of lead shot and debris from the bank, and shot and cartridge wads taken from Angela's body. All these items were subjected to painstaking examination, tests, and inquiries.

Brian Arnold, a firearms expert at the laboratory, reported that the shotgun was a 12-bore with external firing hammers and no safety catches. Although wet, rusty and covered with silt, it was in good working order. The barrels had been shortened to 18⅝ inches. There was a fired cartridge in the right barrel and a live one in the left. These were identified as Eley paper cased trapshooting sevens, the same as those discovered at Hart's home. When opened and examined, the intact cartridges were found to contain shot and wads identical to those taken from Angela's body. Analysis of the shot revealed that, although made up as trapshooting, the cartridges in fact contained gameshot. The difference between the two types of cartridge is that gameshot is softer, containing only .5 per cent of antimony hardener compared with the one per cent used in trapshot. The finding of this oddity led to contact being made with the manufacturers and Sidney Hands, technical manager of Imperial Metal Industries Ammunition Division, was asked to examine the shot and wads. He gave the opinion that they had come from a gameshooting cartridge but admitted that an error could have been made in loading the cartridges. He added that the box containing them showed that they had been packaged on June 22 1976, which meant that the ammunition had been manufactured between two and seven days earlier.

Arnold's report also said that the left hammer of the gun was found cocked and had been wedged open for safety. After cleaning the working parts, he had fired the weapon several times and established that the right trigger required a pronounced pressure of 6½ pounds to fire. The trigger of the left, unfired, barrel required 3½ pounds. He next tried, by striking the gun in various ways, to cause the hammers to drop without touching the triggers. He found that the only way this could be made to happen was by striking the butt of the gun violently against a hard surface. To achieve this effect he had had to use such force that the toe of the buttstock was chipped. A microscopic comparison of the fired cartridge taken from the right barrel with those with which Arnold tested the gun showed that the used cartridge had been discharged in that barrel. A similar comparison of marks on the gun and on the sawn-off barrels showed that they had formerly been part of the same weapon. Tests with a similar gun and identical glass proved that the muzzles of the shortened barrels had been one inch from the screen when the shot was fired.

Arnold also wrote that the pistol was a .22 French self-loader in good working condition. A microscopic comparison of marks on the fired cartridge case found by Paice with those made on test rounds Arnold fired in the gun showed that the Paice cartridge had been discharged in the same pistol.

Other scientists at the laboratory, Dr Roger Davis and his colleague Brian Heard, examined the shattered glass screen, the shotgun and the stolen Austin A40 car. The laminated screen was found to consist of three sheets of glass separated by clear plastic. It had a relatively uncommon refractive index. More than a thousand particles of glass with the same index were found in the unfired barrel of the shotgun and other fragments, which had evidently been carried on Hart's clothing, were found in the car.

Armed with this evidence, Sewell set the legal processes in motion. Hart and Stacey appeared at Richmond Magistrates' Court on April 4 1977 and were committed for trial at London's Central Criminal Court – the Old Bailey. Among the charges, Hart was accused of murder, of the theft of the shotgun and pistol and of the theft of a Ford Escort car. With Stacey, he was also charged with dishonestly obtaining property.

At the opening of the trial, on November 3 1977, only a

week short of a year after the murder, Stacey pleaded guilty to six counts of criminal deception and asked for 22 other offences to be taken into consideration. She was sentenced to three years' imprisonment on each of the charges, these terms to run concurrently.

Hart pleaded not guilty to the charge of murder but guilty to six counts of criminal deception and asked for 39 other offences to be taken into consideration. Incredibly, despite the quality of the evidence produced against him, one person on the jury remained unconvinced that he had callously killed Angela. Nevertheless, by a majority of 11 to one, he was convicted of murder. On that charge he was sentenced to life imprisonment, with a recommendation that he should remain in prison for a minimum of 25 years. He was also given concurrent sentences of 10 years for robbery, five years on each of three charges of burglary, theft and possessing a firearm, three years for shortening the barrel of a shotgun contrary to the Firearms Act of 1968, and two years for taking a conveyance without authority. Perhaps amusingly, his driving licence was endorsed on the 'conveyance' charge. Hart appealed, unsuccessfully, against the convictions and sentences.

Police persistence, aided by the skills and equipment of specialists at the Metropolitan Police Forensic Science Laboratory, had enabled justice to be done. The judge, the Right Honourable Justice Melford Stevenson, paid tribute to the police achievement in 'an investigation of very great difficulty'. Five thousand people had been interviewed and 15,000 house-to-house inquiries made. One hundred and thirty persons had been detained, of whom 67 were later charged with various offences. 'The debt which the community owes to the police cannot be overstated and I hope that this will be remembered by all whose duty it is to consider these matters,' Stevenson added. The Director of Public Prosecutions associated himself with the judge's remarks. The Commissioner of Police for the Metropolis, Sir Robert Mark, presented a book (containing a collection of his speeches) to the leader of the police investigating team. On the flyleaf he wrote 'To Jimmy Sewell, for a job well done'.

Barclays Bank gave the police a £25,000 reward which Sewell was permitted to distribute at his discretion. The bank also rewarded Tony Paice, the observant car cleaner, a female witness who produced a sketch of the bank raider, and other individuals.

Born in Coxhoe, County Durham, Deputy Assistant Commissioner James Sewell retired from the Metropolitan Police Force in 1984 after 31 years' service which he began as a 22-year-old trainee constable. In 1986 he was appointed head of security to the Guinness brewing company. When I interviewed him in his Portman Square office in December of that year, his recollections of the Hart and Stacey case were clear despite the more immediate pressures being placed upon him in consequence of the opening of an official inquiry into the company's financial affairs. He said he regarded the forensic contribution as 'memorable, because of the exceptional circumstances'.

I asked him why, in his opinion, Hart had killed so needlessly. Pointing out that the man was a hard and violent criminal, Sewell gave me his theory: that Angela had put some money in the tray but Hart demanded more – 'It was to be his big job.' Angela, a strong-minded girl, may then have told him to clear off and Hart, instantly enraged, had fired at her.

Sewell also revealed a previously undisclosed thought – that had Hart claimed that he fired at the glass believing the shot would not penetrate the screen, he might have been convicted only of manslaughter.

When I asked why, in his view, Hart had confessed after claiming innocence throughout five days of questioning, Sewell answered 'I think he knew I wasn't going to give in and that we would get him in the end.' Again there was a supplementary observation: the significant point that, had the Police and Criminal Evidence Act of 1984 been in force in 1976, it would not have been permissible to detain Hart for questioning for so long a period. He might, in consequence, have evaded conviction for the murder.

Curious about Stacey's false confession that she had driven Hart to the scene of the shooting, I asked why a girl, however criminally disposed, would make such a self-incriminating statement. Brushing a hand over his close-cropped hair (he was known affectionately among his police contemporaries as 'Hedgehog'), Sewell smiled. 'The Bonnie and Clyde syndrome,' he said.

INTRODUCTION

FACED WITH DAILY NEWS REPORTS of increasing crimes of violence, coupled with minority – but vociferous and persistent – demands for the imposition of more stringent limitations on the powers of the police, the soundly-principled citizen might well feel driven to conclude that there seems little prospect of achieving alleviation in this age of aggression.

Although understandable, such reasoning would not take proper account of the deterrent contribution that is made, in conjunction with the efforts of detectives, by forensic science. There is evidence that, in the absence of personal conscience or self-restraint, one of the most effective ways of dissuading potential law-breakers is to shorten the odds against their capture, conviction and punishment.

The measurement of crime is ancillary to the purpose of this book. My primary object here is to describe the foundation and subsequent endeavours of the Metropolitan Police Forensic Science Laboratory (MPFSL), noting something of the history that foreran it and outlining the advances that have been made in techniques and capability during its first half-century. (An example of the accomplishments may be seen in an enhanced sensitivity which can now be applied to the detection of certain drugs in body samples such as blood, urine, or liver. Under favourable circumstances about 100 picograms of drug per millilitre of urine can be analysed – an attainment described by a former director of the laboratory as roughly equivalent to seeing, with the unaided eye, a mouse on the surface of the moon.)

The laboratory's functions are clearly defined. Before persons who are believed to be wrongdoers can be brought to justice, there is a requirement additional to the tasks of their physical discovery and detention. Those who are guilty must be shown, beyond reasonable doubt, to have been responsible for, or involved in, the misdeeds under inquiry. Similarly, the innocent must be exculpated.

From nowhere come testimonies more telling in these respects than those which issue from the upper floors of the greyly brooding building close to the vellum-hued palace of The Most Reverend His Grace Robert Cantuar in London's Lambeth Road. Employing equipment, training and experience that are envied in similar, but less fortunate, quarters, the laboratory's multidisciplinary teams, totalling some 210 scientists supported by about 40 clerical and other staff, work to unravel the mysteries of human turpitude, be it simple or sophisticated. Neutrality is their code and detachment their *modus operandi*. As my interviews with them revealed, few of the establishment's biologists, chemists, pharmacologists, physicists or toxicologists could recall noticing the appearance or reactions of the defendants they were impeaching during the process of providing expert evidence and undergoing cross-examination in court.

It is pertinent to mention that, from time to time, a spectre is raised (usually by the legal representatives of those accused of offences) alleging that, because it is financed via police funds, the laboratory is operated solely for the purpose of producing evidence to support charges the police are proposing to bring. To ensure absolute impartiality, it has been said, the laboratory should function as an independent body, paid for directly from the public purse. Whatever may be their organizational merits, such arguments exhibit a woeful misconception and mistrust of the ethical standards of men and women whose reputations and careers depend upon the precision and veracity of their work. Moreover, access to their facilities and findings is available to scientists engaged for the defence of individuals under suspicion.

The growth of the forensic caseload provides an index of the escalation of wickedness and stupidity. In 1966 the laboratory dealt with a total of 6,464 cases. In 1987 – a mere 21 years on – it handled 27,979. Of those, by far the largest number

(12,515) were offences involving dangerous drugs and 7,110 were drunken motorists. Cases of murder and manslaughter (they are grouped together in the laboratory's records) increased from 152 in 1966 to 283 in 1987, assaults and woundings from 138 to 529, robbery with violence from 88 to 522, and rape from 191 to 574.

There is another startling fact behind these figures. During the period mentioned, the geographical area served by the laboratory underwent massive shrinkage. Following reorganizations agreed between Scotland Yard and the Home Office, the main forensic requirements of the Bedfordshire, Berkshire, Buckinghamshire, Cambridgeshire, Hampshire, and Suffolk police were transferred from the MPFSL to Home Office centres in 1967, those of the Surrey force in 1980, those of Sussex in 1981 and those of Kent, Essex and Hertfordshire in 1982. These movements reduced the London laboratory's territorial field to that of the metropolis (including the city). The relatively minor effect on its caseload is an indictment of a place where crime and its perpetrators are concentrated.

Although my empathy with their problems and responsibilities will be obvious, it must be made clear that this monograph is in no sense a public relations project on behalf of the police or the laboratory. No attempt has been made to conceal historical details which the zealous image-builder would almost certainly prefer to have suppressed. Neither the writing nor its publication entailed any financial outlay on the part of either body.

Accuracy and objectivity are of fundamental importance in works of this kind. The former was safeguarded by access to official records and extensive contacts with investigators. The latter was aided by my being neither scientist nor police officer – having no foot in either camp facilitated an impartial view of both.

PHILIP PAUL

PART ONE

The Historical Background

CHAPTER 1
Beginnings

FORENSIC SCIENCE IS THE BODY of knowledge behind expert evidence that is called for in the processes of law. No name stands unchallengeably above others in its evolution. Initially, its skills and applications emerged gradually from the exercise of other abilities rather than taking the form of a new and purposely-created discipline.

Like medicine, law may be said to be as old as society itself. Mankind's early comprehension of the advantages of living in groups was soon followed by realization of the need for codes aimed at restraining antisocial activity. Thus, law was born. Similarly, the search for food uncovered substances which lessened pain and promoted health as well as others that caused suffering and death. When individuals began to specialize in such knowledge, the community medicine man had arrived.

Sadly, the written history of humanity dates back only some five thousand years, when literate civilizations had developed in Egypt, Sumeria, Babylon, India, and China. Ancient Egyptian papyri reveal that there was an extensive knowledge of medicine and a definite system of law. Punishments for crime included amputation of offenders' ears, noses, hands or feet. It is believed that the regulations in force at the time were derived from the precepts of Imhotep, grand vizier, chief justice and physician to King Zoser about 3,000 BC. Imhotep might fairly be described as the first medico-legal expert.

The oldest written code of law is probably that of Hammurabi, inscribed on stone in Babylon about 2,000 BC.

Its penal provisions included removal of the hands, or even the lives, of inefficient surgeons. The earliest record of a murder trial is thought to be that found in Sumeria on a clay tablet dating back to about 1,850 BC.

Although more advanced, Roman legislation was founded on the Greek legal code which, drawing on the scientific methods of Hippocrates, gave medicine a more rational basis. The teachings of Hippocrates have influenced the ethical outlook of the medical profession for more than 2,000 years. Galen, Celsus and others, both Greek and Roman, perpetuated the rational methods of the Greek physicians. On occasions, factual medical findings reached standards that were admissible under strict codes of legal procedure. Following his murder in 44 BC, the corpse of Julius Caesar was examined by a physician who stated that, of the 23 wounds sustained by the deceased, only one, in the chest, had been fatal.

Emerging from the decline of Rome between AD 529 and 564, the Justinian Code provided for regulation of the practice of medicine, including proof of competence by examination, limitation of the number of practitioners in each town and penalties for malpractice. With the dictum that the medical expert is not used to greatest advantage if he is regarded simply as an ordinary witness appearing for one side or the other, the code also indicated the status and function of such experts more clearly than ever before. The Justinian enactments provided the ancient world's highest point of achievement in the way of defined forensic medicine.

There are grounds for belief that in medieval times Chinese forensic medicine was far in advance of contemporary European practice. A book compiled in the first half of the 13th century was entitled *Hsi Yuan Lu*, meaning, literally, 'the washing away of wrongs', but more liberally translated as 'Instructions to coroners'. Based on earlier works, it continued in use until relatively recently. Offering comprehensive guidance on medico-legal procedure, it described the need for careful examination of wounds on bodies when checking the validity of confessions and warned examiners not to be deterred by the unpleasant state of cadavers. The difficulties caused by decomposition were discussed, as were the dangers of being misled by counterfeit wounds. The importance of examining the locus was stated in an adage: 'The difference of a hair will be the difference of a thousand li'. A li is a Chinese mile (about 633 yards) or a weight of some three-fifths of a gram.

In Europe the collapse of Rome was followed by a long period of stagnation during which the lamps of civilization and progressive thinking burned low. Then, in 1507, under the auspices of the Bishop of Bamberg, a comprehensive penal code was established. It was swiftly adopted by several neighbouring German states and was the starting point for forensic medicine as it is now constituted. Twenty-six years later came the more important *Constitutio Criminalis Carolina*, or *Caroline Code*, published by the emperor Charles V as the law to be observed throughout his extensive empire. Both of these early Germanic codes specified that expert medical testimony had to be obtained for the guidance of judges in cases of suspected murder, wounding, poisoning, hanging, drowning, infanticide and abortion. The *Caroline Code* was followed by a gradual awakening from the intellectual slumber in which Europe had lain for so long. As science and logic gained acceptance, the travesties of witchcraft and trial by ordeal began to wane.

One of the first known medico-legal exponents was a French barber's apprentice-become-surgeon, Ambroise Paré, who died aged 80 in 1590. Largely self-taught, he became the leading surgical expert of his time. Constantly avid for knowledge, he led the way in describing, in scientific terms, the injuries inflicted by firearms. He learned to trace the whereabouts of bullets in victims by ascertaining their positions when hit and then palpating appropriate areas of their bodies.

Three Italians also figured in early forensic evolution. Paolo Zacchias (1584-1659), personal physician to two Popes, acquired a reputation as mastermind of the legal medicine of his day. Giovanni Lancisi (1654-1720) was among the earliest of those who took a scientific interest in sudden and unexpected death. By means of systematic autopsies, he succeeded in identifying cerebral haemorrhage as a cause of swift demise. Giovanni Morgagni (1682-1771) is considered to have been the originator of modern morbid anatomy. The discovery of oxygen in the 1770s was followed by new comprehension of the mysteries of combustion and respiration. There was also steady progress in chemical toxicology.

In December 1839 a Monsieur Lafarge, until then in perfect health, was staying in Paris on business. He ate a cake sent to him by his attractive young wife and was immediately taken ill. His condition worsened after his return home and he died in January 1840.

After an unsatisfactory *post mortem* the authorities consulted a Spaniard named Orfila (1787-1853) who had achieved prominence after pursuing medical studies in Paris. Orfila was able to demonstrate the presence of lethal quantities of arsenic in the viscera. It was proved that Madame Lafarge had purchased arsenic shortly before the onset of her husband's illness. She was put on trial. The court was convinced by the evidence and she was sent to penal servitude.

Another outstanding contributor at the time of notable scientific advancement was Belgian astronomer Lambert Adolphe Jacques Quételet (1796-1874) of Ghent. His statistical works on crime and his *Physique Sociale*, a quantitative examination of human activity that introduced the new study of sociology, drew praise from Florence Nightingale and others. Quételet also wrote a massive work entitled *Anthropométrie ou mesure des différentes facultés de l'homme*, which had direct relevance to forensic science.

Chemist Felix Leblanc and medic-cum-lawyer Ambroise Tardieu impressed their 19th-century contemporaries with their research on asphyxia. Leblanc described carbon monoxide poisoning in 1842.

Schools for the study of forensic sciences were set up in Paris in 1795, in Vienna in 1804 and in Berlin in 1850. Each was blessed with intellectual independence and a reputation for total integrity. It was to a leading light of the Vienna school, a man named Von Hofmann, that fell one of the major forensic investigations of the time. On January 30 1889, the Archduke Rudolf, heir to the throne of the Austro-Hungarian empire, killed himself after shooting his mistress, Baroness Maria Vetsera. Von Hofmann gave the opinion that abnormalities in the archduke's skull justified the view that he was mentally unstable.

In May 1897, the death in a fire of the Princess of Alençon, along with several members of the French nobility, provided the originating basis for forensic odontology. The unfortunate victims of the conflagration were among the few who could afford dental care in those days. This enabled their badly burnt bodies to be identified.

A sister of the princess, Elizabeth, Empress of Austria, was the subject of forensic inquiry when she died the following year after receiving an apparently trivial wound from a shoemaker's awl wielded by an anarchist. It was discovered that she had suffered a haemopericardium.

Events during the second half of the 19th century illustrate the interdependence of scientific specialisms. But for the invention of the condensor of the microscope in 1873 and its improvement by the addition of oil immersion in 1878 (both by E K Abbe of Jena) biologists would have had to wait much longer to uncover nature's secrets in respect of the agents of infectious disease.

Jules Bordet (1870-1961) made discoveries which resulted in the triumph of *in vitro* (test tube) techniques in biological laboratories. His later successes led to the introduction of serodiagnosis in forensic medicine. Bordet received the Nobel Prize in 1919.

Although Orfila had earlier noted the phenomenon, it was another researcher, named Mégnin, who proved that insect attacks on human remains tend to occur in a definite sequence. Mégnin recorded his findings in a monograph entitled *La Faune des Cadavres*.

Despite the quickening of developments, forensic science did not make the speedy progress that might have been expected in the first quarter of the 20th century. One reason for this was the reluctance of those engaged in the field to place their trust in discoveries until there was totally convincing proof of their reliability. This was, no doubt, the reason why the stupendous discovery, in 1900, of the existence of several distinct groupings of human blood did not find its true place in forensic medicine for almost two decades, despite its much swifter acceptance in the clinical world. Despite its drawbacks, this tendency always to err on the side of caution, which continues today, has contributed significantly to the rarely-challenged standing of forensic science.

But it must be admitted that there have been some unhappy reverses of fortune. Perhaps one of the most deplorable was the tragic affair of Captain Alfred Dreyfus, a probationer on the French General Staff. In September 1894 French counterespionage agents recovered an incriminating secret message from a wastepaper basket in the German embassy. Amateur handwriting analysts decided that it had been written by Dreyfus. The document was then referred to a commission of three 'qualified' experts. The head of the Criminal Investigation Department, Alphonse Bertillon, joined the group. When the experts disagreed over their findings, Bertillon insisted that Dreyfus was the culprit. Condemned to imprisonment for life, loss of rank and degradation, Dreyfus was deported to Devil's Island. Because of pressure of public opinion, he was retried in 1899 but was again convicted. Only in 1906, when the guilty person, a man named Esterhazy, confessed, was the truth revealed. Bertillon's incorrect application of Quételet's treatises was considered to have been responsible for this grave injustice.

Soon after the second World War the reputation of French toxicology suffered a largely undeserved setback because of the administrative mishandling of a case in which a widow, Marie Besnard, was accused of poisoning her mother, most of the members of her family and some friends with arsenic – a total of 13 killings. She underwent three trials and five years of preventive imprisonment before being acquitted. Competent forensic experts, who were not engaged until the legal problems had become hopelessly entangled, found some consolation in the fact that the case shed new light on the behaviour of arsenic in buried bodies.

Comparable problems beset an investigation into the death of Wilma Montesi, a 16-year-old Italian girl whose body was found on a beach near Rome. A bungled autopsy led to a national scandal.

In Britain, the most discussed post-war case of suspected

miscarriage of justice has been that of Timothy John Evans, a mentally-retarded tenant of the notorious later-convicted and executed women-killer, John Reginald Halliday Christie. Evans suffered the death penalty for a murder which was afterwards seen as likely to have been one of Christie's crimes. Public concern included no criticism of the forensic findings.

But we are approaching the present too quickly. We must not overlook a significant early development in the process of attempting to identify and classify criminals. The work of the same Alphonse Bertillon of whom we have already heard, this system became known as anthropometry or, more colloquially, 'Bertillonage'.

By the middle of the 19th century the French Sûreté (Security) – founded by a former criminal named Eugène François Vidocq – had acquired an international reputation for the speed with which it apprehended criminals who fled to Paris. This efficiency was attained by two basic means: the employment of numbers of former criminals as officers of the force and the establishment of a photographic 'library' of convicted wrongdoers. Upwards of 80,000 photographs were soon accumulated but they were not of uniform quality. Some were unclear (photography was then in its infancy) while the usefulness of others was diminished by their subjects' deliberate distortion of their faces when the pictures were taken.

Although he was the son of a distinguished physician and statistician, Alphonse Bertillon was a poor performer at school and suffered expulsion for bad behaviour. He was pale, dismal, taciturn and unpopular. It was only because of his father's good connections that he gained an appointment as an assistant clerk in the Paris Prefecture of Police. There, his boring task of copying out the monotonous descriptions of prisoners – 'tall', 'small', 'average', 'ordinary', 'no distinguishing features' – added to his innate miserableness.

In 1879 he became interested in the works of Quételet and an Italian psychiatrist, Cesare Lombroso. Seeking to clarify the physiology and psychology of crime, Lombroso had visited prisons and insane asylums. After measuring the skulls of many criminals, he had concluded that offenders were marked by specific anomalies in the shape of the head, placing them closer to the animal realm than law-abiding men. Thus, as physiological 'throwbacks', criminals were born, not made.

Having gained the amused acquiescence of his superiors, Bertillon began measuring the convicts who were brought in for registration. Ignoring the gibes of his fellow clerks, he went on recording the dimensional details of heads, arms, fingers, and feet.

Promotion to the rank of clerk gave him the confidence to submit a special report to the prefect of police. If 11 measurements of a criminal were taken, he claimed, the odds against finding another with precisely the same sizes were 4,191,304 to one. If 14 measurements were taken, the chances became 286,435,456 to one. Such a system would, he averred, provide absolute security against trickery and mistakes. By grouping the records into specific categories, it would be possible to turn up the details of individuals with rapidity. Unable to make sense of Bertillon's pedantic, repetitive and ill-expressed report, the prefect, Louis Andrieux, a politician, passed it to the head of the Sûreté, a talented and successful policeman named Gustave Macé. Macé told Andrieux that the police had more important things to do than toy with theorists' experiments. Andrieux told Bertillon's father that unless his son concentrated his attention on his routine duties it would be necessary to discharge him. But Bertillon senior read his son's report and was convinced of its validity. 'This is applied science,' he told Alphonse. 'It will mean a revolution in the police world.' He tried to persuade Andrieux to reconsider, but the prefect was adamant.

Three years passed and a new prefect, Jean Camecasse, was appointed. Through a lawyer friend intermediary, Bertillon senior prevailed upon Camecasse to grant his son's theories a trial. Camecasse gave young Bertillon three months to establish the worth of his scheme.

Towards the end of that term Bertillon's file of measurements had grown to 1,800 cards. But, as might have been expected in so short a time, there was no second capture of a convict who had been measured before. Then one day, with his hopes fading, Bertillon was noting down the details of a prisoner who claimed that his name was Dupont. The length of 'Dupont's' head fell in the category of 'medium' and took Bertillon to the corresponding section of his files. The breadth of the head reduced the number of files he had to search to nine, the length of the middle finger to three, of the small finger to a single file containing only 50 cards. Moments later, Bertillon was looking at a card containing measurements identical to those of 'Dupont' but the man's recorded name was Martin. He had been arrested earlier for stealing bottles. His voice trembling with excitement, Bertillon exclaimed 'I've seen you before. You were arrested on December 15 for the theft of bottles. At that time you called yourself Martin.' There was a stunned silence in the room. The other clerks stared at Bertillon. The policeman who had detained 'Dupont' was dumbfounded. 'So what? So I was,' the prisoner snarled. Bertillon's theory had been vindicated. This triumph, which was later featured in the Paris newspapers, only just preceded the death of his much-gratified father.

Given an office of his own and several assistants, Bertillon identified another former convict within a month, during the following three months six more, in the next three months 15 and during the remainder of the year 26 prisoners whose true identities had slipped undetected through the old system. During 1884, 300 previously convicted criminals were detected by means of the new records.

In 1888, established in new headquarters in the attics of a courthouse, Bertillon acquired the title of Director of the Police Identification Service. His fame spread abroad when a distinguished Parisian journalist wrote 'Bertillonage, based upon the measurements of certain unchanging parts of the skeleton, is the greatest and most brilliant invention the 19th century has produced in the field of criminology. Thanks to a French genius, errors of identification will soon cease to exist, not only in France but also in the entire world.'

But Bertillon did not allow himself to rest on these laurels. Some time previously he had begun taking his own photographs of criminals and, by cutting up the pictures, assembling categories of eyes, ears and noses. Having acquired the prefecture's photographic studio as part of his domain, he drew up new rules for the taking of prisoners' portraits. Henceforth, he ordered, two pictures were to be taken of each individual, one profile and one full face. They were to be taken from the same distance, using the same lighting and with heads held in identical positions. Subjects were seated in a specially-designed chair to assist the photographers in meeting these requirements. The resulting pictures were pasted onto the cards bearing the anthropometric measurements. Along with these arrangements, Bertillon introduced a system of coding by letters which represented standardized words and phrases describing all visible characteristics of the human head.

By these means, which Bertillon called the *portrait parlé*, the French police were provided with the most precise descriptions of criminals ever possessed. Anthropometry soon became an integral part of their system. Among the foreign visitors who came to learn about it was an Englishman, Edmund Spearman, who had close connections with the British Home Office.

In 1892, the use of anthropometry resulted in the conviction of a notorious anarchist named Ravachol, who planted three bombs which exploded in Paris. He also committed several murders and robberies and had earlier been arrested on theft charges. He went to the guillotine. The case was a much-celebrated triumph for Bertillon and, with his later successes, brought about his rise to leadership of the CID in Paris. Anthropometry – and Bertillon – had gained their places in forensic history.

But far more enduring than Bertillon's techniques were the efforts of a German lawyer and another Frenchman. They were Hans Gross (1847-1915) and Edmond Locard (1877-1966).

In 1893, 46-year-old Gross, a professor of criminal law in the University of Graz, published a masterly work entitled *Handbuch für Untersuchungsrichter*. Repeatedly stressing the value of science to the detective, the book was reproduced in numerous editions. The first translation into English was published in 1907 as *Criminal Investigation*. It was revised and reissued many times. In 1968, paying tribute to Gross, Dr

Hamish Walls, a senior British forensic scientist, declared 'The whole craft of detection still bears his stamp.'

Locard, of the University of Lyons, also entered forensic annals in consequence of his advocacy of scientific methods. Many procedures still in use owe their origins to the Institute of Criminalistics which he founded as a one-room laboratory for the Rhône prefecture of police in 1910 and which later rose to the status of a university department. Again like Gross, Locard was 46 when his major work, entitled *Traité de Criminalistique*, was published in 1923. Many of his pupils, from countries all over the world, later produced outstanding achievements in their homelands.

One of Locard's guiding principles was the contention that 'every contact leaves a trace', meaning that anything touched or unknowingly left at or collected from the scene of a crime or accident, be it only the treading of feet, the momentary brushing of a garment against other materials, or the shedding or acquisition of a single hair, flake of skin, or other fragment, leaves a record. There are, of course, occasions when the detection of such traces is beyond current capabilities, but the frontiers of discovery are not static. Locard is believed to have been the person who coined the term 'criminalistics', meaning the science of contact traces.

In Britain early progress was slow and tedious. In 1788 Dr Samuel Farr published a volume entitled *Elements of Medical Jurisprudence*. This was offered as 'a succinct and compendious description of such tokens in the human body as are requisite to determine the Judgment of a Coroner and Courts of Law in cases of Divorce, Rape, Murder, etc, to which are added Directions for Preserving the Public Health.'

The work aroused little interest but, fortunately, other things were stirring. In 1789 Andrew Duncan (1744-1828) was appointed professor of the Institutes of Medicine at Edinburgh University. He began to give lectures on medical jurisprudence and public hygiene.

Despite considerable criticism and opposition, the first British chair of medical jurisprudence was created at Edinburgh in 1807. Duncan's son, also named Andrew, became its first incumbent.

Interest in the subject gradually spread to England. In 1816 the first creditable book on forensic medicine to be published in English was produced by Dr Male, of Birmingham. At about the same time courses of lectures in the subject were started by London doctors Harrison (in a medical theatre at Windmill Street), Elliotson (in an anatomical theatre at Southwark) and John Gordon Smith (at Westminster Hospital and London University). The fortunes of Harrison and Elliotson are not recorded but it is known that Smith died at the age of 41 after 15 months' incarceration in a debtors' prison.

In 1822 Robert Christison (1797-1882) became professor of medical jurisprudence at Edinburgh. He was Britain's first toxicologist and figured as medicolegal adviser to the Crown in many important cases, including investigation of the notorious Burke and Hare murders. A contemporary tribute to his abilities reads 'As a witness he was remarkable for a lucid precision of statement, which left no shadow of doubt in the mind of the Court, Counsel or Jury as to his views. Another noteworthy characteristic was the candour and impartiality he invariably displayed.' Christison transferred to the chair of materia medica in 1832 and remained there for 30 years.

In London in 1834 Alfred Swaine Taylor was appointed professor of medical jurisprudence at Guy's Hospital Medical School. Two years later he published the first of many editions of his *Elements of Medical Jurisprudence*. This was followed by two further distinguished works, *Poisons* (in 1848) and *Principles and Practice of Medical Jurisprudence* (1865). Ten years after Taylor's appointment at Guy's, King's College appointed Dr William Guy as professor of forensic medicine.

The earliest European laboratory concerned solely with forensic science is believed to have been one headed by R A Reiss, a Swiss-naturalized German, whose teaching of photography in the University of Lausanne was changed to a course on forensic photography in 1902. Soon afterwards this became the Lausanne Institute of Police Science. A forensic laboratory was opened in Dresden in 1915 and another in Vienna in 1923. Sweden, Finland and Holland each had laboratories before 1925.

Although later than those in Europe, institutional forensic

developments in the USA preceded those in Britain. The Los Angeles forensic science laboratory was established in 1923 and the Federal Bureau of Investigation started its laboratory in 1932.

Before specialist laboratories came into being, detectives had to turn for scientific help to people whose forensic activities were a sideline to their primary occupations. The first problem facing the policeman was often the question of where to go for the assistance he needed. British names from that era include those of Dr Ainsworth Mitchell, who is remembered for outstanding work on the identification of inks, and Sir William Willcox, who conducted the toxicological analysis in the case of the London murderer Dr Crippen.

While knowledge and acceptance of forensic science slowly gained ground worldwide, understanding of the various specialisms involved in its application was also growing.

CHAPTER 2
Fingerprints

IN THE EARLY 1860s, William Herschel, a British administrative official working in the Hooghly district of India, suffered sleepless nights as he grappled with a seemingly insoluble problem. Responsible for the payment of allowances to superannuated Indian soldiers, he had become aware that some of the recipients of this beneficence were in the habit of slipping back for 'second helpings' after they had received their rightful dues. The difficulty was that, to European eyes, most of the men were indistinguishable from one another. Nearly all had the same coloured hair and eyes and a great many bore the same names. Most were illiterate and incapable of inscribing their signatures. How, Herschel wondered, could be put a stop to the swindling?

Although he was later unable to say precisely why such a seeming triviality had captured his attention, he suddenly became conscious of the imprints left by dirty fingers on wood, glass and paper. He was aware that Chinese traders in Bengal sometimes sealed documents with the imprint of their thumbs.

Seeking a way to obviate the delays that seemed inescapable in a country where people customarily paid little heed to agreements, Herschel made an Indian supplier of road-building materials put his palm-print on a delivery contract. Then, out of curiosity, he began collecting 'hand marks' in a notebook. The pages were soon filled with prints of his own fingers and those of many friends. As he studied these markings he began to realize that every print had a unique pattern of its own; no two were the same. He lost no time in applying this discovery to the pensioner ex-soldiers, each of whom was required to place the prints of two fingers against their names in Herschel's lists and to repeat this process in a register when drawing their money. The 'second helpings' attempts stopped abruptly.

After maintaining this practice for some time, Herschel made further observations. He noted that, even after five, 10, 15 or more years, the pattern of individual fingerprints never changed. Although men grew older and faces and bodies were affected by sickness or the passing years, the unique patterns etched into the skin of their fingers did not alter.

Seized by thoughts of the purpose that might be served by this phenomenon in the identification of criminals, Herschel wrote to the inspector general of the prisons of Bengal. Having described his discovery, he asked that his findings be put to the test in other state institutions. Although gently phrased, the reply made little attempt to conceal the writer's view that Herschel's state of health (he had been suffering from dysentery and fever) was affecting his powers of judgment. Greatly disappointed, Herschel made no further attempt to focus official attention on his thinking about 'hand marks'. Still unwell, he returned to England in 1879, aged 46, to recuperate.

The following year his attention was drawn to a contribution published by the scientific journal *Nature*. Written from Japan by an acidic Scottish physician named Henry Faulds, it described the deliberately-imprinted finger marks he had found on old oriental pottery and revealed that this had led him to make a study of the papillary lines on their living owners. Initially his interest had been to discover whether the patterns bore any relationship to race or ethnic origins. Then, after a robbery had been committed at a neighbour's home, prints of sooty fingers left by the intruder were found on a whitewashed wall. When the police told him they had apprehended the thief, Faulds asked their permission to take the accused man's fingerprints. They did not match the wall prints. The true interloper was found a little later. Again Faulds took fingerprints. They tallied with those found on the wall.

Faulds revealed that he had subsequently learned that fingers did not need to be inky, sooty, or dirty to leave prints. He had discovered that sweat glands in the skin produced secretions which left detectable marks on objects that were touched.

These were facts that might well have applications in the investigation of criminal offences, Faulds told *Nature*. '... bloody finger marks or impressions on clay, glass, etc ... may lead to the scientific identification of criminals ... Other cases might occur in medico-legal investigations, as when the hands only of some mutilated victim were found ... There can be no doubt as to the advantage of having, beside their photographs, a nature-copy of the forever-unchangeable finger furrows of important criminals ...'

After reading these remarks Herschel hastened to despatch his own message to *Nature*. He pointed out that he had used fingerprints for identification purposes many years before the 'discovery' claimed by Faulds. It was only the lack of official interest and his delicate physical condition that had prevented him from making these facts generally known.

Infuriated by Herschel's comments, the tetchy Faulds resolved to return to England. He prepared his way by writing to scientists in Britain, including Charles Darwin, to the Home Secretary and to the Commissioner of Police in London. Informed by a friend that Scotland Yard did not consider him to be altogether trustworthy, Faulds next wrote to the Prefect of Police in Paris, Louis Andrieux. As we have already learned, that worthy was not a ready recipient of new notions, but he was then on the point of being replaced by Jean Camecasse. And Camecasse was altogether more open-minded and enterprising ...

It was a financially-independent scientist, Sir Francis Galton, a cousin of Charles Darwin, who first championed fingerprinting in Britain. Asked by the Royal Institution to provide a report on Bertillonage, Galton had been to Paris, met Bertillon and studied his system. He was not totally convinced by it. 'Incorrectness lay in treating ... different dimensions of the same person as independent variables, which they are not,' he wrote. 'A tall man is much more likely to have a long arm, foot or finger than a short one ... still, the system was most ingenious and very interesting ...'

With his customary thoroughness, Galton did not leave things there. His subsequent probings brought to light the Faulds/Herschel correspondence with *Nature*. Galton made contact with Herschel and was given the details of the latter's theories. It was immediately clear to Galton that here was something of far greater value than Bertillonage.

Three years later his collection of prints was larger than Herschel's. Each print was photographically enlarged, to facilitate examination and comparison. After much research and analysis, Galton calculated that the chances against any human being possessing ten fingerprints that were identical to those of anyone else in the world amounted to 64,000,000,000 to one.

Later, he evolved a rudimentary system of classification of fingerprints, based on four groupings derived from the positions of the triangular formations which he saw were the basis of the patterns. In 1891 *Nature* published a paper he wrote on the subject. It included an acknowledgement of his indebtedness to Herschel. In 1892 he published a detailed treatise in a book entitled *Fingerprints*. The emergence of this historical work coincided with the rising of red brick, towered and gabled buildings near the Palace of Westminster on the northern bank of the Thames. This fortress-like edifice was to become known as New Scotland Yard, the headquarters of the London police.

In 1893 the British Home Secretary, Herbert Asquith, read Galton's book and appointed a committee to examine both fingerprinting and Bertillonage. The following year the committee's voluminous report included an unexpected recommendation – that all ten fingerprints of every convict should be placed on file but that these were to be accompanied by an abbreviated adaptation of Bertillonage, arranged under Bertillon's 'superior' method of classification.

The detailed problems of classifying fingerprints – by then known as dactyloscopy – remained unsolved for a further three years. In 1894 Edward Henry, then Inspector General of the province of Bengal, visited Galton during a period of leave in London and was given a suitcase crammed with finger patterns. After careful study of this material Henry made his individual contribution to fingerprinting history by devising a system of cataloguing which enabled specific prints to be swiftly traced amidst millions of others. Based on divisions within five fundamental patterns – known as plain arches, tented arches, radial loops, ulnar loops and whorls – the searcher needed only a brief period of instruction and the provision of a magnifying glass and a needle (the latter to help in counting ridges) to be equipped to use the process.

Soon after Henry had introduced his system to the Bengalese police the Governor General ordered anthropometry to be dropped and dactyloscopy to replace it in criminal records throughout British India. Reports of its success there reached London in the midst of the troubles – marching mobs of unemployed and increasing crime – that beset the capital after the Boer War.

The deliberations of a committee of inquiry led by Lord Belper were followed by a recommendation that Bertillonage be replaced by dactyloscopy in English criminal records. Henry was appointed Acting Police Commissioner of London. Drawing on his experience in India, he conveyed his enthusiasm for dactyloscopy to Scotland Yard. In just one year the new fingerprint department there identified 1,722 convicts – four times the maximum ever achieved by anthropometry.

The reliability of fingerprinting was soon established in the criminal courts. Its validity was additionally confirmed by the failure of an attempt to obliterate the papillary patterns by having the skin removed from the fingers. This was tried by a Chicago gangster named Jack Klutas. His attempt was discovered after he had been shot dead by police. It was seen that surgery had been carried out on each of his fingers but the skin growing back over the wounds carried the same figurations that Klutas had had before.

A more determined attempt at obliteration was made by another American criminal, named Robert Philipps. Skin grafting by a disreputable doctor required Philipps to spend three weeks with his fingers fastened against transplant sites on his chest. The results did not prevent the police from identifying him. The age of unmistakable criminal identification had dawned.

The first murderer brought to justice – life imprisonment – with the aid of fingerprinting was Francesca Rojas, an attractive 25-year-old woman living in Necochea, in the province of Buenos Aires. The case was a personal triumph for a police officer, Juan Vucetich, a Croat who emigrated to Argentina in 1884 and who, by 1891, had become head of the police statistical bureau in that land. Having read of Galton's work, Vucetich realized that dactyloscopy was by far the most reliable method of providing incontrovertible evidence and, against the wishes of his superiors, he set up a fingerprint system in the La Plata Bureau of Investigation.

In 1892 Rojas' two illegitimate children, a boy aged five and a girl of four, were found brutally murdered and the woman with a wound in her neck. At first she accused a peasant neighbour of the killings but confessed after her bloody thumbprint was discovered on a doorframe. Her explanation was that she had wanted to be free for the attentions of her lover, who disliked the children.

Although Vucetich introduced his own, highly successful, system of classifying fingerprints, his over-ambitious dream that the entire population of Argentina should be fingerprinted clashed with the easy-going Latin temperament. Riots broke out. In 1917 Vucetich was banished to another city and his work dismantled. Eight years later, dying from the combined ravages of cancer and tuberculosis, he wrote to a friend 'I shall not see this year out, I fear. My work is destroyed and perhaps will be forgotten ... Nobody will ever remember me ...'

Henry's system of ten-finger classification was effective in facilitating searches of formal fingerprint files, but it is the single print left at the scenes of crimes that is the task most frequently encountered by investigators. Searches of ten-finger collections would impose an onerous burden in such circumstances. In 1930 Scotland Yard adopted a single print system devised by Chief Inspector Harry Battley, then the head of the fingerprint bureau. This system comprises ten numbered files, each referring to individual digits as they appear in the ten-finger records. Although Henry's general formula of classification is followed, greater attention is paid to details of ridges, cores, and deltas. The laws of most countries demand the achievement of specific minima in respect of points of comparison between the prints on record and those found during inquiries or taken from suspects. In English criminal courts, 16 points of matching characteristics are required in a single print or 10 + 10 in two prints or two parts of the same print, before identification is deemed to have been established.

Obviously the prints kept in records are taken from carefully inked impressions, but the latent prints left in the course of crime and made by perspiration or natural skin oils may be indistinct or fragmentary. A helpful assistance in such cases was introduced by French forensic scientist Edmond Locard. He discovered that individual sweat pore openings in the skin differ in size, shape and position from person to person and, like the ridges and hollows that make finger-prints, are permanent.

It must here be added that, as is logical, the fingerprinting work of London's police is customarily carried out by 'scenes of crime' officers ('SOCOs') and is associated with the criminal records kept at Scotland Yard – work with which the forensic laboratory is normally not involved. In more complex cases, where special efforts or equipment are required, the laboratory is able to employ high technology, including laser illumination.

The days of manual checking of fingerprint files are virtually over – a matter of no regret to the officers who spent two weeks checking through the entire collection during inquiries into the 'Black Panther' murders of 1975. A year later Scotland Yard installed a national fingerprint computer called Videofile, containing 2,500,000 prints of convicted criminals. Needless to say, that number has increased greatly since then.

CHAPTER 3

Firearms

THE SCIENTIFIC EXAMINATION OF EVIDENCE relating to the suspected illegal use of firearms is another matter. This is one of the functions undertaken within the forensic laboratory.

In Britain, these endeavours – sometimes mistakenly described as 'ballistics' – are thought to have begun with the Bow Street Runners – the far-from-respectable band which was, for a time, responsible for upholding London's law and order.

In 1835 one of the last of the Runners, Henry Goddard, noticed that a bullet taken from a murder victim's body carried a curious ridge. In the home of a suspect he found a bullet mould of a kind that was then in common use. The mould had a flaw, a slight gouge which corresponded to the ridge on the bullet. Faced with this evidence, the owner of the mould confessed to the crime.

As the years went by it became commonplace for gunsmiths to be called into courts to give 'expert' evidence as to the use and performance of weapons. During the 19th century, when cartridges and breech-loading were developed, gun barrels began to be produced with rifling – spiralling grooves cut into the inner surface which cause the departing bullets to rotate, preventing them from tumbling end over end in flight and giving much greater accuracy to their placing on targets. Different manufacturers developed specific types of rifling, some using five, and others six, grooves, some using wide and others narrow 'lands' (the prominences between the grooves) and some varying the angle and direction of the twist, so determining whether the bullets rotated to the left or right.

In the spring of 1899, Professor Lacassagne, of Lyons, discovered seven longitudinal grooves in a bullet he had removed from a corpse. Shown revolvers owned by a number of suspects, he found one with seven grooves in the barrel. Its owner was convicted of murder. Nowadays, of course, such 'evidence' would not be considered conclusive. Later specialists took matters considerably further, firing test bullets from suspects' guns into specially softened receptacles so that, undamaged, they could be compared, microscopically, with the missiles recovered at the scenes of crimes.

In 1913 another French professor, of forensic medicine, published an article noting that the firing pin and breechblock of every firearm leave typical markings of seams and unevenness on the base of fired cartridges and that the extractor and ejector of automatic weapons also imprint identifiable traces. His findings were engulfed by the outbreak of World War I.

In 1920 a New Yorker named Charles Waite began to catalogue data on the construction, calibre, twist and proportions of grooves and lands and the angle and direction of rifling of all the types of guns manufactured in the USA since the 1850s. After three years of work he had learned that there was no type of gun which was identical to any other in every detail and could tell police the weapon from which an American-made bullet had been fired. His jubilation declined when he learned that, in one year alone, over half a million foreign-made guns – of which he had no knowledge at all – had been brought into the USA at just one port: New York.

A man of great determination, Waite spent a year in Europe collecting data of the same type that he had gathered at home. An Austrian weapons manufacturer told him '...it will never be possible to make one weapon precisely like another. There are always tiny deviations. Study a razor blade under a microscope ... You will see that its cutting edge is not smooth; it consists of a great many teeth which differ in arrangement and size in every blade ...' Waite found several people who helped him continue his work with the aid of microscopy, a technique that was new to him. An American optician, Max

Poser, developed a special microscope, fitted with bullet holders and measurement scales, which enabled the most subtle markings and dimensions to be examined and recorded. With a physicist, John Fisher, and a chemist, Philip Gravelle, Waite opened, in New York, the world's first bureau devoted to these purposes.

After photographing thousands of bullets that had been fired into cotton-wool containers, Gravelle concluded that the barrel of every gun inscribed upon the bullets passing through it markings unique to that weapon – its 'fingerprint'. He went on to invent an ingenious optical linking of two microscopes, by means of which he was able to examine simultaneously the many times magnified details of two bullets. Each missile could be rotated mechanically so that entire surfaces could be checked. These side-by-side comparisons removed human error from judgment of similarity or dissimilarity.

In 1925 Waite acquired a new recruit in the person of a physician, Calvin Goddard, who had earlier risen to the position of deputy director of Johns Hopkins Hospital. A former major in the medical corps, Goddard was fascinated by guns. He became an expert user of Gravelle's comparison microscope, easily identifying each of the bullets fired from weapons of the same type made with the same tools. When Waite died of a heart attack in 1926, Goddard took over the leadership of the team. Armed with supreme confidence and the undeniable efficiency of the comparison microscope, he set about persuading police and lawyers that his studies had produced an exact science. His scientifically proven testimonies caused sensations at several trials. His confirmation that two accidentally-discovered Thompson submachine guns were the weapons used by Al Capone's mobsters in the 1929 'St Valentine's Day Massacre' of rival gangsters in a Chicago garage sent one of the killers to life imprisonment. Two other suspects were gunned to death in 'revenge' murders.

Later, at the invitation of an influential group of public-spirited citizens, Goddard accepted the directorship of a newly-created scientific crime detection laboratory on the campus of Northwestern University in Evanston, Illinois. One of its aims was to train young, uncorrupted, policemen in forensic techniques. It was an appointment carrying the risk of attack by Chicago's widespread criminal fraternity. Thereafter, Goddard always carried a loaded pistol. His dedication was total: in 1934, when the economic depression swept away the laboratory's financial support, he worked for a year without pay. His ultimate goal – the creation of a national laboratory of firearms studies in Washington – reached realization when J Edgar Hoover set up a special department of the kind in the Federal Bureau of Investigation.

The comparison microscope was used in Egypt before it was adopted in Europe. Sydney Smith, a characterful pioneer of forensic medicine who was then leading a department of the Egyptian Ministry of Justice, had one made after reading about the achievements in the USA. The scientific evidence he was able to give at a trial led to the conviction of terrorists who had assassinated Sir Lee Stack, commander-in-chief of the Egyptian army.

Smith's account of the case in the *British Medical Journal* (*BMJ*) came to the attention of London gunmaker Robert Churchill, a man accustomed to advising police and legal experts on firearms technicalities. In court, Churchill modelled his style of giving evidence on that of the famous pathologist with whom he sometimes appeared, Sir Bernard Spilsbury. Churchill acted with alacrity on the information he gleaned from the *BMJ*. First he had a comparison microscope constructed to his order. Then he hastened to America and contacted Goddard, with whom he had lengthy conversations. Fate had decreed that the new device and its associated forensic skill reached England just in time to play a key part in solving the vicious murder of an Essex village policeman, Constable George William Gutteridge, in 1927.

Gutteridge's body, with four bullet wounds, was found by the roadside. Two shots had been fired deliberately into his eyes after he had fallen. There was, at the time, a superstition that the last sight a man saw registered photographically on the retina of the eyes; Rudyard Kipling had written a short story about the belief. Tests showed that these wounds had been inflicted by bullets from obsolete 'black powder' cartridges which had not been made for many years. The other shots had come from modern rounds, using smokeless powder. Firearms experts reported that the bullets were of .455 calibre and had been fired from a Colt, Webley or Smith and Wesson revolver. Although the bullets had been deformed by impact, Churchill, using the microscope with comparison shots fired from revolvers of all three makes, was able to show that they had come from a Webley. A Webley pistol was found in Hammersmith, London, but the comparison microscope disclosed that it could not have been the weapon used in the killing. Then a car, stolen from a doctor shortly before the murder, was found abandoned. There were heavy bloodstains on the running board beside the driver's seat and, inside, a policeman discovered an empty cartridge case.

The Scotland Yard detective in charge of inquiries, Chief Inspector Berrett, found it difficult to put Gutteridge's terrible eye wounds out of his mind. He combed the criminal records for details of villains known for coarse savagery and soon came upon the name of Frederick Guy Browne, a felon who had served several terms of imprisonment with violent defiance. Berrett watched Browne's activities in a small garage in Battersea, London, and pounced when Browne sold a stolen car. In another car there Berrett discovered a Webley revolver and ammunition. Again Churchill's comparison microscope was used. It showed that the murder weapon had been found but, because the bullets removed from the victim were deformed, Churchill refused to offer them as evidence. He pointed out that this was to be the first time a British jury would be asked to accept the findings of a comparison microscope; the evidence put before them had to be perfect. The difficulty was overcome when marks on the empty cartridge were seen, under the microscope, to tally exactly with the pattern on the breechblock of the Webley, while checks of the breechblocks of 1,374 other pistols failed to locate one whose markings resembled those on the cartridge.

Meanwhile, Berrett had arranged the arrest of an associate of Browne's, named Kennedy. Kennedy tried to shoot the officers who arrived to detain him but his gun misfired. At the police station he blurted out a confession. He and Browne had stolen the car, he said, and Browne had shot the policeman after the officer had stopped and was questioning them.

Forensic history was made in April 1928, when the case came to trial in London's famous Central Criminal Court – the Old Bailey. The evidence obtained by the comparison microscope received sensational headline treatment in the press. Despite the vehemently-expressed misgivings of sceptics – who included George Bernard Shaw – about the new situation in which accused persons' lives could be ended by the slender thread of proof obtained from a miscroscope, it was shown that Churchill had eliminated error from his findings.

Browne and Kennedy were hanged in Pentonville and Wandsworth prisons on May 31 1928.

CHAPTER 4
Serology

NO OUTLINE OF THE HISTORY of forensic science would be complete without some reference to developments that led to techniques which now make a major contribution towards the detection of crime.

Since it was in 1628 – more than 350 years ago – that the English physician William Harvey discovered the circulation of blood in the human body, it is a somewhat surprising reflection that, only two lifetimes ago, no means existed whereby it could be established beyond question whether stains found at the scenes of suspected violence were or were not the residue of blood.

Advances in microscopy and the finding that blood consists of erythrocytes (red corpuscles), leucocytes (white corpuscles), and a watery fluid (serum) prompted the thought that bloodstains might be identified under the microscope because of the characteristic shapes of the red cells. Unfortunately, these shapes disappear when blood dries and the great majority of the stains requiring forensic examination are dry.

A range of experiments applying different combinations of chemicals to stains produced little progress. In one example it was found that, while traces of blood reacted significantly to the application of hydrogen peroxide, so did the similar stains left by other substances, among them rust, semen and shoe polish.

There were other difficulties too. Even when blood could be positively identified there was no way of proving that it was of human origin. Some of the accused whose clothing was found to be bloodstained produced an effective defence by claiming that the marks had come from the killing of an animal or the handling of raw meat.

It was in 1901 that a German scientist, Paul Uhlenhuth, an assistant professor at Greifswald University, achieved a breakthrough. Working from earlier discoveries that the inoculation of animals with diphtheria toxin produced protective antibodies in their blood serum, he found that the injection into rabbits of protein from chickens' eggs and the later mixing of rabbit serum with the white of egg caused the egg proteins to separate from the otherwise clear solution as a cloudy precipitate. Pursuing his experiments over a few months, Uhlenhuth found that he could produce rabbit serums that were effective in precipitating proteins in the blood of many types of animals, including human. Thus, he was able to identify, swiftly, blood of almost any origin. His method had a single flaw: blood from closely-related animals could not be distinguished because of the similarity of the proteins. This proved to be the case in respect of blood from human beings and apes.

Tests showed that Uhlenhuth's method worked equally well on dried bloodstains of different ages and with very small samples. But despite repeated proofs of the scientific validity of the technique, several years passed before it was generally adopted by sceptical criminologists.

Research was unveiling other secrets. Among them was the discovery that all human blood is not of a single type, that there are divisions into distinct groups, some of which are biologically incompatible. It was the repeated observation that the blood serum of some individuals caused the agglutination ('clumping') of the red corpuscles of others that opened the way to more knowledge. But death, as well as time, was the price of progress. In 1871 daring physicians who carried out 263 transfusions of blood from healthy donors to ailing recipients reported that only 117 of the patients survived the experience.

In 1900, 33-year-old Karl Landsteiner, assistant to a professor at Vienna University, experimenting with mixtures of his own blood and that of five colleagues, began to unravel the mysteries of human blood grouping. He established that human blood can be classified into four main types. These became known as groups A, B, AB and O. The value of Landsteiner's work was publicly recognized in 1930, with the award of a Nobel Prize. He was then living in New York and working at the Rockefeller Institute. His endeavours, like those of Marconi, the 'father' of wireless, opened the door to a continuing trail of experimental trial and error by a range of successors, gradually advancing the frontiers of understanding. Again like radio, many of the major developments in forensic science have been made possible by the invention of increasingly sophisticated instrumentation. As a former director of the Metropolitan Police laboratory, Dr Hamish Walls, wrote in *Expert Witness*, his autobiography published in 1972: 'Much of forensic science may be simply applied commonsense, but one does have to collect some scientific data to apply it to. It is this data-collection which is getting more and more technical, even esoteric. We started 35 years ago with test tubes; now we use gas chromatography and electron beams. A modern forensic laboratory is full of mysterious boxes of electronic gadgetry automatically printing out slips of paper and drawing wiggly lines on charts. Most of these mysterious machines were not invented, or at least not available commercially, until after World War II. Now they are spreading like dry rot and keep on proving themselves indispensable everywhere. The forensic scientist trying to keep up with their proliferation is like the Red Queen – he has to run as hard as he can to keep in the same place.'

The breakthrough of the age came with success in isolating cells which could have originated only from specific individuals. This field of inquiry concentrates on patterns of deoxyribonucleic acid (DNA), the component in human chromosomes which contains everyone's genetic code. But difficulties arise from the fact that red cells, the dominant constituent of blood, contain no DNA and stains may not contain sufficient white cells to enable testing to be carried out effectively. Semen may be more promising because spermatozoa are loaded with DNA.

The value of such research can be appreciated when it is

realized that, in Britain alone, more than a million people share even the least common blood group – AB. Some 47% of UK residents have group O blood, 42% have group A. More complex, and therefore more specifically identifiable, blood grouping systems have been developed. Some, like the ABO, are connected with the outer membranes of the red blood cells while others arise from subtle variations in the properties of the blood fluids.

One blood characteristic is particularly helpful in forensic investigations connected with areas in which there are concentrations of coloured people. As far as is at present known, the haemoglobin (the red pigment which gives blood its colour and enables it to supply oxygen to the body tissues) of nearly all white Europeans is identical, but a mutant variety, known as haemoglobin S, also exists. The gene with which it is connected confers the benefit of increased resistance to malaria. But anyone inheriting it from both parents is likely to die at an early age, from sickle cell anaemia. Evolutionary processes have caused the gene to disappear in countries where there is no malaria, but it persists in countries where this malady is endemic.

It follows that, in Britain, the gene is present in immigrants from tropical countries but not in the indigenous populace. This fact serves the purposes of forensic science because the sickling characteristic is detectable in the haemoglobin extracted from the stains left by dried blood. On occasion the forensic investigation of violence among coloured people has been assisted by the fact that, although the blood of both victims and assailants has been of the same group, they were distinguishable because one showed the sickling trait while the other did not.

But the study of blood for criminological purposes is anything but simple. One problem arises from the presence of antigens – substances which stimulate the production of protective antibodies. It has been found that one such antigen is caused by bacteria which produce material similar to A, B and other blood group substances, creating the danger that blood containing it could be incorrectly categorized after basic testing. In 1963, Pierre Moureau, Professor of Forensic

Medicine at Liège University, was consulted in connection with inquiries into the death of a child whose body had been in water for some time. The police had reason to suspect the mother, whose blood was group O. Moureau's tests showed that the child's blood contained A and B antigens. An O group mother cannot have an AB group child. Further tests conducted by Moureau led to the finding that the B antigen had been acquired – in other words that the blood group had changed after death.

In another case a segment of a dismembered female torso recovered from the Thames and carrying cuts which showed conclusively that it fitted together with another part of the body discovered nearby was found to contain blood of a group different from that in the second fragment. Again further tests showed that the apparent contradiction was of bacteriological origin.

In 1940, working with assistants, Landsteiner identified another antigen. As this finding followed experiments involving the injection of rhesus monkey blood into rabbits and guinea pigs, it was given the name Rhesus (Rh). The injected animals produced an anti-Rhesus antibody which also agglutinated human cells and enabled people to be categorized as Rh positive and Rh negative.

Some scientists take the view that serology (a word derived from the ancient Sanskrit *sara*, meaning 'to flow') may still be on the threshold of major discoveries in the analysis of body fluids. But much progress has been made since the early, pathfinding breakthroughs. For example, in many instances it is now possible to determine which bloodstains are of female, and which of male, origin. This is achieved by radioimmunoassay, a specialized technique for measuring the relative quantities of male and female sex hormones, and thereby finding the sex of the person who lost the blood, in bloodstains.

In the investigation of suspected crime, it is often valuable to be able to prove that blood could not have originated from a particular individual. Serological expertise exonerates the innocent as well as identifying the guilty. In 1961 the work of a Scotland Yard laboratory scientist, Bryan Culliford, saved a suspect from gaol. Tests showed that alien stains found on the victim of an attack were of group A while the accused man was of group B. In her distress, the woman who had been assaulted had chosen a blameless individual at an identification parade. Thanks to the evidence provided by Culliford, the case was dismissed.

The routine forensic investigation of suspected bloodstains is carried out by means of the 'precipitin test', using a technique called electrophoresis. A small amount of a solution prepared from the suspected stain is placed in a hollow in a film of jelly on a glass plate. A similar quantity of biological reagent, called anti-serum, is placed in another hollow in the film. When an electric current is passed through the plate, protein molecules in the solution and the anti-serum migrate in opposite directions through the jelly. The plate is arranged so that the molecules meet and react together.

Electrophoresis is also used for the identification of polymorphic (isoenzyme) forms of enzymes. Enzymes, another component of blood, are the complex proteins that control the variety of biological reactions which take place in our bodies. In these cases, short lengths of bloodstained thread are moistened and pressed into a jellified coating on a glass plate. An electric current passed through the plate causes the proteins to migrate through the jelly at speeds that vary according to the protein type. When certain chemicals are applied to the plate the proteins can be seen to have separated into a series of bands. Differing band patterns indicate different forms of enzymes. At first, when a starch-based jelly was used, only three commonly occurring types of enzymes were known but the introduction of an advanced method, called isoelectric focusing, enabled 10 types to be classified. Like others, the technique enables more blood grouping systems to be applied to each sample tested, thereby narrowing down the source from which the blood could have come.

As has been indicated, the serologist is concerned not only with blood but also with all the bodily fluids which may have a bearing on forensic inquiry, such as saliva, semen, sweat, tears, gall, mother's milk and vaginal secretions. Blood groups can be determined from secretory spots of each of these fluids. Thus, the rapist who loses no blood in the course of his attack may be identified from the semen he leaves behind him and the blood groups of persons who have licked and sealed envelopes can sometimes be determined from traces of their saliva on the flaps.

The forensic science laboratory is equipped to identify and analyse many other substances from the tiny fragments that may be available. These include dust, hairs, fibres, soil, paint, glass, metallic particles and gunshot residues. Even fish scales, candlewax, and flour have featured in the probings.

Unless they can contrive to operate in a virtual vacuum, leaving no microscopic trace of their presence, 20th-century criminals face a formidable battery of skills and equipment by means of which they may be identified with their misdeeds.

CHAPTER 5
Toxicology

THE STORY OF POISONS BEGAN when man first learned of substances that are biologically inimical to the human system. The facts of their employment are scattered through the pages of history, as insidious expressions of hatred and enmity, as part of Machiavellian schemes for gain or advantage and as judicial methods of execution. Among the names that spring to mind are those of Socrates, the Greek philosopher whose advanced teachings are said to have led, in 399 BC, to a sentence of death by drinking a fatal draught prepared from the umbelliferous plant hemlock, and the infamous Spanish/ Italian Borgias, whose crimes, including several murders by the clandestine administration of lethal toxins, echo from the 16th century.

A hundred years later, the English novelist and criminologist Henry Fielding called for methods of making poisons visible so that those who used them for homicide could be brought to justice. Doctors told him it could not be done. They were right then, but the time was to come when, with advancing scientific knowledge, the cadavers of the victims could be made to yield their tragic secrets – when dead men (and women) began to tell tales.

In Socrates' days there was general knowledge of a few vegetable poisons like hemlock and henbane, but people were also becoming familiar with the metallic poison called arsenic. During the ages that followed, and particularly after the eighth-century Arab alchemist Gber had succeeded in converting it into an odourless, tasteless white powder (arsenous oxide), arsenic became the poisoner's favourite potion. There is no way of estimating the numbers who perished, without arousing the least suspicion, from its surreptitious administration. Certainly many hundreds of Europeans suffered an agonizing end in consequence of its unsuspecting ingestion, enduring symptoms that the physicians of the day sometimes ascribed to cholera, then one of the most prevalent diseases. Arsenic became the selected *modus operandi* among ladies with murderous intent. Two 16th-century schemers, Teofania de Adamo and Marie Madeline, Marquise de Brinvilliers, were responsible, directly and indirectly, for many killings by means of sprinklings in food and beverages. Only by gross carelessness in the acquisition, possession, or deployment of the poison were their less-successful imitators brought to book, for more than a century was to pass before it began to be possible to identify arsenic in bodily remains. Meanwhile the deadly dust became known as *poudre de succession* – 'inheritance powder'.

In 1787 a Königsberg professor of medicine, Johann Metzger, discovered that a layer of arsenous oxide formed on copper plates held over the vapours rising from heated substances containing arsenic. When white arsenic was heated with charcoal in a test tube the vapours were converted back into metallic arsenic, which deposited metallic flakes like tiny mirrors on the cooler upper parts of the tube. Nearly 20 years later, another German experimenter, Valentin Rose of Berlin's Faculty of Medicine, applied Metzger's discovery to a process of testing for the presence of arsenic in the human stomach and intestines. After boiling pieces of these organs in distilled water, Rose repeatedly filtered the resultant liquid and treated it with nitric acid to destroy the remnants of the organs themselves. After adding potassium carbonate and lime water, he produced a precipitate which he dried and then heated over charcoal in a test tube. When arsenic was present, the metallic 'mirrors' were formed.

It was Mathieu Orfila, the Spaniard mentioned in chapter one, who achieved the first outstanding international reputation for successful toxicological research. Born on the island of Minorca, he studied in Valencia and Barcelona before becoming a doctor of medicine in Paris at the age of 24. Two years later he published the first part of a two-volume work titled *Traité des poisons ... ou Toxicologie générale*. It was seized upon eagerly throughout Europe by everyone concerned with questions of poisons and was acclaimed by doctors, lawyers, and police. Other valuable books followed and Orfila was nominated dean of the Paris Medical Faculty in 1831, aged 44.

By administering the poison to dogs, he had shown that arsenic passed from the stomach and intestines into the liver, spleen, kidneys and nerves. When no poison was found in the stomach, its presence could frequently be traced in the other organs. By subjecting human and animal tissue to the destructive effects of saltpetre, he proved that removal of the structures which had absorbed the poison enabled it to be detected more readily. But occasionally, even after he had personally administered poison to dogs in the presence of his students, he found it impossible to find any trace of it in their bodies. Despite his best endeavours, he could not solve the problem.

The simple procedure required to detect the smallest trace of arsenic brought immortal recognition to its discoverer, an impoverished English chemist named James Marsh, who was employed at the Royal Arsenal in Woolwich. Marsh was 44 when, in 1832, he was asked to help investigate the murder by poisoning of an 80-year-old Plumstead farmer named George Bodle. Statements made by a maid and a retail pharmacist indicated that a grandson, John, who was known to be eager to receive an inheritance from the old man, had purchased and administered arsenic. Because there was no other competent chemist in the area, Marsh was asked to examine the dead man's intestines and a suspect brew of coffee. Both yielded the telltale signs of arsenic. The coroner's jury was convinced that murder had been committed and the suspect was duly charged with the crime. But the jury at the trial was not so readily persuaded and made it plain that they regarded Marsh's scientific evidence as fanciful and incomprehensible. Spectators' cheers greeted its 'Not guilty' finding. Ten years later, John Bodle, who had meanwhile been sentenced to seven years' imprisonment for fraud and to deportation to the colonies for blackmail, confessed to the murder of his grandfather.

But Marsh had not been idle all that time. Resentful of the acquittal, he had determined to find a method of demonstrating the presence of arsenic by making it so visible that even the least intelligent of jurors would be forced to accept the fact. He began with some research in the Woolwich Arsenal library. There he read of the method used by a Swedish chemist, Karl Scheele, for producing the colourless, inflammable, garlic-odoured, poisonous gas called arsine. The technique involves the mixing of sulphuric or hydrochloric acid with any fluid containing arsenic. The addition of zinc brings about a reaction which produces hydrogen. This again reacts with arsenic in any compound, producing the gas.

Applying the same system, Marsh made a U-shaped glass tube with one end open and a tapering nozzle at the other. In the nozzle he suspended a piece of zinc. The fluid to be examined was placed in the open end and acid added. When the fluid level reached the zinc even the most minute trace of arsenic produced arsine, which could be ignited as it escaped through the nozzle. By holding a cold porcelain bowl against the flame, Marsh obtained a precipitate of metallic arsenic in the form of a black deposit. The technique enabled the last trace of arsenic in the suspect fluid to be collected on the bowl. With refinement the procedure proved capable of detecting a thousandth of a milligram (three hundred thousandths of an ounce) of arsenic added to the test fluid. When Marsh described his achievement in the *Edinburgh Philosophical Journal* for October 1836 his name entered the annals of chemical history.

But the extreme sensitivity of the device also produced a snag. There was consternation among chemists when it was found that the apparatus produced arsenic deposits even though no arsenic had been added to test solutions. More and more experiments revealed the presence of arsenic where no one suspected it. Even the bones of people who had died naturally showed traces of the poison. Gradually the truth dawned – that arsenic is an extremely common element, minute traces of which might be found almost anywhere. But the agitation was increased when arsenic was discovered in samples of earth taken from some Paris graveyards.

Orfila decided to scrutinize the problem. He examined human bones taken from various mortuaries and soil from fields and cemeteries. He gave the opinion that, in future tests for suspected arsenic poisoning, it would be necessary to test the earth in the vicinity of the grave. If the arsenic content of the soil was large and that of the corpse small, the possibility of *post mortem* arsenical infiltration had to be considered. On the other hand, the absence of arsenic in the soil but its presence in a body would argue strongly in favour of deliberate or accidental poisoning. The individual circumstances, including the condition of the coffin, were all-important, he stressed.

The source and quantity of arsenic found in the corpse of 48-year-old Eliza Barrow became an issue of life or death for bald, diminutive, 40-year-old Frederick Henry Seddon, the man accused of her murder in 1911. It was also the central concern in his trial – a classic in the history of poisonings.

Possessing substantial holdings of securities, cash and jewellery, the corpulent Eliza took up occupation of the third floor of Seddon's London home at a rent of 12 shillings a week. Within a year he had persuaded her to make over to him virtually all of her valuables, including a tenement house, in exchange for the payment of a regular annuity for the remainder of her life. That 'remainder' turned out to be short. A few months later she was dead and buried in the cemetery at Finchley, north London.

A suspicious cousin went to the police and inquiries were begun. These uncovered a mass of *prima facie* evidence. The body was exhumed and found to contain lethal quantities of arsenic. Seddon and his wife were arrested, he charged with murder and she with complicity. Eliza had died just three weeks after their daughter Maggie had bought a package of arsenic-coated flypapers. Throughout that, for her, agonizing period, Eliza had been tended by Mrs Seddon.

Opened at the Old Bailey in March 1912, the trial developed into a fiercely-contested legal struggle. Seddon was defended by the formidable Edward Marshall Hall, but the prosecution's case was founded on the meticulous laboratory work of an outstanding forensic scientist, Dr William Willcox. He set about preparing precise calculations of the amount of arsenic in the body, with the aim of refuting any defence contention that the poison had entered by means other than deliberate administration. First he weighed the exhumed corpse in the mortuary and the organs he had in his laboratory. Together they totalled 60 pounds. Eliza's last lifetime weight had been 140 pounds. The loss was due to evaporation of water from the tissues. Making hundreds of tests with the Marsh apparatus, Willcox obtained results showing that the stomach contained 7.3 milligrams of arsenic, the intestines 41 milligrams and the liver 11.13 milligrams. Working on the accepted standard that muscles account for two-fifths of total body weight, he concluded that the woman's muscles contained 67.2 milligrams of arsenic. In the hair he found an average of 18 milligrams per 100 grams of hair. Altogether his calculations totalled 131.57 milligrams – ample proof of fatal poisoning.

Challenging this damning testimony, Hall cross-examined Willcox about his method of reckoning the quantity of arsenic in the corpse. Willcox was forced to agree that he had based his findings on large multiplications of the quantities of poison he had found in pieces of the various organs. Pressed further, he also admitted that, when so multiplied, the smallest error in a basic finding would be grossly magnified.

Plainly impressed by this argument, the jury was swayed still more by Hall's next manoeuvre. Answering his questions, Willcox said that he had found one-eightieth of a milligram of arsenic in the hair nearest the scalp and a quarter as much in the furthest ends. Hall then pounced. Pointing out that it had been scientifically established that arsenic took several weeks to enter the roots of human hair and 10 months to penetrate six inches of its length, he asked how it could have been possible for the poison to reach the ends of Eliza's hair in just over two weeks. Did the Willcox findings not show that the woman had ingested arsenic a year before her death?

It seemed that Hall had scored a vital point. But the expert's mind was racing as he responded to the lawyer's continuing questions. The court was hushed when he explained that, before he had taken the hair for analysis, it had been 'lying in the coffin and was more or less soaked in the juices of the body'. Angrily, Hall dismissed the statement as a concocted excuse. But, back at his laboratory, Willcox took hair from a corpse that was known to be free of arsenic and laid it in the juices from Eliza's coffin. A few days later tests showed that the hair had absorbed a large quantity of arsenic – he had been right in maintaining that Eliza's hair had been permeated by the escaping poison outside her body.

The point was made in court and Hall's attempt at defence collapsed. Although his wife was acquitted, the acquisitive Seddon was convicted of the murder and was hanged at Pentonville prison on April 18 1912.

Arsenic was not the only metallic or mineral poison to engage the investigative and experimental talents of emerging toxicologists. Others included lead, phosphorus, sulphur, mercury, and antimony. And meanwhile the gradual unravelling of mysteries surrounding the initially small group of vegetable poisons uncovered more problems and even created new toxins. Taken in small doses, some were medicinally helpful. For example, the analgesic morphine was first extracted from opium by Sertürner, a German apothecary, in 1805. Later, many poisons were drawn from exotic plants. With the same basic alkali resemblance and all affecting the nervous system of man and animals, they were given the name alkaloids. Fourteen years after Sertürner's discovery, the toxicologists Caventou and Pelletier gained the stimulant strychnine from *nux vomica*, the seed of the pulpy fruit of an East Indies tree. Twelve months later other toxicologists, Desosse and Runge, found, respectively, the febrifuge quinine in the bark of the cinchona tree and the stimulant caffeine in coffee beans. In 1826 the toxicologist Giesecke discovered the poisonous principle – conine – in hemlock. In 1828 the toxicologists Possell and Reimann extracted the poison nicotine from tobacco. Five years later another toxicologist, Mein, discovered the dilatant and analgesic atropine in *atropa belladonna* (deadly nightshade). Eventually some 2,000 different alkaloids, including such things as the anaesthetic cocaine and the sedatives hyoscyamine and hyoscine were developed. As they found their way into the hands of the general public, many of these useful but deadly substances were employed to bring about the deaths of people who stood in the way of human schemes. Few of the early killers were convicted of their crimes because it was not until 1850 that researchers began to discover chemical reagents which could be used to detect the presence of alkaloids in dead bodies.

The fact that there was no means of disclosing the presence of morphine in cadavers was the problem that faced the French Prosecutor General, de Broe, when, in 1823, he accused a young Parisian medical practitioner, Edmé Castaing, of poisoning two patients, the brothers Hippolyte and Auguste Ballet, with the new drug. Both men had previously been in good health and both had been medically attended only by Castaing. Soon after their deaths, the doctor had repaid his many debts, loaned his mother 30,000 francs and invested 100,000 francs in stocks and shares. In the total absence of scientific proof of the presence of the poison in the corpses, it was only de Broe's eloquence in urging the jury to concentrate on the other evidence against Castaing that persuaded them to convict the doctor of the killings. Sadly, the publicity that was given to the case throughout Europe undoubtedly led others to use the untraceable poison for murder.

But as progress was made with laboratory techniques to prove the presence of cadaveric alkaloids, the legal net was slowly tightened around miscreants who misused the drugs for their nefarious purposes. It was hyoscine that, in 1910, Dr William Willcox discovered in the scanty remains, found buried beneath the cellar of her north London home, of Cora Crippen (née Kunigunde Mackamotzki), wife of Dr Hawley Harvey Crippen, now immortalized as the first murderer to be brought to justice with the help of radio. Only 13 years after 21-year-old Guglielmo Marconi had given the first public demonstration of wireless, to the chief engineer of the Post Office in London, a message was sent to Scotland Yard from mid-Atlantic by the observant captain of the SS *Montrose*, the ship on which Crippen and his mistress, Ethel le Neve (who was disguised as a boy), were fleeing to Canada. Crippen was hanged. The evidence given by Dr Willcox in the case detailed a new method of identifying alkaloids by processes producing individual forms of crystals from each drug.

During the 1930s, 40s, and 50s, the pharmaceutical factories of Europe and the USA poured out torrents of synthetic alkaloids but, generally speaking, methods of identifying their presence in the dead kept pace with this progress. By 1955 there were 30 different means of testing for morphine alone. The newly-developed techniques included x-ray crystallography, x-ray structural analysis, ultra-violet and infra-red spectroscopy, and paper chromatography.

Sadly, the lifetimes of men like Willcox and his talented contemporaries were not of sufficient duration to enable them to see the astonishing progress that was made around the middle of the century. The photometer, which had been used to detect tiny amounts of carbon monoxide, was adapted to uncover similarly minute quantities of other poisons. Coupled with electronic measuring instruments, the device permitted the amounts of many poisons to be read on dials. This new ability to identify infinitesimally small traces of toxins enabled new light to be shed on the old problem of the natural arsenic content of the human body. It was found that micrograms of the poison could be identified in the blood, heart, lungs, liver, spleen, hair and fingernails of every normal person, as well as in the milk of nursing mothers. It was calculated that the average human body contains arsenic totalling about one ten-millionth of the body weight. People who came into contact with quantities of arsenic in the course of their work, such as winegrowers using arsenical insecticides and persons who ate large quantities of seafood, were found to have up to three times the usual quantity of arsenic in their urine. Similar analyses showed that 50% of all soil contains between five and ten milligrams of arsenic per kilogram of earth.

A few years later the discoveries of nuclear science were put to service in forensic toxicology. By radiochemical techniques, bombarding hair with neutrons, the arsenic it contained was made radioactive. The quantity of arsenic present was then determined by measuring the radiation.

Killing and curing have rarely been more closely linked than they were through discovery of the powerful hypnotic and sedative compounds known as barbiturates. It was in a romantic mood rarely seen among scientists that, in 1863, the German professor of organic chemistry Adolf Baeyer named his newly-synthetized acid after a female friend called Barbara. Four decades later Emil Fischer and Joseph von Mering learned that two derivatives, known as barbital and phenobarbital, were effective sedatives. Because the initial idea had come to him in Verona, Mering called barbital Veronal. Phenobarbital was given the name Luminal. Both products acquired swift popularity among the suicidal.

By the 1930s the task of detecting barbiturates in corpses had become a major problem for toxicologists. The ever-growing demand for sedatives in the war and post-war years and the heightened tensions of the atomic age greatly increased their workload. A large number of barbituric acid derivatives were developed, licensed and marketed. By 1948 the world production of these drugs totalled 300 tons. In England in 1954 the number of suicides directly attributable to the misuse of barbiturates was a dozen times greater than it had been 16 years earlier. By the time researchers had evolved techniques for the reliable detection of barbiturates, another family of potential poisons had arrived on the scene – the tranquillizers. These were eagerly pressed into service by family doctors beseiged by tense and depressed patients. Again toxicological explorers had to redouble their efforts to enable the investigation of suspected abuse to have any prospect of success.

The study of toxins is indeed a complex pursuit in which the discovery of answers often creates new queries. Underlying all is the fundamental question: what is a poison? Some, taken in small quantities, are essential to life. Others, in like amounts, are positively beneficial to health. But some are so virulent that no qualification is needed in their description. Poisonousness would appear to be as much a function as it is a property.

It is a realm in which there is no greater truism than Alexander Pope's 'A little learning is a dangerous thing'. The employment of this level of understanding by a male nurse in Yorkshire brought about the death of his wife, his life imprisonment for murder and the creation of a milestone in forensic toxicology.

Mrs Elizabeth Barlow, in her thirties, was found dead in the bath at her small, terraced home at Thornbury Crescent, Bradford, just before midnight on May 3 1937. She was lying on her right side with her arms bent as in sleep. Her husband, Kenneth, told the family doctor, who had been called by neighbours, that he had found her in the bath when he had awakened and realized she had not come to bed. He had tried to lift her but she was too heavy. After emptying the bath of water, he had tried to apply artificial respiration as she lay there. An investigating policeman's suspicions were aroused by the facts that, despite these alleged rescue attempts, there was no water on the bathroom floor, Barlow's pyjamas were dry and a little pool of water rested in the crook of the woman's right elbow.

A *post mortem* showed that Mrs Barlow had died from drowning. There were no signs of violence. She was about two months pregnant. The pupils of her eyes were extraordinarily dilated but there was no evidence of disease, although sweat-soaked lady's pyjamas and vomit-soiled bedclothes confirmed her husband's story that she had been unwell before taking her final bath. The combination of sweating, vomiting and dilated pupils implied that she had drowned because she had become unconscious, perhaps in a hypoglycaemic coma. Hypoglycaemia is a condition opposite to diabetes – too low a blood sugar level, from which diabetics suffer if they take too much insulin and/or too little food. But Mrs Barlow was not diabetic. Exhaustive laboratory analyses of samples of the vomit, urine, blood, digestive tract, liver, spleen, lungs and brain revealed no trace of any known poison.

Using a magnifying glass under strong lights, pathologist David Price examined the entire body, inch by inch. The task was made more difficult because the skin was heavily spotted with moles, freckles and acne. After two hours of painstaking searching he found two tiny injection marks on each of the buttocks. Two hypodermic syringes had been found in the kitchen of the house. Barlow had explained their presence by saying he had given himself injections of penicillin because of a carbuncle. He had never given injections to his wife, he said.

Price took pieces of skin, fat and muscle from the area of the injection marks. Subjected to a series of elaborate biochemical and animal experiments, these small samples, weighing just six ounces, yielded 84 units of insulin – an amount vastly in excess of the total quantity, spread throughout the body, which could have been produced normally by the pancreas of a woman of Mrs Barlow's weight – 75 pounds.

Police inquiries at the hospital where Barlow worked revealed that he was often put in charge of insulin injections. Two of his colleagues there informed detectives that Barlow had told them that insulin could be used to commit the perfect murder because it dissolved in the blood and left no trace. Faced with these facts, Barlow admitted that he had given injections to his wife but claimed that they had been of ergonovine, an abortifacient, to end her pregnancy because she did not want the baby. But ergonovine had been one of the first poisonous drugs for which the toxicologists had searched in the samples taken from the body, without success. Barlow lost the freedom to practise more of his 'little learning'.

And, still, no one knows it all. As Dr Hamish Walls wrote in his autobiography, from which I quoted an extract in chapter four, 'Toxicology will deserve to be called a science only when we can answer the question: what makes a poison a poison? To do so we will need to know a great deal more than we do yet about the ultimate intracellular chemistry of how poisons act … The exploration of this field has only just begun.'

PART TWO

Scotland Yard's Laboratory:
the first fifty years

CHAPTER 6
The Met gets its lab

WITH PROGRESSIVE DEVELOPMENT OF THE techniques described in Part One, many of the police authorities of Europe established their own forensic science laboratories. Scotland also took this course. In London the forces of law and order showed their scepticism by doing nothing.

It was a humble constable in charge of police pay sheets who, totally unofficially, introduced forensic science to Scotland Yard in the late 1920s. A Devonian, his name was Cyril Cuthbert. While official book-keeping provided his living, it was the study of works on criminalistic medicine that occupied his mind. He made personal sacrifices to purchase books by authors such as pathologist Sydney Smith and chemist Ainsworth Mitchell. With increasing knowledge, he gained valuable contacts among doctors interested in medical jurisprudence and with institutions like the Government Chemist's Laboratory.

Police colleagues who learned of his personal interests began to consult him about cases that were causing them difficulty. Cuthbert advised them gladly and his help was often of practical value. Before joining the police he had had an uncompleted medical training and some dental tuition, as well as attending evening classes in chemistry. He taught himself how to apply simple skills, such as the reagent presumptive test for blood and the deciphering of erased writing. When faced with problems beyond his capability, he referred officers to experts outside the police organization.

While their use of his abilities was encouraging, the attitude of his administrative superior was anything but. On several occasions he was reprimanded for spending time on efforts unconnected with his official duties. But Cuthbert was a determined man. Despite being transferred to work in the Criminal Records Office, he continued his studies and went on with his unofficial advisory function. He spent 35 shillings – a significant sum from his pay of £3.10s (£3.50p) a week – on acquiring a secondhand microscope. This, with other small items of apparatus, was carefully stored in the police section house where Cuthbert, then a bachelor, lived. The equipment could not be kept at his place of work because the detective inspector to whom he reported had given strict instructions that no official time or space was to be devoted to his 'hobby'.

There came an occasion when, during his off-duty hours, Cuthbert helped a colleague to identify original written matter on a document that had been tampered with. Soon afterwards he was ordered to report to the office of the Assistant Commissioner, Sir Norman Kendall. There, he was angrily informed of a message from a senior police officer in Folkestone, requesting that a written statement be supplied by Cyril Cuthbert, 'of the Metropolitan Police Laboratory', who would also be required to attend court to give evidence regarding his examination of the incriminating document.

Cuthbert was given a severe talking to and the request from Folkestone was refused. But that officer was not so easily disposed of and Cuthbert was finally compelled to attend the court as a witness. There was more trouble when he also had to attend the Kent quarter sessions, to which the case was committed. Hurt by his sufferings, Cuthbert told a friend that he would have resigned from the police if he could have found another job.

But help was at hand. When the accused person was found guilty at the quarter sessions, glowing tribute was paid to Cuthbert's skill and expertise. His evidence had, he was told, been presented magnificently and it was to be hoped that 'the appropriate authorities' in London would be made aware of his valuable work.

Understandably, some faces were reddened by receipt of this message at Scotland Yard. Here was a dilemma indeed!

How did one deal with a situation in which a police officer had been both rebuked and commended for the same action? News of the happenings reached the ears of the Commissioner, the forthright Lord Trenchard, who had declared in his first report that crime was divided into two categories – preventable and detectable. His immediate reaction to the Cuthbert affair was a demand to be shown the 'Metropolitan Police Laboratory', of whose existence he was unaware.

Hastily, Cuthbert's few items of apparatus were placed on display in a cupboard in the photographic department, Cuthbert was clad in a white coat borrowed from a nearby hospital and the Commissioner's inspection was arranged.

Appalled by the pitiful inadequacy of what he saw, Trenchard turned his concentrated attention to the task of creating a genuine laboratory, which he had realized was essential for the efficient working of his force. A massive correspondence ensued between Trenchard and the Home Office. Trenchard's persistence paid off. It was agreed that the new establishment should be created, housed at Hendon in conjunction with the police college that was in the process of establishment there in the former country club run by pioneer aviator Claude Grahame-White. The college was the brainchild of Arthur (later Sir Arthur) Dixon, an assistant secretary at the Home Office and a keen amateur microscopist. His proposals included a recommendation that the curriculum should embrace some instruction in microscopy, physiology, chemistry and medico-legal matters. Cuthbert was promoted and put in charge of supervising the contractors who were engaged to install the apparatus.

Trenchard offered the directorship of the new laboratory to several eminent experts, including the legendary Sir Bernard Spilsbury and Sydney Smith, but the salary and conditions attached to the appointment were not sufficiently attractive to gain the full-time services of those already distinguished in the field.

The post was eventually accepted by 41-year-old Dr James Davidson, an enterprising young pathologist who was a lecturer in forensic medicine at Edinburgh University and a former house surgeon at Edinburgh Royal Infirmary. His salary at the laboratory was £1,000 a year plus a special non-pensionable allowance of £60 which was approved by the Home Office 'in view of the difficulty in obtaining suitable accommodation within easy access of the laboratory'. A note in the personnel files of the time reads 'Appointment subject to three months' notice on either side and liable to termination at the age of 60 and will not in any case continue after the age of 65.' Davidson's holiday entitlement was listed as '36 days, increasing to 48 days after 10 years' service'. He reached that maximum but his services were 'terminated by the Commissioner on reorganization of the laboratory' in March 1946.

Referring to Davidson's appointment, an unnamed journalist on the *Scottish Daily Express* wrote 'I met a shy, smiling young man yesterday, whose words in a few months may decide whether certain men will live or die ...' Another paper added the comment 'It is Dr Davidson's opinion that, just as police officers and members of the force are assisted in their work by some knowledge of law procedure, so those engaged in the detection of modern crime should have some knowledge of the channels along which investigations might be pursued in the laboratory.' The *News of the World* waxed lyrical: 'Donning the mantle of Sherlock Holmes, the policeman of tomorrow will lay aside his truncheon for the test tube and call to his aid all the resources of science in the war on crime. The police students, fine, upright young men, are indeed fortunate in the opportunities which the new laboratory will afford them.' A statement issued by Scotland Yard announced that Davidson's duties would be '... to assist in the investigations of criminal cases, to give instruction in scientific methods of crime detection to students at the College and at Peel House, and to other members of the force, and to undertake research work.'

The *Illustrated London News* printed his portrait among others under the headings 'Personalities of the week' and 'People in the public eye'. The centre spot was devoted to a medal being struck to commemorate the 25th anniversary of George the Fifth's accession to the throne. Other portraits included those of the dramatist Sir Arthur Pinero, who had recently died, Mlle Hélène Boucher, holder of the women's world airspeed record, who had been killed in an aeroplane accident near Versailles, and Sir Archibald Page, who had been appointed chairman of the Central Electricity Board.

Despite the stern scepticism that was known to exist among many senior officers, the *Police Review* was eulogistic about the new venture. 'The laboratories of the Metropolitan Police College are a fine example of how much can be achieved in a short time,' began an article contributed by Dr H B Fraser. 'In under a month a large, empty building has been converted into a well laid out and generously equipped scientific department.

'This department is really subdivided into two; on the one hand there is the lecture and instruction room where the students ... receive their training in elementary anatomy, physiology, chemistry and physics, and on the other the laboratories of the CID, where the routine scientific work is carried out.

'The instruction laboratory ... can hold a class of 64 students and is the only example of its kind in any European Police Force. The laboratory is equipped with an epidiascope for the projection of slides, printed sheets or photographs and a micro-projector for microscopic slides. The benches themselves are equipped with a water supply and sink, a bunsen burner and a bench light for each student. There are also some 20 microscopes (capable of magnification up to 300 diameters) ...

'Such a course in elementary microscopy ... is of value not so much in converting each of the students into a pseudo-expert in the subject – an aim which it could never hope to achieve – but in enabling him to appreciate what clues and what evidence may be of importance to the expert in those subjects. The value of such knowledge is inestimable in the intelligent investigation of crime.'

Describing the two chemical laboratories, two biology laboratories, technicians' laboratory, photographic darkroom, chemical store and exhibits room which made up the scientific section, Dr Fraser declared that the establishment was 'exceedingly well equipped with physico-chemical instruments'. He mentioned in particular 'one of the latest type reversion spectroscopes ... which can be used not only for qualitative but for quantitative analysis of blood spectra – for example in cases of coal gas poisoning the actual amount of carbon-monoxy haemoglobin produced can be estimated'; a comparator rack; a 'modern type colorimeter'; a fume cupboard with gas generators; an electrically-heated water bath; an electric furnace; a drying oven; a distilled-water still; a centrifugal separator and chainomatic balances for accurate weighing. 'An interesting experiment has been carried out in the construction of the balance room in order to obtain rigidity,' he added. 'The floor has been so designed that it is independent of the floor of the rest of the building, from which it is insulated by pitch. The reason for this precaution is the propinquity of the college gymnasium.'

Among the photographic equipment he noted x-ray apparatus and an ultra-violet lamp 'which will show up stains and writing which are invisible in ordinary artificial or daylight. Letters written in urine or other invisible "inks" can easily be read in this light and it can be used for the detection of urine and seminal stains on clothing.' There was also 'a very fine spectrograph' which could be applied to the detection of coining – 'minute particles of metallic dust can be analysed ... where ordinary chemical analysis would be impossible or at least very difficult ...'

The instruments in the biological laboratories would 'delight the eye of any scientific worker,' Dr Fraser stated. There were several high-powered microscopes with oil immersion lenses, some of them binocular; photomicrographic apparatus which could deal with the highest power magnifications; a microscope fitted with an ultrapak condenser which made opaque objects 'stand out in high relief with amazing clarity – a sample of dusty blue serge looked like a primeval forest tree, bearing strange and exotic fruit' and a comparison microscope for the examination of fired bullets.

'Nothing appeared to be missing although the time in which the equipment has been obtained and arranged is so short,' he summed up. 'The whole department is a tribute to the foresight with which it was planned and the energy with which the fitting and equipment have been carried out.'

Applauding the appointment of a Scot as the laboratory's first head, Scotland's *People's Journal* permitted itself observations which, half a century on, have a comical ring. Opening with the reflection that the new setup might have the effect of making every detective a Sherlock Holmes, the paper went on 'Criminals will in future not only have to contend with mechanical aids such as motor transport, wireless, &c, but all the resources of the laboratory into the bargain.' Davidson's work would probably make him the nearest approach to Holmes in real life, the article affirmed, adding 'Curiously enough, he is not unlike the great hero of fiction, both in appearance and manner. He is a tall, fair-haired man with sharp, intelligent features, a man of few words, of shy and retiring disposition, obviously keen on his job and a master of his subject.'

More intentionally amusing were the efforts of some cartoonists. The irrepressible Low produced a scene showing the fronts of two suburban homes. On a pathway was a corpse with a dark stain oozing from the vicinity of a knife protruding from the chest. Two constables were crouching nearby, holding test tubes and a microscope. One policeman was remarking to the other 'I think we may conclude that all our tests go to prove that this is a bloodstain.' Shown pointing at a villainous-looking individual carrying a bag marked 'Swag', another constable exclaimed 'Move on there; don't disturb our studies!' In *Punch* another artist showed Sherlock Holmes, wearing a dressing gown and constable's helmet, pouring liquid into a clinical beaker. Dr Watson, seated nearby, exclaimed 'Holmes, you astound me!'

Like other papers, the *People's Journal* made mention of the fact that, as an assistant to Sydney Smith, then Professor of Forensic Medicine at Edinburgh University, Davidson had played a key role in solving a case which had become known as 'the Aberdeen sack murder'. Discovery of a hair in a sack containing the body of eight-year-old Helen Priestley was part of the evidence that led to the conviction and life imprisonment of Mrs Jeannie Donald.

Within a month of the opening of the laboratory, Davidson's evidence at an inquest solved a mystery surrounding the death of a man at a Hastings, Sussex, rifle range. Twenty-four-year-old engineer Spencer Bransby was one of four men at the range when he fell dead, shot in the head. Though the tragedy was clearly an accident, no one was sure who had fired the fatal shot. Producing microscopic comparison photographs of the bullet taken from the corpse and those from test shots fired with the four rifles, Davidson showed that the bullet which killed Bransby had come from the rifle used by Frank Coates, of Elphinstone Road, Hastings. Coates said 'I thought Bransby was firing himself. I heard him say "That's hit it" and thought he was speaking of his own shooting. Then he fell from the darkness into the light. I had fired just before he fell, but I saw nothing in the line of my sight.' Returning a verdict of accidental death, the coroner said no one was to blame unless it was Bransby himself for his keenness in jumping up to observe the effect of a shot.

The laboratory was officially opened by the Home Secretary, Sir John Gilmour, on April 10 1935. A prestigious gathering assembled for the occasion in the conference hall of the college. In addition to Trenchard, Sir John and Dr Davidson, those on the flower-decked platform included Lord Atkin (Lord of Appeal), Lord Dawson of Penn, Lord Horder, Lord Snell, Sir Edwin Deller, Sir John Moylan, Sir Robert Robertson, Sir Russell Scott, Sir Frank Smith, Sir Bernard Spilsbury, Sir Hugh Turnbull and Sir Henry Wellcome.

Speaking with candour, the Home Secretary said that the provision of the laboratory was the beginning of a department which should have been established many years earlier. 'I hope by its means we shall solve some of our problems and lay the foundation of a more rapid and certain detection of crime,' he said. 'Sometimes a few hairs or a little dust might be of the highest importance and require a peculiar and particular attention.'

Emphasizing that he was speaking as a judge, Lord Atkin said 'Anybody who makes himself familiar with what has been done elsewhere must have some feeling of shame at the lack of what has been done here.' It was 'a sound thing' that men who were going to take part in police work should be made familiar with the process and powers of science because science, which gave its evidence impartially, was more closely allied to the truth than anything else. He added the hope that the opening of the laboratory was a first step towards establishment of a national medico-legal institute. As a branch of London University, such an institute would enable coroners, prison doctors, advocates, police officers and even judges to train for diplomas. Evidence coming from such an institute would possibly be more favourably received by juries than evidence which might be construed as police evidence.

Lord Dawson wished that the laboratory might provide 'a rallying ground' for discussion for police students and others professionally interested in criminal problems.

Revealing that there had been some thought for the future, Gilmour announced that to provide for the laboratory's development in the national interest, a body of experts – to be known as the Advisory Committee on the Scientific Investigation of Crime – had been appointed to consider its work, with special regard to the desirability of close and effective contact with police institutions in Britain and overseas and with any medico-legal or scientific institute which might be constituted for teaching and research in forensic medicine or other relevant sciences. Under Trenchard's chairmanship, the committee consisted of their lordships Atkin and Dawson, Sir Russell Scott (Permanent Under Secretary of State at the Home Office), Sir Edwin Deller (Principal of the University of London), Sir Bernard Spilsbury, Sir Frank Smith (Secretary of the Department of Scientific and Industrial Research), Sir Frederick Menzies and Sir Arthur McNalty (Chief Medical Officers of the London County Council and the Ministry of Health, respectively), Sir Robert Robertson (Government Chemist) and Dr Hugh Lett (Senior Surgeon to London Hospital). Sadly, the committee did not emulate Trenchard's individual success. It was finally adjourned, *sine die*, in 1938.

After the formal opening ceremony, the visitors, who included senior policemen from various parts of the country, coroners, distinguished members of the legal and medical professions and representatives from London medical schools, were given tea in the dining hall and escorted on tours of the laboratory. Lengthy press reports of the occasion appeared the following day, in the *Times*, the *Daily Telegraph*, the *Daily Mail*, the *Morning Post*, the *Daily Sketch* and the *Daily Herald*.

Following a half-century of monetary inflation, it is an astonishing reflection that the annual operating budget of £500 (for equipment, reagents, etc) first assigned to the laboratory proved to be more than adequate. Davidson began with a staff of five: Lewis Charles Nickolls (a chemist from the Government Chemist's Laboratory), Cuthbert (as police liaison officer), a technician, a clerk-typist and a cleaner. Nickolls was to become the third director of the laboratory, from 1951 to 1964. The man who eventually served as its fourth, from 1964 to 1968, Dr Hamish Walls, was taken on within a year of the opening because of his experience in use of the spectrograph. During the same period another chemist, C G Daubney, was also engaged.

'The association [with the Hendon college] did us no good,' Walls recalled in a paper published by the Forensic Science Society's *Journal* in 1976, 'because the college was for several reasons – some better than others – very unpopular with the rank and file of the police.

'For the first 10 years [the laboratory] never really prospered. The "Old Guard" at Scotland Yard were suspicious of it and for a time very little of even such work as it did came from the Metropolitan Police. Even officers who wanted to use it had to submit to a frustrating amount of unnecessary red tape before doing so. The laboratory failed to win the confidence of the people that mattered and who should have been its best customers, such as the Director of Public Prosecutions.'

Officialdom was not unaware of the difficulties. 'Even before the war suggestions appeared on confidential files that a fresh start should be made with a new director and staff,' Walls' paper went on. 'Moreover, Sir Philip Game, who succeeded Lord Trenchard as Commissioner at the end of 1935, was anti-lab. He suggested going back to calling in outside experts as required, wanted the laboratory put in charge of a police superintendent and thought for example that all seminal stains ought to be examined and reported on by the divisional police surgeons. The Home Office not surprisingly found his ideas "retrograde" and in 1941 suggested that the laboratory should be removed from direct police control and made officially what it in fact almost was – the south eastern regional one. However, rather astonishingly in the circumstances, this suggestion was strongly and successfully resisted by the Commissioner. With hindsight, it is surprising that the outbreak of war was not made an opportunity to close the laboratory altogether. However, in the event, there was no change until 1946, when Dr H S Holden came as director and the entire senior staff were replaced.'

The man who had been at the root of it all, Cyril Cuthbert – who had fagged for and often been 'slippered' (beaten) by another pupil named Oswald (later Sir Oswald) Mosley at Exeter Grammar School – rose to the rank of superintendent in 1949, retired from the police in 1951 and died at his home at Haywards Heath, Sussex, in 1984. It was a measure of his personal qualities that, in his book *Science and the Detection of Crime*, published by Hutchinson and Co Ltd in 1958 and, in paperback, by Arrow Books in 1962, he made no mention of his early sufferings and passed over his unique place in the history of forensic science at Scotland Yard. During an interview in 1981 he confessed 'I never wanted to join the police. I am the world's worst police officer that has ever been. I served for 28½ years without arresting a single person or summonsing anybody.' During the 1939-45 war he was commandant of enemy aliens' internment camps in the Isle of Man. From 1956 to 1970 he was secretary of St George's Hospital Medical School, at Hyde Park Corner. But, for the sake of accuracy, it is worthy of record that, contrary to statements made in books by Cuthbert and John McCafferty, the laboratory was not closed during the war. Although the work of the Hendon Police College was suspended during that time, the labours of the laboratory went on.

When Davidson was discharged from the laboratory in 1946 he was, as noted above, succeeded as director by Dr Holden, then the officer in charge of the Home Office laboratory at Nottingham. Known as 'H₂S', Holden, who joined at a salary of £1,800 a year, brought several of his Nottingham staff with him, causing a complete change of senior scientists at the laboratory. Only Walls and Daubney had remained of the pre-war staff and both then moved to appointments elsewhere. In 1947 the laboratory gained a recruit who was to distinguish herself in forensic science: Miss Margaret Pereira. Having established a reputation as a world authority on blood grouping, Miss Pereira finally rose to become controller of the Home Office Forensic Science Service, based in Westminster.

During its first decade the laboratory never dealt with more than 400 cases a year – a gentle average of less than eight a week – but from 1946 onwards there was continuous growth in the workload. When Nickolls took over as director in December 1951, the staff had increased to ten and the annual caseload to 854, of which 778 were crime (including 76 drug cases) and 76 drunk-driving.

Nickolls stamped his personality on the place, becoming known as 'Old Nick'. Some of his staff also developed personal idiosyncracies. One, named Eric Sweet, achieved some notoriety as an eccentric. When attending court hearings in connection with evidence regarding sex offences, he always wore yellow socks. When the matters being dealt with involved evidence on blood grouping, his socks would always be red. Nickolls retired in 1964 and died in 1971.

CHAPTER 7
People and places

THE GROWING DEMANDS FOR ITS services drew attention to the unsuitability of the laboratory's suburban location. Recalling the problems of those days during a talk with me a few months before her retirement from her Home Office appointment, in 1988, Margaret Pereira said that, as the Metropolitan Police were not then as liberally equipped with motor vehicles as they are today, exhibits (items requiring forensic examination) were often sent to Hendon by train. This was a slow and cumbersome process, particularly with large articles. In 1948, two years after 'H₂S' Holden had taken over as its second director, the laboratory was moved to more appropriately situated quarters on the fifth, sixth and, later, seventh floors of the North Building at Scotland Yard's headquarters on the Victoria Embankment at Westminster. It was there, the following year, that a minor tragedy occurred which blemished the otherwise remarkable record of an organization noted for its safe handling of objects and substances that endanger human life.

Two youths, Trevor Humphrey Byast and Frederick Alfred Thompson, had been arrested and charged with stealing foodstuffs from a mobile canteen and with the illegal possession of a .38 revolver and ammunition. They confessed to other offences, including safebreaking, using an explosive, at a school in Hornsey, north London. They had with them some powder which they admitted was intended for safeblowing. Similar powder was found in Byast's bedroom.

Sent to the laboratory for testing, the powder was received

by Detective Sergeant John McCafferty on July 28 1949 and was passed to 38-year-old Eric Hucknall, a Senior Experimental Officer, the same day. Hucknall made a microscopic examination of a minute quantity and took the remainder, in four sample containers, into the main chemical room, where he instructed an assistant, 21-year-old John William Gordon Smith, to carry out some tests on it. In accordance with normal procedure, the four samples were put well away from the analytical bench. Having completed his work on three of the containers, Smith picked up the fourth, took it to his test bench, extracted a small amount of powder for examination and was replacing the stopper in the bottle when it exploded. He sustained severe injuries to his left hand and lacerations to his left eye, face and upper body. Working immediately opposite him, Hucknall was also cut by flying glass. A miniature crater was blasted into the teak workbench, a range of glassware was smashed, and a small fire started. The conflagration was quickly extinguished by other members of the staff and Smith and Hucknall were rushed to hospital, where Smith suffered amputation of his left hand and forearm. Happily, lessons were learned and the accident has never been repeated.

Director Holden is remembered by Margaret Pereira as 'a highly regarded palaeobotanist but a strange character who was extraordinarily mean with his personal expenditure'. She recalled, for example, his habit of proffering packets containing a single cigarette and the alacrity with which he would then accept the offer 'No, have one of mine' from impecunious young assistants. He had, however, been 'extremely supportive' of the continuing studies which brought her a first-class honours degree in 1953.

As has been noted in the previous chapter, 'Old Nick' Nickolls followed Holden as director, holding the post for 13 years after his appointment in December 1951. Of the six men who have headed the laboratory to date, he was the only one without a doctorate. It seems that a tradition of frugality was at that time being handed on by the occupants of this office, because Margaret Pereira recalls Nickolls as 'a terrible Scrooge. We had to go on and on pressing and pressing to get any new piece of equipment; you'd have thought he had to pay for it himself.'

Nickolls' successor remembers him differently. In his book *Expert Witness*, published in 1972, Hamish Walls, exercising his considerable powers of description, depicts his predecessor thus: 'He was rather perceptive and even tender-hearted, but concealed this quite ferociously under a carapace of feigned toughness and disengagement. I think that much was explained when one knew that he had found himself in the trenches in France during the 1914-18 war as a sensitive lad of 17 ... He was not an easy-going man ... He had a caustically witty tongue; for example, his opinion of a certain doctor of our acquaintance was "If I had three broken legs and saw Dr So-and-So coming to treat me, I could still run faster than he could ..." His profanity was the most luridly ingenious I have ever heard; his method of summoning a more junior member of the staff was a reverberation of colourful obscenities rolling down the laboratory corridor, with no offence intended or taken ... In spite of that, he was no linguist. I can remember an evening when the laboratory was opened to visitors after a dinner ... attended by a number of high-ranking foreign police officers ... Nickolls was showing a senior French official some apparatus set up for arson investigation and was explaining (?) it by repeating loudly "Arson! Arson!" pronounced nasally as if it were a French word, finally getting quite cross with the visitor's bewildered incomprehension. The French for arson is l'incendie criminel.'

In fairness it must be recorded that Walls' affirmation of 'no offence taken' in respect of Nickolls' style of summoning staff was not entirely correct. Shortly before her 3½-years-early retirement from the laboratory in 1987, I talked with Dawn Banks, a well-rounded, bright and jovial personality who served as personal assistant to Nickolls, Walls, and Walls' successor. Even after an interval of almost a quarter of a century, she still smouldered at the recollection of Nickolls demanding her presence by bawling her surname along the passageways. 'It used to make me so wild that I deliberately didn't answer,' she confessed. 'But that only made him shout louder! However, he was very capable. You had to be on your toes.' Having joined the staff as a clerical assistant at Scotland Yard, she had transferred to the laboratory in 1953. 'At that time the only shorthand typist here was a male, named Billy Sadler,' she told me. 'The lab was not thought to be a suitable place for female clerical staff!' Born in India – her father was an engineer in the British army – and divorced in 1972, she said she was looking forward to a quiet life in a new home she was buying in South Wales.

During his four years as director, Edinburgh-born Walls, a protégé of James Davidson, earned the gratitude of Margaret Pereira and her colleagues. 'We were able, not to go wild, but to reasonably equip the laboratory to make our lives easier, even to the extent of commissioning some things to be made, like the comparison microscope,' she remembered.

Seventy-nine-year-old Walls' own reflections on his time in forensic science were mixed when I talked with him at his home near Crystal Palace, south London, in December 1986. A tall, spare, lonely and quietly-spoken figure suffering from painful back trouble, he did not hesitate in answering my question whether, were he to have his time over again, he would choose the same career path. 'No,' he said, 'I would rather be an architect.' The greatest problem during his incumbency at the laboratory had been a shortage of qualified professional staff, he asserted. During one particularly busy period it had become necessary to ask for the assistance of one of the Home Office laboratories. With hindsight, his advice to any forensic scientist 'working with the police breathing down their neck' was: 'Keep calm.'*

The staffing problem did not remain static. As the inflow of work increased, the time needed to deal with cases – a matter of concern to police officers responsible for keeping suspects in detention and preparing evidence for their trials – began to lengthen. It became clear that, if the laboratory was to have any prospect of fulfilling its multiplying obligations in the foreseeable future, more staff in the scientific grades, and room to accommodate and equip them, were essential.

As forensic caseloads are obviously linked with the

---

* Dr Walls died in August 1988.

incidence of crime, the question of the overall longer term adequacy for police purposes of the Victoria Embankment buildings also came under review. In 1964 it was announced that the Metropolitan Police had taken a lease on a triangular arrangement of Devon granite-faced structures being erected on a site bounded by Victoria Street, Broadway and Dacre Street, Westminster. Construction within the 21-storey tower block, nine-storey block fronting to Victoria Street and seven-storey linking block was adapted to meet the specific requirements of the force. The result was a totally air-conditioned, purpose-designed environment. Following the move from Victoria Embankment, work began on converting the old buildings for use as offices by some Members of Parliament. They were reopened for that purpose in 1975, the alterations having cost an estimated £2,400,000 – as the *Daily Telegraph* pointed out 'An average of £6,500 for each of the 128 MPs and 130 secretaries'. Its report added 'The former room of Police Commissioner Viscount Trenchard, with wallpaper of the period and velvet curtains, is the new conference room.'

But circumstances made it necessary for the laboratory's relocation to precede both the total police departure from Victoria Embankment and the finding of a lasting new abode in which its mounting tasks could be discharged with dispatch. Planned as a temporary measure, its third home, for the nine years from 1965 to 1974, was in a building in Richbell Place, off Bloomsbury's Theobald's Road. It was far from ideal 'but it had its advantages', Margaret Pereira quipped. 'For one thing, we had more lavatories!'

During the Richbell Place period, in September 1968, Walls was succeeded as director by 41-year-old Oxford graduate Dr Raymond Lionel Williams. As an incumbent who was to hold the directorship for nearly two decades – far longer than the terms of office of any of his predecessors – the earlier career of this self-described ' "foreigner" with no previous experience of forensic science' is of interest.

Bournemouth-born and an only child, Williams sprang from a father and paternal grandfather who were both trousermakers. But from grammar school onwards he had wanted to get into chemistry, he told me during an interview in his flora-crowded office shortly before his retirement in November 1987.

During his early years, his 'whole outlook and perspective' had been changed by a post-doctorate fellowship he was awarded to the University of California, he confided. 'The whole idea was to promote an understanding and experience of the United States. One of the obligations was to travel for a period of time so that you could get a feel of the country, away from your actual area of expertise. I had 15 months there – 12 months at the university and three months travelling. I was given 700 dollars to cover the cost of travel. I bought an old car and drove north and south, ending up in New York on the way back to the United Kingdom. Then I had to prepare a heavy report on what I had seen.' The experience gave him 'a much more rational view of the position of the United Kingdom in the world'.

On his return home, in the mid-fifties, he found that a bleak situation prevailed for scientists. After some months of unemployment he was appointed to a senior research fellowship in the civil service and was allocated to the analytical group of the Ministry of Supply explosives research and development establishment at Waltham Abbey: 'Again one of the very fortunate happenings in my life. Many things have been examples of serendipity as far as I am concerned.'

His leader in that appointment was Lionel Bellamy, an expert on molecular microscopy. 'A very refreshing and unorthodox character; it was a great joy to work for him. We did a tremendous amount of research and published many papers.'

With Williams' marriage came the need of a matrimonial home – not easy of attainment in the post-war period of shortages. Accommodation was obtained by transferring his services from research to an analytical function, which qualified him for a house on the ministry estate. His primary task then became the analysis of explosives and propellants and the surveillance of stocks of ammunition, to determine whether they were safe for continued storage or should be destroyed. This brought him promotion from Senior Scientific

Officer to Principal Scientific Officer and the responsibility of supervising a group – his first step into management. No personal danger was incurred, he assured me, because precautionary measures were always taken: 'When you're looking at nitroglycerine you don't carry it around by the bucketful but only handle tiny amounts in the right containers and store them in the right magazines.'

For several domestic reasons, mainly because his mother had become seriously ill, he next sought and was granted a transfer to the Admiralty materials laboratory at Halton Heath, west of Bournemouth, where he was concerned with analysis of the atmosphere in nuclear submarines – a vitally important function on behalf of crews who might spend 30 or more days in uninterrupted submerged cruising. Later, while awaiting completion of another transfer, to running the materials group, he was for a time in charge of two divisions of the laboratory, controlling the work of 70 scientists.

These switches of responsibility had not created any functional problems for him, he said. 'You were still using analytical chemistry but were looking at a different sort of analyte – at long, deep, mucky molecules rather than fairly refined ones. After all, nitrocellulose is a polymer and to go from that to, say, polystyrene is not too different.'

About three years later he had been made aware that the directorship of the Metropolitan Police laboratory was becoming vacant and his application had succeeded. Despite his lack of acquaintance with the forensic world, he suffered no manifestations of resentment from his subordinates. 'In retrospect I was told they were thankful it was the devil they didn't know rather than certain people from within their sphere of operations!'

Preparations were already in progress for the move to what was intended to be the laboratory's permanent home in a purpose-built police support headquarters building planned for construction in Lambeth Road. But even then it was known that the new accommodation was going to be too small. As Williams put it, 'You could look at the rate of growth of input into the laboratory and extrapolate and say with considerable certainty that the place was going to be saturated within a short period of its occupancy.' It had been a matter of finance, he explained, in terms of the sum the Home Office was prepared to authorize. In Williams' view the then Commissioner of Police for the Metropolis, Sir Joseph Simpson, had become 'fed up with the argy-bargy and the time delaying uncertainty of administration arguments and had finally decided to crystallize the situation.' Some additional space was, in fact, wrung out of the official arbiters, but Williams did not succeed with his contention that it was nonsensical to assign a significant proportion of a prime-sited central London building to the warehousing of police stores when such things could have been dispensed with equal efficiency from prefabricated huts in the north and south of the capital. Having been persuaded to 'move in and see how things go', the laboratory had been waiting for more space ever since, Williams commented wryly. They had, however, recently secured approval for an expansion downwards from the presently-occupied two upper floors of the premises.

On taking over leadership of the laboratory he had found the organization 'totally badly structured,' he went on. 'There was no concept of line management as I had known it in Waltham Abbey days. Virtually every decision of every sort was being referred to the director.' He had experienced no union or individual opposition to his reorganization – 'getting it into the right sort of units with the right responsibilities'. The co-operation of the staff had been excellent, even though forensic scientists were 'very much individualists'. But administration was only a part of the director's functions, he stressed; it was of great importance that close attention should always be paid to anything new coming up on the horizon. He took pride in having been largely responsible for bringing scanning microscopy into the forensic world in its proper form and for having encouraged other developments, such as immunoassay.

I asked him whether, as scientific progress becomes more complex, the task of leadership in such fields as forensic investigation is also growing more intricate. He thought not. 'My feeling has always been that all fundamental science is really essentially simple, but then gets elaborate clothing built around it, rather like an onion. The seed that starts it off should be very simple. We all rely on models by which you can draw an analogy. If you can understand this basic model you ought to be able at least to talk to your experts with some degree of understanding.'

Answering a question about the disappointments he had encountered during his 19 years at the laboratory, Williams said that his greatest regret was that the value of forensic science had never been fully acknowledged by the Home Office or the government. It was not only a matter that the salaries paid to professional and administrative grades in the civil service were greater than those received by scientific staff. The trend of officialdom over the past few years had been to believe that anybody could do forensic work; in consequence, the responsibilities of the scientific expert were sometimes ignored.

When I inquired what he would say if asked to leave a piece of succinct advice for his successor, he said that this was not an action he would dare, or care, to take. 'It is up to every individual to manage according to their own standards. But I think one would prefer to run a fairly easy-going setup, in the sense that it is no good using a disciplinarian system. It is much better to persuade and to listen to what other people have to say first of all. Obviously, you have got to make up your own mind sooner or later, but very often people see problems from a totally different angle. You can be quite unappreciative of this and might possibly change your thinking if you were aware of it.

'The other thing of which scientists are sometimes unaware is that we are only one factor in the operation of a police force. Although it might seem glaringly obvious to me that I must have so much money and so much space, it might well be that there are other very serious and profound reasons elsewhere which prevent this happening. It is useful to understand this if you're having a fight, because it helps you to know what the strengths and weaknesses of your rivals' cases are. You have to appreciate that it is not just what goes on here that dictates how you operate. One of the nice things about having worked in other organizations is that you do understand that there are other important factors.'

It was clear that the frustrations he had suffered had not destroyed his sense of humour. When I asked how he intended to occupy his leisure in retirement, he said that he hoped to spend more time in court. 'Listening to expertly-rendered forensic evidence?' I queried. 'No, playing tennis' he replied.

Small and slim, with straight, swept-back, thinning and greying dark hair and quick in speech and movement, Williams has a talent for descriptive terminology. Describing his animation when indicating how a matrix of evidential connections can come together and point clearly in one direction, *Sunday Times* writer Malcolm Brown reported 'Williams' highest praise for a piece of scientific deduction is that it is "elegant".' Calling this 'a slight misquotation', Williams told me that his meaning was that he would take pleasure from achieving an end 'using something very simple which gave you exactly what you were looking for with the minimum of effort'. The route to 'elegance' that he had in mind was to pick up something which didn't cost very much and of which it could be said 'Why the hell didn't we think of this before?'

Many things had to be thought of in preparing for relocation in the laboratory's share of the new building in Lambeth. Section-by-section schemes were drawn up by senior staff, including Margaret Pereira. For her, it was history repeating itself, because she had already contributed towards fitting the laboratory into its Victoria Embankment and Richbell Place quarters. Looking back on her involvement with the layout of the biology section at Lambeth, she told me that, had she had the opportunity of seeing the Home Office laboratory at Chorley before drawing up her design, she would have recommended inclusion of some of the ideas which had since been adopted in most Home Office forensic establishments. She mentioned, as an example, the use of reinforced glazing rather than solid walls for internal partitioning, a system which admitted more light and stimulated a friendly atmosphere.

Accompanied by its improvements and imperfections, the move to Lambeth took place in 1974. 'At that time the new site seemed like a palace but within five years the accommodation has become too small and moves are afoot to provide yet more space,' Williams wrote later.

Turning again to personalities, I asked Margaret Pereira what, in her estimation, had been the greatest success of her outstanding career. My underlying thought was that she would nominate one of the many cases in which her constantly-advancing expertise in serology had produced evidence which provided the key to some otherwise intractable mystery. Instead, with little hesitation, she exclaimed 'My long fight to break through the sex barrier.' Explaining, she said 'My career was totally limited by being a woman. When I got my degree in 1953 I had six years of forensic experience behind me, but I was not allowed to become an expert witness and had to train new members of staff and then act as their assistant. I was very cross and embittered.' Faced with her protests, Nickolls had told her that he was entirely opposed to putting a woman into the witness box because he believed she would break down and weep under cross-examination. She would also be going through the menopause, he told the 25-year-old, when she certainly wouldn't be able to cope. 'By this time I probably knew more about the blood field than anyone else in the laboratory, but I was not allowed to give evidence about it.'

Nickolls was, in her view, representing the establishment attitude rather than pursuing any deeply-held personal conviction of his own. He finally relented on the 'expert witness' issue after he had heard her capabilities with the spoken word during a visit to the laboratory by members of the Medico-Legal Society.

Public discussion of abhorrent sexual aberrations would never cause her embarrassment, she assured me. 'I have been concentrating on those things; they are almost bread and butter to me. When you work on them every day they become commonplace. It is other people who are embarrassed.'

In this connection she remembered that her breakthrough into court procedure had soon produced another problem. The day after giving forensic data in the prosecution of two homosexuals she was called to the director's office and told that the judge had complained that he had been highly discomposed by hearing a woman giving evidence in such a case. For her part, aside from the shock of receiving such a judicial reaction, she had found the proceedings amusing. The active male had pleaded not guilty to the charge, while the passive partner had admitted the offence. The former claimed that, after he had gone into an alleyway to urinate, the second individual had entered the passageway backwards, with his trousers down! Because of her presence, said the judge, the court had felt unable to put any penetrating questions to probe the reality of this story.

Yet the outcome pleased her: 'For some years after that I didn't do any more of these boring sex cases but concentrated on the big, bloody murders, which were more interesting.' Another memory of her witness-box appearances concerned a murder case in which Quintin Hogg (now Lord Hailsham) was conducting the defence. He was clearly ready for a challenge, but he lost his case.

An engineer's daughter who married an engineer, she left the Metropolitan Police laboratory in March 1976 to become deputy director of the Home Office forensic science establishment at Aldermaston. She described her entry into the forensic world as 'totally by accident, as a lot of jobs are'. It suited her because she had always enjoyed a search: 'I am quite tenacious once I am onto something. I like to see things through to the end.' Her 'quite unexpected' and rapid rise, via directorships at Aldermaston and Chepstow, to the administrative pinnacle as the officer in charge of the six (formerly eight) Home Office forensic science laboratories throughout the country was 'an evolution rather than a sudden transition' which had followed her increasing involvement in management. She became controller in 1982. In her early days, attainment of the rank of Principal Scientific Officer had been the highest goal she had envisaged.

When I asked whether she had enjoyed her responsibilities with the Home Office, she answered that it was necessary to choose her words carefully – 'I must be a good civil servant!' It had, however, been 'a terrible job, far worse than I ever foresaw'. The service had, she explained, been extremely difficult to run with all the setbacks and restraints that had been imposed. Not least among her worries had been Treasury-inspired efforts to downgrade all the staff. The questions that had arisen concerning the quality of work done by a former Home Office forensic scientist had also contributed to her problems. She had had 'a lot of battles'.

At least one of her male colleagues at the Metropolitan Police laboratory sympathized with the resentment she felt concerning the obstruction she suffered during her early days there. Chemist David Ellen told me that, when he began work at the laboratory as an Assistant Experimental Officer in October 1953, 'Margaret had got her results, a good honours degree, which qualified you for promotion to the Scientific Officer class. They were the honours types, while we were not. But she was told that such promotion would involve being a reporting officer and going to court and a woman couldn't be allowed to do that, especially in biology. So she was offered promotion in the Experimental Officer class.' The injustice of the situation had been highlighted by the contemporaneous recruitment, straight from university, of a male honours graduate who had been given immediate Scientific Officer status.

Fifty-six-year-old bachelor Ellen was the oldest remaining scientific inhabitant of the laboratory when I talked with him there in May 1986. His departure to Adelaide, South Australia, on a two-year contract for forensic work, was imminent. He told me that his first task in the 1950s had been to examine motor cars for erased engine and body numbers. In the car-starved years after the war, vehicles of pre-war manufacture sold for three times their original price, creating many opportunities for thieves and con-men.

Of the experiences during his 14 years in chemical investigation, one that lingered in his memory was the deaths at sea of two heavily over-insured racehorses. Their bodies had, quite properly, been dumped overboard in mid-Atlantic. During the inquiries, a police officer talked with a crewman who had helped with disposal of the carcasses. After remarking on the waste entailed in abandoning the harness, he received the answer 'Oh, it wasn't left on the horses. I've got it.' On examining a halter, Ellen found a food stain. A test of the stain revealed the presence of strychnine, then a much-favoured substance for killing animals.

On another toxicological issue, Ellen remembered his work in the widely-publicized case of Dr John Bodkin Adams, an Eastbourne, Sussex, general medical practitioner who was accused of killing some elderly, ailing female patients after becoming a beneficiary in their wills.

After transferring to the Documents Section on its foundation in 1968, Ellen became its head in 1974. At the time of writing, this unit employs 14 scientists. 'We have nothing to do with the pseudo-science of graphology,' Ellen stated firmly. 'And another mistake that is commonly made is that we are the section that keeps the laboratory's records!' His training in the section's work was obtained from its previous head, Max Fryd, now over 80 and still working as a document examiner from his home near Farnham, Surrey. Ellen described his team's functions as 'Varied, but mostly connected with suspected fraud – cheques and more complicated matters. We also deal with quite a number of anonymous letters and cases requiring comparisons of handwriting.'

In December 1969 and January 1970 the section had the task of examining notes purporting to have come from 55-year-old Wimbledon housewife Muriel McKay, kidnapped by Trinidad-born brothers Arthur and Nizam Hosein in mistake for the wife of Australian newspaper tycoon Rupert Murdoch. The notes were found to be genuine, showing that, at the time, the unfortunate woman was surviving her ordeal. But her captors finally disposed of her so effectively that her body has never been found. Caught when trying to collect the ransom money, the Hoseins were sentenced to life imprisonment in October 1970.

Terrorist bombing plans, the chemistry, physical absorption and dye content of inks, and the surprising individualism of typewriter typefaces are other matters examined by the Documents Section. The laboratory led the world, Ellen claimed, in the study of indented impressions – marks left on material under the paper being written on. In co-operation with the London College of Printing, the laboratory developed a method called ESDA (Electrostatic Detection Apparatus) which has been adopted internationally for reading impressions invisible to the naked eye. It exploits the fact that impressions, however slight, cause lasting effects on paper – 'probably internal damage to the fibres', said Ellen. He explained that the ESDA technique consists of putting the document to be examined on a metal box, into which it is sucked by vacuum and covered with a thin layer of plastic. The top surface is then charged with a high voltage on a thin wire, producing an effect which delineates the impressions with photocopying toner. The device has been highly successful in several investigations of terrorist activity. Ellen is the author of a book, *The Scientific Examination of Documents*, published by Ellis Horwood.

Williams' successor as director, 46-year-old Dr Brian Sheard, took office at the laboratory in January 1988. Born in Dewsbury, Yorkshire, he was for 14 years research manager with the pharmaceuticals division of Imperial Chemical Industries plc, based at Macclesfield, in his home county. As, on his arrival, Williams had been, a 'foreigner' to forensic science, he was immediately confronted by the same difficulty that faced his predecessor – how to carry ever-growing case and workloads with staff, accommodation and equipment resources which do not keep pace with demand. Symptomatic of the problem, a few weeks after his arrival the correspondence columns of the *Guardian* included letters from London solicitors complaining of delays in the provision of forensic evidence to support charges being made against their clients. 'One has only to spend a morning in any London magistrates' court to realize that defendants both in custody and on bail are encountering excessive delays caused by the absence of crucial forensic evidence,' wrote Brian Spiro of Simons Muirhead and Burton, of Bedford Street. He went on to allege that 'police bail' was being granted for periods of up to six months due to the backlog of work in the forensic laboratory. Richard Hallmark of the Brixton firm Hallmark Atkinson Wynter claimed to have a client who had waited 24 weeks for the analysis of suspected drugs and another, facing a murder charge, who had been waiting for more than six months for fingerprint and other scientific evidence.

It seems unlikely that Dr Sheard will ever find it necessary to search for administrative quandaries to solve.

CHAPTER 8

Police and scientists: a vital relationship

FACTS CANNOT BE GAINSAID. Nor, in a work of this nature, may they be hidden or ignored. For these reasons it is necessary to consider the past and present condition of a cardinal component in the machinery of detecting and ascribing crime in London: the relationship between the police of the metropolis and their forensic scientist colleagues. It is a subject of which the impartial observer, belonging to neither camp – in this instance myself – may, perhaps, claim to see the least prejudiced picture.

Little purpose would be served by introducing any lengthy discussion as to the desirability or otherwise of a revised administrative system under which the laboratory could be removed from direct association with the police. Whilst possibly ameliorating the anxieties sometimes expressed by lawyers defending those accused of criminal offences, such an arrangement would be unlikely to aid the laboratory's efficiency or economy. It could certainly not improve upon the present scrupulous standards of impartiality that are observed by its scientists. Since any change of this kind appears improbable within the foreseeable future, the topic merits no further space here.

Nevertheless, it must be acknowledged that the decision to establish the laboratory at the college at Hendon did nothing to smooth the way towards its acceptance by the 'old guard' of the capital's police. As has already been mentioned, many officers viewed the arrival of the college with deep mistrust. Undoubtedly, the fact that the laboratory was created within the college precincts was a factor in leading the already entrenched critics to see the scientific newcomer in a similar light.

It is not difficult to appreciate the innate delicacy of a working partnership involving, on the one hand, people schooled in militaristic disciplines, whose thoughts and actions are governed by an all-embracing code of rigidly-applied regulations and, on the other, persons trained and qualified in pursuits that are often incomprehensible to the layman, specialists educated to be constantly questioning traditional concepts and seeking always to advance the frontiers of human knowledge.

At the functional level there is obviously some possibility that forensic scientists may appear to be an uppish elite who are so enveloped by their own specialisms that they give insufficient attention to the more down-to-earth problems of the police. Similarly, the scientists may sometimes be tempted to see police officers as tiresome and unappreciative of the precision required in the work of expert forensic witnesses.

The early years of this relationship were undoubtedly very difficult. The faults were by no means all attributable to the anti-laboratory prejudices within the force. The first director of the laboratory, Dr James Davidson, was more than once heard by his colleagues to give vent to his feelings about policemen in moments of exasperation, rolling his r's with Scottish emphasis as he exclaimed 'These crreaturres ...!'

Something of the other side of the coin was conveyed in a book published in 1975 – *Mac, I've Got a Murder* – by John McCafferty, who was recruited, after 13 years on the Metropolitan force, as a detective sergeant, from the CID to be deputy to Detective Chief Inspector Cyril Cuthbert, the laboratory's first police liaison officer. McCafferty worked at the laboratory for 26 years, switching from liaison duties and reaching the rank of Principal Scientific Officer in charge of the Firearms Section before his retirement.

An open admirer of Cuthbert – '[He] was an exceptionally gifted officer. He had an eye for mistakes and was superb at administration' – he was less impressed by the setup in the laboratory. So far from endorsing the eulogy published by the

Police Review, he described the commencement of operations as 'primitive' and added 'Equipment and chemical stock wouldn't have fetched more than £200 or £300 in a sale.'

It was 'not unknown' for frictions to develop between police officers and scientists, McCafferty declared. He had 'found it difficult to ignore completely the sideways glances or the grunted responses to the most civil questions on my part concerning, for instance, a technique being used to examine an exhibit that had been brought to the laboratory or a request from a detective kicking his heels outside.' He confessed that he had 'fumed' when a senior scientist objected to his addressing a female member of the staff by her first name. 'I found myself thinking ... that if we couldn't get liaison working *inside* the laboratory, how in God's name were we to achieve the other half of this vital partnership,' he wrote.

But his first attendance, with Cuthbert, at a scene of crime showed him that there were problems to be faced on the other side as well. A woman had been found battered to death behind the counter of her north London shop. When Cuthbert and McCafferty arrived: 'The body was ... obscured by no less than 15 investigators – detectives, pathologist, fingerprint and photographic staff, assistants and so on.' 'We won't be going in there yet awhile,' Cuthbert told him. 'There seems to be very little point in making the figure up to 17.'

It was, McCafferty observed, 'A sorry but classic illustration of an investigating officer not fully realizing the value of a minute examination not only of the body and clothing but also of every inch of the surrounding area for anything that the scientists could get to work on.'

McCafferty also recounted a story describing an innocent failing on his part and the unambiguous language that is important in the world of science. Divisional Detective Inspector Shelley Symes, investigating the disappearance of Chelsea hotel resident Mrs Durand Deacon, had interviewed a suspect, John George Haigh, who had told him that he had disposed of Mrs Deacon and others by dissolving their bodies in sulphuric acid. Haigh's impudent contention that, as no bodies could be found, he could not be charged with the killings, proved fallacious, because remains identified as belonging to the unfortunate woman led to his conviction and execution for her murder. But, before these events, Symes found it difficult to believe Haigh's statement. He telephoned McCafferty and asked whether a human body could be dissolved in sulphuric acid. Knowing of a toxicological process in which acid was used to dispose of body tissue in searches for poisons, McCafferty answered that it was possible, providing that sufficient acid was available for the purpose.

A few hours later he was confronted by a furiously angry senior chemist. 'He accused me of grossly misleading a police officer, of telling him something that was wholly untrue scientifically and of putting him completely and utterly on the wrong track so far as his inquiries were concerned.'.

It appeared that, unsuccessful in reaching McCafferty with a second telephone call, Symes had spoken with the chemist and told him what McCafferty had said. 'The chemist had hit the roof. It couldn't be done, he said. You couldn't dissolve a body that way. To a scientist, you see, the word "dissolve" means just that. If, for example, you put a substance like sugar into tea or salt into water, the liquid becomes clear and stays clear after the substance has dissolved. I had accepted the word loosely: in layman's language it could also be taken to mean "disappear" or "digest", but not to a chemist.'

Parts of Haigh's yard at Crawley, Sussex, were found to be covered with sludge resembling river mud. It was the undissolved remains of his victims. Dentures identified as having been made for Mrs Durand Deacon had resisted the acid and were found in the mire.

As a liaison officer, McCafferty was conscious of his duty to bring policemen and scientists together. Realizing that much needed to be done to educate police officers as to what was going on in scientific minds, he was also aware of the necessity to acquaint the scientists with the problems confronting the police. Tending towards the belief that most misunderstandings were the fault of the experts – a predictable point of view on the part of a police officer – he accused them of having 'a habit of hiding behind their expertise at times, of not expressing it to their police colleagues in terms that a layman could understand. It was almost as though they felt there would be a loss of dignity if they did – that in some way it would rob them of their mystique.'

Clearly no slouch at seizing examples to prove his points, he declared '... the question can be more important than the answer, as the correct answer to the wrong question solves nothing ... Haigh might have got away with it for a while at least, if the first question, as put to me, had been answered by a scientist. If Shelley Symes had said to the senior chemist "I have a man here who says he has dissolved bodies in sulphuric acid", the chemist's reaction might well have been "Well, for Pete's sake, I'll be pleased if he'll tell me how he does it, because I can't do it".'

In the laboratory's work, it was necessary to know why a police officer was asking his questions, McCafferty affirmed; '... a good fifty per cent of the time he turns out to be asking the wrong ones.' Science had reached a stage at which an interpreter was vital: 'The scientist is so divorced from the layman's thinking that quite ordinary expressions used by the man in the street have an entirely different, specialized meaning in the scientific world, which of course has its own highly specialized and complicated language. Often questions are not asked solely to avoid the appearance of ignorance, when in fact you often have to ask simple questions to avoid *being* ignorant.'

Expanding on this theme, he added 'I am a hundred per cent certain that in many cases not only the jury but also the judge did not – could not – understand technical evidence and as a result ignored or understressed it when the time came for assessing what the case was all about ... I believe that if the jury had been able to comprehend the true importance of what a scientist was saying, there would, in many cases, have been a conviction and not an acquittal.'

But, in the early days, his police colleagues had by no means been blameless. Even after they 'came round to our way of thinking', scientific tests would be nullified because officers had failed to grasp exactly what was needed of them. 'For instance, we taught police that the clothing of a criminal would probably be contaminated with traces of material from the scene of his crime. These could be too minute to see, but could prove ample for the scientist to identify with control samples of material from the scene of the crime. Thus, in theory, all the officer had to do was to bring the clothing and the samples to the laboratory, where a scientific examination would determine whether or not he had the right suspect.'

In practice, things had not, at the beginning, been that simple. Lacking facilities for packing exhibits, officers had had to beg or buy, from their own pockets, such things as wrapping paper and boxes. On occasion they had used old envelopes or newspaper. Many exhibits of powdery substances had leaked away through the unsealed gaps at envelope corners.

It had not been easy to convey guidance on these matters to all officers, McCafferty reported, but it had been harder still to get official purse strings opened to enable suitable packaging and containers to be provided. Happily, this had eventually been achieved and ample material was now made available.

The passage of years has done much to lubricate the association of the disparate partners in London's forensic science service. Improved education on the one hand and greater understanding on the other have brought about a more harmonious, and therefore more effective, working relationship which must redound to the credit of all. Had that progress not been made, the task of combating the growth of crime in the capital would be far more formidable than it is.

CHAPTER 9
Staff, structure, skills and hazards

THE METROPOLITAN POLICE FORENSIC SCIENCE LABORA-
TORY is part of Scotland Yard's 'C' (Criminal Investigations)
department. At the time of writing the laboratory has a
complement of 210 scientists, of whom 150 are graduates.
Fifty have a doctorate degree. The clerical and other
supporting staff total 40. Although employed by the police, all
are civilians. Their terms and conditions of service follow Civil
Service practice, but they are not civil servants in the strictest
sense because their salaries are not paid wholly from
Exchequer funds. Their range of seniority conforms with the
grading system of the Civil Service. It is headed by the
director, as a Deputy Chief Scientific Officer (equivalent to a
Deputy Assistant Commissioner, fourth in line from the
Commissioner, the head of the force). The laboratory's four
deputy directors hold the rank of Senior Principal Scientific
Officer and their scientific assistants range downwards at six
levels: Principal Scientific Officer, Senior Scientific Officer,
Higher Scientific Officer, Scientific Officer, Assistant
Scientific Officer and Laboratory Assistant.

The scientific staff are further categorized into four groups
related to the principal tasks each performs. These are (1)
reporting officers, (2) research workers, (3) specialists, and (4)
assistants. Reporting officers are responsible for deciding what
is to be done with material submitted to the laboratory, for
directing the work of other grades and for giving evidence in
court. Research workers are involved in short term 'trouble
shooting' or long term development work. Specialists provide

a service to reporting officers, having developed skills in relation to certain equipment, such as the scanning electron microscope and mass spectrometer. Assistants carry out the bulk of the bench work, under the supervision of the other officers.

Functionally, the laboratory organization is separated into four divisions, General and Administration, Chemistry I, Chemistry II and Biology. Each is headed by a deputy director.

Employing 27 scientists, five photographers and three fingerprint officers, the General and Administration Division is responsible for work on suspect documents (examinations for the discovery of forgeries or falsifications, the comparison of handwriting and typescript, etc.); for the examination, testing and comparison of bullets, firearms and other weapons; for the detection of marks and latent evidence in serious crime; for photographic work (including the production of evidence to show that specific films were shot in particular cameras) and for the provision of information, computer, and library services.

The two chemistry divisions employ a total of 124 scientists. Chemistry I deals with criminalistics (the comparison of glass, paint and other contact traces); the examination of footwear and manufacturing marks; the indexation of marks from unsolved crimes; physics and metallurgy (the investigation of traffic accidents, counterfeiting, fraud and malicious damage; tachographs and erased numbers on vehicles engines); geology (the comparison of soils); investigation of the causes of fires and development work and support services.

Chemistry II is responsible for work on drugs and toxicology (the analysis of body organs for the identification of poisons, the checking of chemicals, suspected food and other substances, etc.); for the examination of blood and urine samples concerning alcohol in relation to road traffic offences; for electron microscopy (dealing with very small traces of paint, gunshot residues and the like) and for research, development and specialized equipment, such as the scanning electron microscope.

The Biology Division is also concerned with research and

development in its field, which encompasses the comparison of contact traces in offences against the person (fibres, body fluids, etc.) and includes the identification and grouping of blood, saliva, semen, etc; botanical examinations (fragments of vegetation, sawdust ballast from safes, etc.) and the maintenance of computerized blood and sexual assault indexes.

Most of the material that is submitted for examination at the laboratory (called 'exhibits') is first retrieved and administratively processed by scenes of crime officers, of whom there are 200. Thirteen police officers (detective sergeants, working under the supervision of a detective inspector) carry out liaison duties at the laboratory. They have a dual role, being (a) intermediaries between officers conducting investigations and the laboratory's scientific staff, and (b) acting as scenes of crime officers.

As well as receiving items submitted for examination, the duties of these individuals include explaining the investigating officers' needs to the scientists and the scientists' requirements to the investigating officers. They also answer inquiries in connection with scientific examinations and arrange court dates, etc. Some of the liaison officers are posted to cover the four Metropolitan Police districts of London, to attend the scenes of serious crimes, such as murder, and to collect and pack items for transmission to the laboratory. The scale of these tasks can be appreciated when it is realized that the geographical area of Metropolitan Police responsibility totals nearly 800 square miles, covering a population in excess of 10 million people.

All items brought to the laboratory by the police are accompanied by a standard proforma, setting out the relevant details. It is the duty of the police liaison staff to check these particulars, to see that no unnecessary items are submitted, to discuss any peculiarities of the case with the investigating officer and to allocate the case to the appropriate division of the laboratory.

The choice of the latter is determined by the nature of the crime, since it is this that creates the crucial evidential items.

In general terms it can be said that anything which is of living origin, however remote, is within the province of biology, whereas an item of inanimate provenance indicates chemistry as the right discipline for its examination. Thus, crimes against the person, producing items such as blood, seminal, or saliva stains, are primarily for the forensic biologist, whilst cases of breaking and entering, with paint or glass as the main contract traces, are the concern of the chemist. There are obvious exceptions to this broad principle, because chemists examine drugs which may have come from plants and biologists may deal with synthetic fibres.

Not infrequently, and especially with very complex cases, all the divisions of the laboratory may be involved. In these instances the case is 'split' and a scientist from each division carries out an examination according to their specialism. Where there is the likelihood of an overlap of interests, for example in the searching of a garment for both bloodstains and paint fragments, this is carried out jointly by the two scientists of the appropriate disciplines in order to avoid possible damage to the exhibit by conflicting methods.

The forensic scientist is usually concerned with finding answers to three questions about the item being examined: (1) What is it? (e.g., is the stain blood?); (2) Is the item found on the suspect identical with a similar one from the scene of the crime? (e.g., is the blood of the same group?); (3) If so, what are the chances that the identity is accidental? (e.g., how common is that particular blood group?)

The scientist therefore carries out such tests as are thought appropriate, writing up the findings in the form of a statement containing a list of the evidential items received and the results of the examination, with a brief statement of the significance of the facts discovered.

Some work in forensic science entails exposure to certain hazards. Apart from the apparent physical dangers which may be encountered at the scenes of crime (for example, during the investigation of suspected arson in severely damaged premises), there are more subtle, but equally ominous, minacities. Chief among these are (a) the risks entailed in handling items taken from persons suffering from infectious and/or obnoxious ailments, such as hepatitis, tuberculosis, venereal disease, scabies, lice, vaginal thrush, trichomoniasis, threadworm, etc., and (b) the inspection or employment of dangerous chemicals. More recently, the menace of Acquired Immune Deficiency Syndrome ('Aids') has appeared on the scene. It imposes a need for particular care when dealing with body fluids in some cases of drug abuse and homosexuality. A comprehensive code of precautions is incorporated in the laboratory's regulations, coupled with a full range of protective clothing, equipment and advice.

These 'dangers of the trade' are shared by male and female scientists alike; no special protection is offered to the fair sex. And, so far from the early days of Margaret Pereira when females were involuntarily 'shielded' from contact with the uglier facts of criminality, the laboratory now employs nearly 100 women, of whom over half are members of the scientific staff.

In common with most countries practising an accusatorial legal system (e.g., Australia, Canada, Denmark, India, Israel, Sweden and the USA) the minimal qualification required in England for the majority of forensic scientists whose duties include appearances in court to present evidence for the prosecution is a bachelor of science degree. (An exception is Pakistan, where such testimony has to be given by the head of the laboratory.)

Many countries practising an inquisitorial legal system (e.g. Argentina, Belgium, Brazil, Finland, France, Germany, Greece, Italy, Japan, Poland, Spain, Switzerland and Yugoslavia) require a similar level of academic qualification for expert witnesses, but some demand higher, and others lower, standards. In nearly every case the further training, in forensic techniques, of scientists recruited into the service is obtained from their superiors in the laboratories.

Describing the collection of this internationally comparative information, in a paper presented to the sixth international meeting of forensic scientists held in Edinburgh in 1972, Dr Raymond Williams, then director of the Metropolitan Police laboratory, said that he had sent a questionnaire to 64 forensic science laboratories, representing 55 of the 78 countries included in the *World List of Forensic Science Laboratories* published by the Forensic Science Society. When only 32 replies were received, the set of questions had been resubmitted to 30 countries through Interpol. This had produced a further 18 responses. The data therefore covered 51 laboratories in 43 countries.

The 'accusatorial system' countries had been much more self-critical than the 'inquisitorial', Williams affirmed. The crucial problems had appeared to be lack of uniformity of forensic skills and methods, coupled with a shortage of training facilities. Since the demand for forensic scientists was relatively small, it would not be sensible to set up separate facilities in universities, he concluded. A more practical solution would be to have national institutes of forensic science, which would undertake both training and research.

CHAPTER 10

Experts in court

ALTHOUGH THE *RAISON D'ÊTRE* of forensic scientists is the provision of evidence to assist the administration of justice, their work does not always lead to appearance in court. Sometimes, when findings point inescapably to guilt, defendants admit their culpability, making it unnecessary for testimony to be given from the witness box. Equally, scientific examination may result in the clearing of a suspect or in the discovery of nothing of value to either side.

When oral evidence has to be given during court hearings, forensic scientists' statements are normally based on written reports which have been provided to the police some time earlier. These record the results of the tests and examinations that have been carried out. In one respect, the delivery of these expert attestations differs profoundly from that of the ordinary witness of fact, in that scientists are not only allowed, but are often asked, to give opinions as to the significance of the material they present.

A distinguished advocate, Leonard Caplan QC, president of the Medico-Legal Society from 1960 to 1963, declared that what the law requires of experts is clarity, relevancy and reliability. They must, he said, remember that, on their own subjects, they are probably better informed than anyone else in court. They must, therefore, eschew unnecessary technical jargon and scrupulously avoid giving the impression that they are trying to 'blind with science'. Explanatory lecturettes must be omitted unless asked for. Most important of all, the court must be left with the feeling that it has listened to a person of absolute integrity whose opinions have been formed with meticulous care and whose declaration of facts is founded on every possible precaution to avoid error.

In his book *Forensic Science*, published by Sweet and Maxwell in 1968, Dr Hamish Walls (director of the Metropolitan Police laboratory from 1964 to 1968) wrote that he considered it a tribute to the quality of expert evidence in Britain that Caplan was able to take for granted a qualification which no reputable expert could even appear to lack – absolute impartiality. 'It is as rare, in the British courts at least, for an expert witness to be attacked on the ground that he is biased as on that he is incompetent,' Walls went on. 'It may be suggested to him that he is mistaken; that, of course, is a possibility which he must always admit, but it is then open to him to draw attention politely to the length of his experience and to the number of confirmatory tests which he has (or should have) made before he testifies to anything factual – reliability again. He must, of course, admit at once the possibility of another expert forming a different opinion from the same facts, but he should modestly but firmly stick to his own; if he cannot honestly do so, he should not have expressed it in the first place. If the witness is a senior and experienced man in his own profession, it can also happen that some previously published statement of his own which seems to be at variance with what he is now saying in the witness box is quoted against him; a famous medical expert in that situation made the classic reply: "Medicine advances with the times and I endeavour to keep pace with its progress".'

A less sanguine view of such medicinal headway was taken by Dr John Havard, a barrister-at-law and medical man who, 19 years later, became secretary of the British Medical Association. In the introduction to his book *The Detection of Secret Homicide*, published by Macmillan & Co Ltd in 1960, he informed his readers that the work was concerned 'simply with the problem of ensuring that deaths resulting from homicide are not disposed of as cases of natural death' and added '... a substantial proportion of cases of homicide are accompanied by an attempt to get the death certified and registered, and to get the body disposed of through the normal channels as a natural death. The inflated publicity accorded to murders where travelling trunks, acid baths, lime burials and other irregular methods of disposal are employed, may lead us to overlook the fact that these methods are rarely used by the resourceful murderer. The number of cases in which the discovery that the body of a murdered person has been disposed of as a natural death has only been made as a result of investigations into a later and recognised murder, allow us to assume that many murderers must be entirely successful in avoiding detection.

'Most crimes are brought to light as a result of a complaint laid by the victim, and it is hardly necessary to point out that it is precisely in homicide that the victim, except in rare instances, is unable to raise the alarm or give information concerning the circumstances.'

Noting that the Coroners' Rules of 1953 recommended that medico-legal autopsies should be carried out by pathologists with suitable qualifications and experience, he asserted that, in most rural areas, the advice was being widely disregarded, because *post mortem* examinations were being made by general practitioners with no special training in forensic pathology. Thus: 'In our courts of law general practitioners and other medical men ... give evidence on medico-legal matters on which they have little knowledge, a practice which would be forbidden in most other European countries today.'

Discussing the belated reception of legal medicine in England, Havard observed 'The most surprising feature of the development of our medico-legal investigative system has been the delay in our recognition of principles which had been accepted on the Continent for many hundreds of years. Medico-legal autopsies were being carried out in the Italian states and the North German towns more than five centuries before any provision existed for the production of medical evidence at coroners' inquests in England. Autopsies in cases of suspected poisoning were carried out in Bologna in 1302, at Sienna in 1348 and had been authorised at Montepellier by 1377. Contemporary with these developments was the limitation by statute of the giving of medical evidence in courts of law to medical men recognised as experienced in medico-legal matters, a principle which still awaits recognition in this country.'

In England, until little more than 100 years ago, coroners' inquests had been 'dictated entirely by the rules which had grown up around the various obsolete institutions which had been attached to sudden death during the medieval period,' he went on. 'As late as 1832 a standard work on medical jurisprudence considered it doubtful if the coroner even had power to order a *post mortem* examination of a body. So, for centuries, coroners and their juries were reaching their verdicts on cases of sudden death almost entirely unencumbered by medical evidence of the cause of death.

'Contemporary with the late reception of medical evidence at coroners' inquests was the delay in the acceptance of the principles of legal medicine by our own medical profession. Chief amongst the reasons for this must have been the reluctance with which our universities abandoned the theoretical approach to the study of medicine in favour of a practical anatomical method. Anatomical dissection, forbidden by the Church since the time of Galen, had been re-introduced on the Continent at least as early as the 13th century, when Thaddeus of Florence is known to have introduced a practical method.'

Bearing in mind that contemporary medical evidence would not have been of great use to the furtherance of justice, it was perhaps as well that English courts had been slow in accepting medical men as expert witnesses, Havard commented. The existence of the coroner's inquest as a medico-legal investigation had become possible only after 1836, when provision was made for the payment of medical witnesses and for *post mortem* examination and toxicological analysis. By that time the need had become imperative owing to the increase in crimes of violence which had followed the industrial revolution. But its effective introduction had still been postponed for a further generation by the obstruction put up by the justices in quarter sessions, a policy which they pursued relentlessly.

One of Havard's 28-year-old statements was updated in a letter he sent to me in August 1988, 11 months before he was due to retire from the BMA. Answering a question I had asked about the current performance of autopsies in rural areas, he wrote '...I think it is unlikely that any *post mortems* are still carried out by general medical practitioners. However, there must be a large number carried out by clinical pathologists with little knowledge of forensic pathology.'

Referring to the situation of expert witnesses vis à vis the law, the perceptive Walls added the following reflection in his book: 'The main cause of any genuine difficulty in which the conscientious and experienced expert witness may find himself is the different mental attitudes of lawyers and scientists. In many years' experience in the witness box, the writer has come to the conclusion that lawyers think of science as a body of facts which, once established, are embodied for evermore in the corpus of knowledge. Science was, of course, never like that, and modern science is even less like it. Science today ... is moving away from the concept of a Universe conforming to a system of rigid absolute laws to one in which all laws are matters of statistical probability. For the scientist, the true business of science is the formulation and testing of hypotheses about the physical world. The testing involves finding out facts, and he accepts provisionally that hypothesis which seems, on a balance of probability, to fit them. They themselves are only a means to an end.

'Now, although it is true that most scientific expert evidence deals with quite elementary facts ascertained by the discipline of science, it is this fundamentally different approach to the value of facts which produces these differences in mental attitudes. Lawyers tend, in the writer's experience, to approach scientific matters with suspicion, and he believes that he has observed this reaction even in the most eminent and brilliant of them. In fact, the scientist's attitude to his science is much more like the lawyer's to his case than the latter seems to realize ...

'The modern view of some philosophers of science is that no hypothesis can ever be *proved* in strict logic; it can always at any time be *disproved* by the discovery of a fact inconsistent with it, but in the absence of any such facts all that we can logically do is to accept it as provisionally established, more or less firmly according to the amount and reliability of the information tending to demonstrate its truth. The situation seems ... very much like that which a jury faces when they are directed to arrive at a verdict. It is certainly that facing the forensic scientist in his laboratory. If the hypothesis has been formulated that this jemmy was used to commit this housebreaking, then one single fact – such as that it is the wrong size for the mark left in the window frame – may suffice to disprove the hypothesis; on the other hand, it can never be proved with logical finality that no other jemmy could have been used; at the best, there may be such a body of facts – matching of scratch marks, coincidence of unusual paints and so forth – tending to establish the truth of the hypothesis that the only practically tenable conclusion is that the hypothesis is proved "beyond all reasonable doubt".'

A more youthful approach to the subject of the divided thinking of lawyers and scientists was included in a 49-page memorandum, *The Criminal Courts, Criminal Law and Evidence*, written in 1981 for the guidance of her colleagues by Dr Ann Priston, a biologist at the Metropolitan Police laboratory. A dedicated part-time student of English law, she wrote 'In conducting any trial the court is trying to get at the truth only in a very limited sense. It is not conducting a scientific investigation but is merely examining that aspect of an incident which the parties ask it to look at, and can only use the evidence which the parties put before it. The inquiry is often limited in scope and depth, and these shortcomings are actively contributed to by the unattractive illogicalities of the law of evidence. Nevertheless the court must make up its mind one way or the other at that time and on the evidence put before it, even though a scientific inquirer would have to conclude "We just don't know." The need for drastic reform is well recognised but the realisation is still a long way off.'

CHAPTER 11

Equipment, earnings and expenditure

IN AN ERA IN which eye-witness accounts are often considered unreliable, when admissions of guilt are more readily set aside and the evidence given by police officers is frequently challenged, the work of the forensic science laboratory assumes ever greater significance. Advances in techniques encourage this development. Crime prevention in the future demands crime detection now.

As has been mentioned, plans are in hand to enlarge the Metropolitan Police laboratory – an essential development if it is to have any possibility of keeping pace with increasing case and workloads. (The term 'caseload' refers to the number of matters to which attention is required and 'workload' to the amount of time and endeavour that are needed to deal with them. As crime becomes more sophisticated, the latter grows even faster than the former, particularly in relation to offences such as the illegal use, possession or movement of dangerous drugs and when scientists are required to make frequent or prolonged attendances at court.)

It is reliably estimated that the Metropolitan Police laboratory's present 55,000 square feet of floor space houses apparatus with a current value of some £3,000,000.

Fundamentally, its work can be segregated into three categories. First, the identification of exhibits (e.g., is the stain blood or the substance a drug?) Second, their analysis (e.g., if it is blood, what is the group; if a drug, which is it and what the percentage of purity?) Third, whence, or from whom, did it come? (e.g., was a bullet fired from a particular weapon or was the blood lost by victim or assailant?)

Since many of the items requiring inspection are small, it follows that action often begins (and sometimes ends) with the prime tool of the forensic scientist: the microscope. In the lay mind, microscopes are visualized as the basic devices encountered in biology classes during schooldays, but the instruments employed in the Metropolitan Police laboratory range from relatively simple stereo microscopes costing about £2,000 to machines with the complexity of the scanning electron microscope (SEM) which, as well as making it possible to identify specks of dust too small to be seen with the naked eye, can characterize metallic particles in such samples. First introduced to the MPFSL in 1970, the two SEMs now installed are valued at some £150,000 each. Altogether more than 100 microscopes, with at least eight different optical configurations, are in use at the Lambeth laboratory.

Comparisons are another forensic function of microscopy. As touched upon earlier, one well-known application of this technique relates to firearms, in terms of establishing whether bullets recovered from bodies or at scenes of crimes were fired in specific weapons. When 'suspect' weapons are available for examination, test shots are discharged into special receptacles. Boxes packed with cotton wool were formerly used to capture, undamaged, such trial firings, but the MPFSL now routinely employs a water tank for the purpose.

An instrument introduced by a leading manufacturer, Leitz, in 1931 and still manufactured today essentially unchanged, is in use in the firearms laboratory. There are two table-top versions, modified for binocular viewing. They can accommodate high-resolution video and photomicrographic processes. A measuring microscope, accurate to 0.01 mm, is used to determine the rifling dimensions on bullets when firearms are not acquired after crimes. An operating microscope on a movable floor-stand enables its user to make effective searches of bulky items like clothing and to examine the interiors of gun barrels.

A chronograph was recently added to the firearms experts' devices. A three-channel unit, this gives full ballistic parameters, such as extreme range, bullet drop and time of flight. The quality of the data provided is assured by two independent readings taken at the muzzles of weapons under test with a third down-range. The system is computer-controlled. A high-speed photoflash unit is available to demonstrate various aspects of weapon function or bullet/shot flight and impact.

Whatever wonders may be attainable by instrumentation, it is necessary to bear in mind that machines are incapable of original thought. They can perform only in accordance with their human operators' instructions. For these reasons certain physical disabilities – for example, colour blindness – would debar their sufferers from some scientific duties in the forensic field. But great advances have been made in instruments to assist the forensic scientist. Nowadays, colour matching (e.g., of flakes of paint) is rarely judged by the eye alone, since the shades perceived are crucially dependent on the illumination and viewing conditions used. Instruments are available to ascertain whether samples are identical or different in colour. One such, called a micro-spectrophotometer, made by Zeiss, is on order for the Metropolitan Police laboratory at a cost of some £70,000. An international convention of colour co-ordinates, agreed by the Commission Internationale de l'Eclairage (CIE), uses a three-figure code to describe a colour on a standard basis that is recognized throughout the world. These figures can provide the foundation for a data store on colour.

Fragments of glass are among the items sent to the laboratory for examination. Their identification is sometimes vital in such tasks as tracking down drivers responsible for 'hit and run' road accidents. Discovery of the refractive index of the glass is a key element in investigations.

Experimenters learned, some years ago, that the refractive index of glass can be ascertained by immersing a particle in oil and heating the oil to a point at which the glass disappears from view under a microscope. At this point the glass and the oil have the same refractive index. The oil is 'calibrated' so its refractive index is known. For some time this process was carried out by wearisome observation of the glass particle and oil, but an automated unit, British made by Foster and

Freeman, of Evesham, Worcestershire, is now available. Developed in consultation with the Home Office Central Research Establishment and the MPFSL (a member of whose staff, chemist/caseworker Pam Hamer, joined the company for two years during its initial marketing) the instrument costs about £10,000 and is called GRIM (an instrument for Glass Refractive Index Measurement).

Linked to a suitable microscope and computerized, it enables the operator to heat the oil electrically, up to about 120°C, while observing a visual display screen showing the ascending temperature alongside an enlarged picture of the sample on a TV screen. The instrument records the exact temperature at the moment the sample disappears. A printed readout of the glass refractive index is provided automatically. The instrument gives very precise temperature readings and, unlike the human observer, does not tire towards the end of the day.

The compositional analyses carried out at the Metropolitan Police laboratory are separated into two classes: organic and inorganic. The larger instrumentation for work in both sectors was acquired over the past 20 years, during Ray Williams' directorship. A few major devices are, however, of earlier vintage. Brian Wheals, the scientist in charge of special services, told me that most of the apparatus used in the laboratory is considered to have a working life of about a decade before becoming obsolescent. This is particularly true of recent instrumentation incorporating computers, which rapidly become superseded because of the swift rate of development in the computing field.

In the field of inorganic analysis the primary instruments are the emission spectrograph, the scanning electron microscope (SEM), the atomic absorption spectrophotometer, the inductively coupled plasma (ICP) spectrometer and the x-ray diffractometer.

The emission spectrograph characterizes the metallic elements in samples by 'exciting' them to high temperatures at which they emit light which is split up through a prism and measured. The equipment, although now over 40 years old, is still used to detect toxic metals in toxicological samples.

Although originally purchased for use by biologists as a high powered microscope, the SEM has since proved very effective in solving a wide range of problems in forensic science. The most important feature of the instrument is the ability to observe the sample and chemically analyse it at the same time. Chemical elements above fluorine in the Periodic Table may be detected and measured in extremely small samples (the norm in forensic science) or in small areas of larger samples. The analysis is non-destructive and can, therefore, be repeated on the same sample at a later date if, for example, a scientific adviser appointed by the defence lawyer in a case wishes to check the original result.

Images of the sample surface may be formed by various types of electron signal, x-ray, or visible light, providing information not obtainable by other methods.

The versatility of the SEM is evident from the following list of routine applications: determination of the order in which two intersecting pen or typing strokes were written on a questioned document; detection and identification of particulate residue deposited on skin and clothing during shootings and bullion robberies; recovery and identification of small bullet and bomb fragments; visualization of fingerprints and microscopy and analysis of a wide range of contact traces associated with crime.

Recently, in a highly successful collaborative project with CAMSCAN, the English manufacturers of the laboratory's SEMs, an automatic particle analysis system has been designed and built. This system is already in use in a number of forensic science laboratories world-wide.

Atomic Absorption spectroscopy is employed for measuring specific elements in samples which have been dissolved out into a liquid solution. Excitation of the elements in a flame or furnace enables the presence of metals to be monitored. An advantage of the technique is that it facilitates quantification of the amount of metal that is present. Although not extensively used now, at one time the technique was widely applied to the analysis of hand swabs from suspects considered to have handled stolen metals, for characterizing lead shot and for the elemental analysis of glass. Its main use today is to ensure that police firearms instructors do not pick up too much lead in their blood as a result of exposure to the lead-fume formed when guns are fired.

ICP spectrometry is a technique for multi-element analysis. Samples are heated to some 10,000°C, causing them to emit characteristic light or energy chiefly in the ultra violet range. The wavelengths of these emissions are then measured, each element having its own, known wavelength. The instrumentation is mainly applied to the analysis of glass. Elemental analysis frequently permits tiny glass fragments to be classified as coming from a window rather than a container – a task which cannot be performed by the refractive index measurement mentioned earlier.

X-ray diffractometry employs a diffractometer to produce characteristic patterns from crystalline solids. Part of its value lies in identifying metals and pigments in paint and in analysing geological (soils and minerals) samples. Originally used for the examination of inorganic materials, it is now applied mostly to the identification of crystalline samples of drugs and their excipients.

The Lambeth laboratory has three x-ray generators, valued at approximately £15,000 each. There are three associated computer systems, each worth some £5,000, and specialized camera equipment valued at about £20,000. A large radiographic unit is also installed. This, with its expensive shielding, is valued at between £20,000 and £30,000. X-ray diffraction is non-destructive; exhibits submitted to the process remain undamaged.

Conventional x-radiography is used in two forms – 'hard' (20-200 kilovolts) and 'soft' (10-15 kilovolts). The former is used to examine items such as vehicle tyres, parts of appliances, gemstones (diamonds, being carbon, offer little resistance to x-rays, enabling false jewels to be easily recognized) and imitation firearms (to check on the degree of obstruction of barrels, etc).

'Soft' x-rays are used to reveal such things as counterfeit banknotes, fraudulent or falsified passports and envelopes which have been steamed open and resealed.

Procedures applied to organic analysis include mass

spectrometry, gas and liquid chromatography and infra red spectroscopy.

The laboratory has three operational systems of mass spectrometry, introduced since 1974. Instruments of the type have existed since the time of the first world war, but the early devices were difficult to operate. The current price of these instruments is about £150,000 each. The technique produces a 'fingerprint' of an organic compound by bombarding it with a beam of electrons, causing the molecules making up the sample to fragment in a particular way. The mass spectrometer enables the breakdown products – positively charged particles – to be separated and identified in terms of their mass-to-charge ratio. The end product is a 'fingerprint' unique to that particular compound.

Mass spectrometry has to be performed under conditions of high vacuum, making the direct introduction of samples somewhat difficult. However, it readily couples up with a separation technique called gas chromatography. Mixtures in solution (frequently drugs or their metabolites extracted from blood or urine) can be injected into the gas chromatograph with a syringe. Individual compounds in the mixture separate during passage through the gas chromatographic column so they enter the mass spectrometer separately, permitting each to be characterized by its specific mass spectrum.

The ability of gas chromatography to analyse complex vapours is of special value in the examination of debris taken from the scenes of suspected arson. For example, petrol contains between 200 and 250 components. Newly developed techniques include the ability to analyse waxes. Oils, greases and waxes used as lubricants in cases of rape and buggery and cosmetics transferred from victim to attacker during struggles are often among the items sent for scrutiny. Polishes containing both flammable solvents and wax and the remains of wax candles are frequently found at the seats of fires and may require analysis. The wax transfer of ink is sometimes used in the forgery of date stamps on documents. In cases of terrorism, the plasticity of certain explosives is due, in part, to the use of hydrocarbon grease. In burglary, anti-climb paints transferred to thieves' clothing contain a proportion of grease.

All these materials are suitable for analysis by gas chromatography.

The MPFSL has many gas chromatographs, which cost between £8,000 and £10,000 per system. A linked computer, with interface and software, costs £20,000.

Another widely used separation technique is liquid chromatography which is analogous to gas chromatography except that a liquid is used as the flowing phase rather than a gas. Whereas gas chromatography requires some volatility for a sample to be analysed, with liquid chromatography only solubility is a prerequisite. Many drug mixtures, dyes and other involatile materials are analysed by liquid chromatography.

Infra-red spectroscopy relies on the fact that all organic and some inorganic molecules absorb infra-red light in slightly different ways. Monitoring the manner in which light is absorbed in the infra-red region enables the investigator to obtain a characteristic spectrum that is rather like a 'fingerprint' of the compound involved.

Computerization began to make a major impact in the laboratory in the mid-1970s. More recently, computers have been linked to video cameras to explore the possibilities of image enhancement and image analysis. An example of this development is the use of a computerized video system to measure typeface styles in cases of suspect documents.

Some of the tests aimed at identifying the blood groupings of body samples are based on immunological factors and the coagulatory properties of serum, but a system of electrophoresis enables the biologist to gather more information from blood, mainly by separating out some of the unusual enzymes it contains. Electrophoresis performs a process in which charged organic compounds are separated on a plate under the influence of a strong electric field. Different compounds move to different positions on the plate. The technique is in use as part of the new DNA profiling procedure.

A special range of equipment is employed by the laboratory's Serious Crimes Unit (SCU), which was created in 1981 as an offshoot of the Photographic Section. Staffed by scientific, photographic and fingerprint experts, the unit is proficient in locating latent evidence that is discoverable only by use of highly-developed instruments and the correct sequencing of appropriate techniques. The SCU has 25 different investigative treatments at its disposal.

The largest and most costly item of the unit's apparatus is an argon-ion-laser device priced at £44,000 plus £20,000 for the necessary cooling attachment. The Lambeth laboratory was the first in Europe to adopt this machine for forensic work. Using 38,000 watts of electrical power, the light emitted from the apparatus could be directed to reach the moon. It is rated as a class four laser – the most dangerous. Protective goggles have to be worn during its operation.

It was an employee of Rank Xerox in Canada, Professor Roland Menzel, who discovered that lasers (the name is an abbreviation of the description – 'light amplification by the stimulated emission of radiation') could be used to detect otherwise invisible fingerprints. Noticing that the light revealed such marks with startling clarity, he learned that the hands that had made them had been contaminated with a red powder which was used in the building. Later developments proved that lasers would show up prints left by the natural deposits from human skin. The principle of the laser's function is the excitement of a tube of argon gas by a high input of electrical power.

As well as the large laser unit, the SCU has a portable machine for transportation to scenes of crime. Portable ultra-violet light equipment is also employed for these purposes.

Vehicles thought to have been used in serious crime are placed in a plastic 'tent' which is filled with the fumes of heated superglue. During the process the substance forms a polymer which shows up latent marks in almost three-dimensional form. The SCU is experimenting with a range of different stains, to cover backgrounds of various colours. 'We sometimes write vehicles off during our searches, but we usually get results,' chief photographer Ken Creer told me during a tour of the unit's quarters.

Demonstrating the laser's ability to reveal clear fingerprints on paper which, to the naked eye, appeared untouched, he showed me how this result is achieved by immersing the paper in liquid nitrogen at a temperature of minus 196°C. 'It is sometimes difficult to explain these techniques when giving evidence in court,' he said. 'For example, if you drop a sheet of paper just after taking it out of a dish of liquid nitrogen, it will shatter to pieces like a porcelain plate.'

The investigators were greatly intrigued when, in 1986, under laser treatment, the back of one of murder victim Tessa Howden's hands revealed the clearly-inscribed word 'Help'. An obvious question arose – had she managed to write the word during the attack in her bedroom at her parents' Surrey home, while her mother and father slept peacefully in the next room? The puzzle was solved when it was learned that the girl had been employed on a local advertising paper doing a 'helpline' service. Tessa had, it seemed, 'doodled' the word on her hand in her office, blissfully unaware of the bizarre implication it was to have in respect of her untimely death. Her killer was sentenced to imprisonment for life.

The salary scales in effect at the Metropolitan Police Forensic Science laboratory in 1988/9 were:

Director	£25,756 – £29,344
Deputy Director	£19,537 – £26,348
Principal Scientific Officer	£15,631 – £21,936
Senior Scientific Officer	£12,024 – £15,823
Higher Scientific Officer	£ 9,687 – £13,005
Scientific Officer	£ 8,284 – £10,622
Assistant Scientific Officer	£ 4,004 – £ 7,816

These are national figures, to which a London weighting of £1,750 is added in each case.

The expenditure figures of the Metropolitan Police Forensic Science laboratory during the five years 1983/4 to 1987/8 were:

Year	Pay £k	Non-pay £k	Total £k
1983/4	4,123	1,747	5,870
1984/5	4,015	1,785	5,800
1985/6	3,983	1,974	5,957
1986/7	4,385	1,091	6,476
1987/8	4,766	2,003	6,769

PART THREE
Results

Author's foreword

EVEN WERE ALL THE facts to be retrievable (which they are not) and judged to hold some interest for the reader (which would be unlikely) there is obviously no possibility of including in this single volume particulars of the many thousands of cases that have been dealt with at the Metropolitan Police Forensic Science Laboratory. What may be less apparent is that selection of examples of the work done by its experts was a far from simple process.

The subjects of the 28 chronicles that follow were not chosen at random. Their preference was based on a number of considerations. An initial requirement was that there should have been a significant forensic contribution to the inquiries. Secondly, while not seeking out occurrences of a sensational nature, it was necessary to give priority to happenings that would merit the attention of the intelligent, although scientifically unembroiled, observer.

Next, thought had to be given to the chronology and vintage of events and to the publicity some have received. Little purpose would be served by repeating oft-told tales to which no further information can be added. On this principle, despite the laboratory's involvement in their investigation, some notorious crimes of yesteryear (such as those committed by Neville George Clevely Heath, John George Haigh, John Reginald Halliday Christie, Brian Donald Hume, and others) have been excluded.

Surprising though it may seem, the availability of adequate records was another factor. (The conscientious forensic scientist is seldom an efficient archivist!) Overall, some effort had also to be made to illustrate the breadth, as well as the depth, of the laboratory's responsibilities.

The material in the ensuing pages deals with various forms of homicide, with child molestation, with the illegal manufacture and importations of drugs, with the investigation of a major fire, with the fatal misuse of motor vehicles and with the help that was provided towards restoration of a damaged art treasure. A few aspects of the laboratory's activities, notably work associated with examinations following acts of terrorism, have had to be excluded for security reasons.

It would be unfeeling to fail to acknowledge the fact that any published description of a crime may revive painful memories for those who were bereaved or otherwise injured by it. To any such victims who may come to read this book I would offer an assurance that the material included here was selected for its forensic merits, not to gratify prurience, and that my self-editing has been carried out with due regard to their natural sensitivities. I hope they will agree with me that public awareness of the evils perpetrated by some members of the human race is a necessary part of lesson-learning towards the reduction of such transgressions in the future.

It may be noticed that my fact-finding interviews were not always conducted with the senior police officers who were responsible for directing inquiries. In some instances I have relied upon, and been assisted by, the co-operation of officers of less elevated rank. The explanation is simple. Although the gathering of information for this work occupied almost three years, it was obviously necessary to put some time limit on that part of the endeavour. In some cases, because of their concentration on police work in hand or of other preoccupations following retirement from the force, it proved very difficult to make contact, within a reasonable period, with officers who had led investigations. In no case did the aides who stood in for them fail to uphold the best traditions of the service.

Where circumstances justified elaboration I have provided considerable detail. Where brevity appeared permissible I have omitted minutiae. But in either case my words can do no more than provide a glimpse of the world in which forensic scientists strive and have their being.

Some readers may be disappointed because there is no

mention of a crime that was of particular interest or concern to them. I can only apologize. There may, perhaps, be another time and place ...

Contract killers

CHAPTER 12

Contract killers

HUMAN VAGARIES BEING WHAT they are, it follows that the
formal requirements of law can seldom be met by the
unquestioning acceptance of accusation or confession. The
motives behind false charges against others are usually easily
uncovered, but covert purpose or unsatisfactory circum-
stance may lurk beneath self-incrimination. For example, it is
not unknown for those charged with offences to withdraw
their earlier admissions of culpability, claiming that those
statements had been made because of unbearable duress
exerted by the police. Sadly, there have been occasions when
such assertions have been found to be valid.

For these various reasons, it is normally necessary to subject
accusations and confessions of criminality to careful
investigation, with the production of such forensic evidence as
may be obtainable.

A case in this category culminated in the trial of 43-year-old
Henry Jeremiah MacKenny, an evildoer known to his cohorts
as 'Harry the bandit' and dubbed 'Big H' by the popular
press. Six feet four inches tall, a keen skin diver and an
arrogant exhibitionist, MacKenny had had his fingers tattooed,
those on his right hand carrying the letters LTFC and those on
his left ESUK, so that their intertwining spelled out an
obscene message.

The case began to unfold with the arrest in 1979, on a
£500,000 robbery charge, of 40-year-old John Childs, an
oft-convicted burglar from east London. During questioning,
Childs broke down and confessed to taking part in six

murders. He had been drinking a bottle of whisky a day to deaden his recollections of these crimes, he told the interrogating officers; he was relieved to get the facts off his chest.

As well as resulting in his own conviction and sentencing to six terms of life imprisonment, Childs' statements led to charges being brought against four other men: MacKenny, who was then said to be of no fixed address; 47-year-old Terence Pinfold, of Ilford, Essex; 41-year-old Leonard Thompson, of Upminster, Essex, and 34-year-old Paul Morton-Thurtle, of Canterbury, Kent.

At the opening of the trial at the Old Bailey in October 1980, the jury was warned that it would be hearing 'unpleasant and revolting' details of the killing, dismemberment and burning of six people, one a 10-year-old boy, each of whom had disappeared without trace.

MacKenny was accused of murdering 35-year-old George Brett, a haulage contractor, and his 10-year-old son Terry; 35-year-old Terence Eve, a toy maker; 36-year-old Robert Brown, a prison absconder; 48-year-old Frederick Sherwood, from Bermondsey, and 35-year-old Ronald Andrews, a roofing contractor from Barkingside, Essex. Pinfold was charged with the murders of George Brett, Eve and Brown and with assisting in the disposal of Terry Brett's body. Thompson was charged with murdering George Brett and Morton-Thurtle was accused of the murder of Sherwood. All four pleaded not guilty.

Presenting the case for the prosecution, David Tudor Price alleged that Andrews had been MacKenny's best friend but MacKenny, assisted by Childs, had shot him because he wanted his wife. MacKenny was said to have told another friend that he should not have killed Andrews because since doing so he had had to keep filling Mrs Andrews with drink to stop her from thinking about her late husband.

MacKenny and Childs had battered and strangled Eve to death, Tudor Price said. Childs had claimed that Pinfold, an associate of MacKenny's in the making of diving suits, had wanted to get rid of Eve and take over his soft toy business.

Describing the proceedings in court the previous day, the

Daily Telegraph for October 8 reported Tudor Price as saying that George Brett's murder had been a 'contract killing' for which Thompson – known to his friends as 'Big Lenny' – had paid £1,800. MacKenny, Childs and Pinfold were each said to have taken £600 from that sum. The background to the affair appeared to be that, in October 1973, there had been a fight between Thompson and Brett, when Thompson had been armed with an axe and Brett with an iron bar, Tudor Price went on. Thompson had ended up in hospital and Brett had later given evidence against him at his trial. Brett's son had been killed simply because, on the spur of the moment, he had accompanied his father when Childs had lured him from his Upminster, Essex, home on the pretext of arranging a business meeting. Both Bretts had, it was said, been shot by MacKenny, using a Sten gun and ammunition supplied by 'Big Lenny'. Childs claimed that he had given the boy a teddy bear to hold before MacKenny had fired into his head while Childs clasped the child in his arms.

The heartless killing of the boy had prompted a row between him and MacKenny, Childs told the court. 'Had I had a gun when MacKenny killed that young boy I would have shot him to pieces. Afterwards it was too late, we were in schtuck.' He had, he added, considered killing MacKenny, by shooting him in the back with a silent crossbow fitted with a nightsight, thinking that this could be done as, silhouetted by lamplight, MacKenny walked down a pathway at his home. Cross-examined by Michael Mansfield, who defended MacKenny, Childs denied that he had bragged to other prisoners about killing. 'There is nothing to boast about. My life is in ruins,' he said. Also denying that he hated MacKenny, Childs declared 'I respect him as a very dangerous person.' Admitting that he had thought about writing a book on the six killings, he denied suggesting 'East End Butcher' as a potential title. The only title he had in mind was 'I Confess'. He added: 'If I wrote a book and if any publisher wished to publish it after my release, it would certainly be for money, to allow me to escape from this country to prevent me from being murdered.'

Among further denials, he refuted allegations that he had

told fellow-prisoners he intended to implicate MacKenny in 11 other murders; that he had been involved in the killing of a black woman who 'went up like paraffin'; that his flat might become a tourist attraction where he would like to take the gate money and that he might end up at Madame Tussaud's next to body-snatchers Burke and Hare, 'which would be great'.

Sherwood's murder, another shooting by MacKenny aided by blows with a hammer by Childs, had, said Tudor Price, been carried out after they had agreed to kill him for £4,000, paid by a deposit of £1,500 and fortnightly instalments of £500.

Brown had been murdered because he had become a danger to MacKenny and Childs after inadvertently witnessing the killing of Eve, the prosecution statement continued. A former professional wrestler who was on the run from Chelmsford prison, he had asked Pinfold for help and had been sent to Childs' home. According to Childs, there had been some difficulty in slaughtering this victim, the court heard. First, Brown had survived two shots into the back of his head and one into his face, fired by MacKenny. Then MacKenny had attacked him with a fireman's axe while Childs stabbed him repeatedly in the chest with a diver's knife. Brown had finally died after Childs drove a sword through his body into the floor.

The principal witness in the prosecution's case against the four, Childs said that he feared for his life since turning Queen's Evidence. 'I am a professional criminal and have broken the code as such – I am open to be killed at any time,' he said. He added that he was also fearful of the 'damage' MacKenny might do to his family.

The information given about the methods used for disposal of the corpses was even more chilling than the details of the killings. It appeared that, in 1972, Pinfold and MacKenny had been using part of a church hall in Haydon Road, Goodmayes, Essex, for making underwater equipment. In June that year, Tudor Price said, Childs had gone to work for Pinfold after being released from prison. He was back in gaol, for burglary, by October, but during his months of freedom the three men had discussed the idea of killing people for money.

When Childs was released again, in August 1974, Eve – known as 'Teddy Bear' – was running his soft toy business in part of the hall premises. Childs said he was murdered when he returned there after making a delivery. Using a length of hosepipe with large iron nuts at either end, MacKenny had struck him repeatedly on the head while Childs hit him in the face with a hammer. MacKenny had finally choked him to death with a rope.

The two killers had then set about cleaning up the bloody scene of their crime, working at it until 7.30 the following morning and including the use of sulphuric acid, Childs' account went on. Eve's body had first been put in a bungalow occupied by MacKenny adjoining the church hall and was afterwards taken, in the boot of MacKenny's car, to Childs' ground-floor flat in council-owned Dolphin House, High Street, Poplar, east London, where polythene sheeting had been installed in a small bedroom in readiness for what was to follow.

Describing the process of dismemberment, Childs said that MacKenny had sawn off one of Eve's legs before they decided to complete the cutting up in the bath. Having called Childs to watch, MacKenny had put a butcher's knife to Eve's throat and, 'with about three motions', sawn completely through to the spinal cord. The head was put temporarily into a plastic dustbin.

It had been decided to put Eve's remains through a butcher's mincing machine which Pinfold had bought for £25, but when MacKenny tried to feed pieces of flesh into the device it had jammed, Childs went on. It turned out that the machine had not been designed to work on the domestic electricity supply. MacKenny had then tried flushing pieces from the body down the toilet with buckets of water, but this procedure had soon been abandoned. It had finally been decided to burn the body in the fireplace and to scatter the ashes from a moving car on the Barking bypass. The mincing machine had been dismantled and the parts thrown into a canal.

The Bretts had also been killed at the Haydon Road factory, their bodies partially dismembered and taken to Childs' flat, where they were similarly cut to pieces and burned in the grate, that process occupying an entire weekend, Childs said.

He added that, before removal of their corpses from the factory, Pinfold had been deliberately smeared with their blood, to ensure that he realized he was physically involved in the murders. Childs affirmed that, after one of the killings, MacKenny had kept an eye as a souvenir. 'He washed it in my sink, then wrapped it in toilet paper.'

Childs said that Brown had been lured to and killed at his Poplar flat. When this victim had been seen to be still alive after the repeated shootings, hacking with axes and stabbings, Childs had 'unsheathed a short sword stick and stabbed him in the belly, running the blade up into his heart'. After dismemberment in the bath, Brown's body had been burned in the grate like the others.

Continuing the gruesome evidence that kept him for several days in the witness box, Childs said that he had enticed Sherwood to MacKenny's bungalow to collect the money for the ostensible purchase of a Rover car Sherwood wished to sell. As Sherwood was counting the cash he had been shot by MacKenny and clubbed with a hammer by Childs. His body had been disposed of in the same way as the others.

Tudor Price said that, in October 1978, Childs had agreed to help MacKenny kill Andrews in exchange for £400 and a silencer for his gun. Posing as a private detective, Childs had lured Andrews to his home, where MacKenny had shot him, using a .38 revolver. The body had been cut up and burned in the 'traditional' way. MacKenny had then driven Andrews' car to a place on the river Nene in Cambridgeshire. Leaving a partly-consumed bottle of vodka in the vehicle to give the impression of a drink-driving accident, he had put the car into the river.

Mrs Sylvia Margo, a friend of Childs', told of his leaving luggage in her loft in June 1979. When removed by the police it was found that two metal boxes and a canvas bag were packed with firearms, ammunition and associated items.

David Pryor, a firearms specialist at the Metropolitan Police Forensic Science Laboratory, compiled a list of the items. There were six hand weapons – a Walther 9mm self-loading pistol, the barrel of which had been shortened to 1½ inches; a Rhoner 8mm self-loading pistol designed to take blank and tear gas cartridges; a Webley Mark VI .455 revolver which had been adapted to take 9mm Parabellum cartridges; a Webley Mark I .455 revolver; another Webley Mark VI .455 with its barrel crudely shortened to four inches, and an Enfield .38 service revolver with its barrel partially cut away and threaded, apparently for a silencer.

There was also a Mark II 9mm Sten sub-machine gun with barrel shortened to four inches, muzzle threaded for attachment of a silencer and butt fitted with a wooden pistol-type grip; a Belgian .22 pump-action repeating rifle with barrel shortened to 18½ inches; four pump-action repeating 12-bore shotguns, all with barrels sawn off to about 14 inches, and a 6.5mm Mannlicher-Schonauer sporting rifle with telescopic sight. The Sten gun had been modified to work correctly as an automatic weapon with underpowered ammunition.

As well as hundreds of rounds of ammunition for these guns, there were waist belt and underarm holsters, spare parts and devices to enable 9mm pistol and .38 revolver cartridges to be dismantled and reassembled.

During a talk with me about the case in December 1987, Pryor said that laboratory examination of debris taken from the fireplace at Childs' flat had revealed two small metal globules which had clearly formed from the molten state. Analysis had shown their elemental composition to be that of bullet lead. The explanation could have been that they had melted out of the bodies as they were burned.

Dr Elizabeth Wilson, a biologist at the laboratory, told the court of her findings from investigatory visits to the Haydon Road factory and bungalow and Childs' flat. Part of the floor covering at the bungalow had consisted of three layers of linoleum, she said. Heavy stains made by human blood had been found on the top and centre layers, with corresponding staining on the lowest. There was also human bloodstaining on floor and skirting boards, on carpet in the hallway, on a bedroom curtain and on the seat of a chair. It had been possible to obtain information about the blood grouping from the stains on the linoleum, some floorboards and a skirting board. This had indicated that all the blood could have come from the same person. It could not, she told me when we discussed the case in December 1987, have come from MacKenny, Childs or Brett.

Her evidence at the trial revealed that her discoveries at the flat had included traces of blood and hair taken from the grate and indications of the presence of blood on plastic sheeting, a bathroom mat and a saw. She had also detected human bloodstaining on a knife, in the handle groove inside a plastic dustbin and in three places on curtain material found in a shed. Grouping reactions had been gained from the stains on the curtain and the dustbin, those on the former showing that the blood there had come from at least two people. One of the groupings tallied with the bloodstains found at the bungalow. The grouping obtained from the stains in the dustbin showed that that blood had come from someone other than the yielders of the bloodstains at the bungalow and on two of the places on the curtain.

Despite the collection of a range of forensic findings which appeared to authenticate parts of Childs' accounts, the officer in charge of the investigation, Detective Chief Superintendent Frank Cater, remained sceptical about the claim that adult human corpses had been totally incinerated in an ordinary domestic fireplace. He asked pathologist Professor James ('Taffy') Cameron whether such cremation would be possible. Cameron replied that he did not know but suggested an experiment to find out. Cater agreed.

The complete carcass of an 11-stone male pig – calculated as the physical equivalent of a fully-developed, average-sized man – was taken to Childs' former home. The original 18-inch grate was missing from the fireplace but a 16-inch replacement was put in. A team of police, fire and medical technicians assembled at the flat and settled down with coffee and sandwiches.

The test began at eight pm, Cameron abandoning his surgical skills and employing 'brute force and ignorance' to cut the animal in pieces with the knife, saw and hammer said to have been used by MacKenny. This took 5½ minutes and was described by Cameron as 'Perfectly simple, requiring no anatomical knowledge.'

The head was burnt first. 'Somebody suggested that we should put an apple in its mouth,' the bluff and jocular 58-year-old Cameron told me when we discussed the affair in his office at London Hospital, Whitechapel, in January 1988. 'The temperature in the fire reached over a thousand degrees but the room temperature never went above 75. It was all properly measured, logged and photographed. But when we put the intestines on, the fire almost went out. Because, as soon as it burnt through, the fluid ran. Later on we were told that MacKenny had washed out and dried the intestines before they were burnt.

'The total burning of the pig took 13 hours. We ended up with remains of ash, bone and whatnot which filled two large plastic bags. We then went over it twice with the hammer, as we were told MacKenny had done, and eventually finished up with a small plastic bag of ash with not a remnant of teeth or bone visible to the naked eye.'

Repeated checks had been made outside the building during the burning, but no smell of roasting pork or other odour had been detected, Cameron added. The residents in the block had not been informed about the venture and the only comment that reached official ears came from an occupant of the flat next to Childs', who remarked, the following morning, on how warm his accommodation had been during the night.

I asked 'Taffy' (a nickname bestowed during his Rugby-playing days, in reference to his birth in Swansea, South Wales) whether the exercise had been a justifiable use of so much of his expert time. He answered that, because of its unprecedented nature, he believed his involvement had been fully warranted. Pouring me another over-generous measure of his north-of-the-border style hospitality, he chucklingly commented 'After all, I came south to educate the Sassenach.' The true code of the pathologist was, he said, captured in the framed message hanging in pride of place above his chair. A quotation from the work of the 17th-century morbid anatomist Giovanni Morgagni, this tells its readers 'Those who have dissected or inspected many bodies have at least learnt to doubt, whilst those who are ignorant of anatomy and do not take the trouble to attend to it are in no doubt at all.'

Following a trial that occupied more than seven weeks, MacKenny was found guilty of murdering the Bretts, Andrews and Sherwood. He was sentenced to imprisonment for life, with a recommendation that he should serve a minimum of 25 years. Pinfold was found guilty of murdering Eve and was sentenced to imprisonment for life. Thompson and Morton-Thurtle were found not guilty and discharged.

In the 'Black Museum', Scotland Yard's famous three-dimensional archive of crime, I examined the weapons and other firearms paraphernalia used by 'Big H' and his cronies. From the carefully-executed work that had been done in adapting the guns for nefarious purposes, it was apparent that they had been in the hands of persons with considerable skill. 'Remember that, apart from his own underwater activities, MacKenny was something of an inventor,' Bill Waddell, curator of the museum, reminded me. 'Among other things, he produced a new type of valve for use with sub-aqua equipment.'

In his chosen sea of iniquity 'Big H' was a diver who plumbed the depths.

CHAPTER 13

The drain blocker who complained

IT WAS EARLY IN the bleak February of 1983 that the tenant of an attic flat in a small house in north London wrote a letter of complaint to his landlord. The house was 23 Cranley Gardens, Muswell Hill. The matters complained of included obstructed drains. The writer was 38-year-old Scottish bachelor, civil service clerk, former trainee butcher and probationary policeman Dennis Andrew Nilsen.

He had a way with words. Among other things, his letter declared 'When I flush my toilet the lavatory pans in the lower flats overflow. Obviously the drains are blocked and unpleasant odours permeate the building. I request not any special favours or unnecessary expenditure, but the basic routine upkeep and maintenance in order to keep my living conditions at a tolerable level.' At that time no one alive, other than Nilsen himself, knew of the extraordinary mode of living that he had come to consider tolerable.

With little delay the landlord called in an expert in the unblocking of drains. Near the house a workman found a deep sewer inspection pit. After descending into this subterranean waterway he discovered what proved to be human fingers and part of a neck.

Initial police inquiries were conducted by Detective Chief Inspector Peter Jay. They led to Nilsen. In the evening of February 9 he arrived home to find Jay and other officers awaiting him. Jay's opening remark was 'We have come about your drains.'

In Nilsen's flat he was told what had been found. Almost

casually, he admitted responsibility. Under arrest and on the way to Hornsey police station, he was asked 'How many bodies are we talking about?' Calmly he answered 'Well, I think about 16.'

During interviews conducted by Detective Chief Superintendent Geoffrey Chambers and other officers over a period of 30 days, producing 157 pages of evidence, Nilsen described his stranglings, between December 1978 and February 1983, of 15 young men he had picked up in public houses. It became clear that a number of others who, like his victims, had accepted his invitations to spend the night with him had survived unharmed. The basis on which Nilsen had chosen those he killed was never discovered. Each of his murdered guests had been in a state of near-helpless intoxication, Nilsen said, before he strangled them, usually with a tie.

With similar frankness he told the police that the remains of three victims had been left in his flat. There, officers found parts of bodies in large black plastic bags in the wardrobe. Some of the pieces were in an advanced stage of decomposition. Each of the bags bore a printed legend: 'Keep Haringey tidy.' In the bathroom were the legs of the last victim, a man named Sinclair. Nilsen had recently completed dismemberment of his lower torso. The finding of Sinclair's hands provided the police with fingerprints which enabled them to be certain of his identity and to lodge the first charge of murder against Nilsen. Known to the police for a number of offences, Sinclair had been due to appear in court on a burglary charge.

A tea chest in the flat held more parts of human bodies. Some Sainsbury's grocery bags, each carrying the message 'Our meat is freshest', contained three human heads. At the local mortuary the various parts were put together, ending with the incomplete assembly of three corpses.

Still talking freely, Nilsen told the police that at his former home at 195 Melrose Avenue, Cricklewood, he had left the remains of 12 earlier victims. Occupying a ground floor flat, he had begun by storing the bodies under the floorboards. When he found that only a limited number of cadavers could be accommodated in this way, he had taken to removing one of the old corpses to make room for each new one. The old bodies, most of which had been under the floor for nearly a year, were dismembered, packed in suitcases and stored in a shed in the garden. When he had accumulated several well-filled suitcases he had begun burning the remains, together with their clothing, on large bonfires, cloaking the smell of burning flesh by throwing rubber tyres into the flames. After this he had used a spade to smash up any remaining bits of bone.

Nilsen told his interrogators that he had once had a bad fright at Melrose Avenue, when a man he was trying to strangle had fought back and escaped. The police were called and an inspector and a sergeant had questioned him while standing on floorboards beneath which lay five dead men. Always articulate, Nilsen had convinced the policemen that the fracas had been no more than a homosexual lovers' tiff.

The time had come, his narrative went on, when the owners of the Melrose Avenue house decided to sell the property. He had quickly cut up and burned all the bodies from under the floor.

With no access to the garden at Cranley Gardens, he had found himself faced with a serious disposal problem. He had tried to overcome it by boiling dismembered parts in a large pot bought from a local ironmonger, afterwards flushing the results down the toilet. In consequence the drains had become blocked. Nilsen had used the same pot to cook a Christmas party curry for himself and his colleagues at their Camden Town office.

When Chambers commented that he could not have disposed of the larger bones in this way, Nilsen agreed and explained that he had thrown some on waste ground behind the Cranley Gardens house. Most of the bones had, he said, been put, with the dead men's clothes, into black plastic waste disposal bags which had been routinely collected by the local dustmen.

Nilsen told the policemen that the first person he had killed at Cranley Gardens – he claimed it as his 13th murder – had said that his name was John, that he was a guardsman and that he came from High Wycombe, Buckinghamshire. From that time and on through the trial, this individual was referred to as

'John the guardsman'. Nilsen said he had met him in an off-licence near Charing Cross station. After drinking together in a nearby public house they had gone to the flat, where Nilsen had cooked a meal and, while drinking throughout the evening, they had watched television. Then, when Nilsen had asked him to leave, his visitor had refused. Wrapping an upholstery strap around his neck, Nilsen had tried to strangle him. But the man had fought back gamely. When he had, at last, gone limp there was blood on the bed where the struggle had taken place. According to Nilsen, this had come from a wound on his guest's head.

By this time, said Nilsen, his dog had been barking excitedly in the next room and he had gone to quieten her. On his return, he had been astonished to see that the man was breathing again. Despite Nilsen's further attempts at strangulation, his heart had continued to beat. Nilsen had then, he asserted, dragged the unconscious individual into the bathroom, laid him in the bath and filled it with water. Bubbles had come from the man's nose and mouth and the water had turned foul with blood, food, and other body emissions. Nilsen said that he had left the corpse in the bath all night and, after pulling the soiled sheets and blankets off the bed, slept with the dog at his feet.

Following inquiries, the police established that 'John the guardsman' had been John Howlett, a young semi-vagrant from High Wycombe who had often been arrested. He had never been a guardsman. His parents were interviewed and a photograph borrowed. When it was shown to Nilsen, he instantly identified it as a portrait of the man he had murdered. Howlett had received treatment at Middlesex Hospital, where details of his blood grouping were obtained. It was of a type found only in some four per cent of the British population. Bloodstained fabric from the bed and liquid present in a femur were examined by Anne Davies, a biologist at the Metropolitan Police Forensic Science Laboratory. In both cases blood grouping reactions identical to those of Howlett were obtained.

Her further forensic work was complicated by the fact that blood from Nilsen and blood thought to have come from

Sinclair were found to be of the same group in several systems although differing in others. At Cranley Gardens she found blood which could have been from Sinclair, but not from Nilsen, on armchairs, on the dressing table, on a bedsheet, on a settee cushion, on a carpet and on the front of the cooker. Blood on other items could have been from Nilsen or Sinclair. Blood of a combination of groups different from both Sinclair's and Nilsen's was found on a grey carpet in the living room and on the bed mattress. Successful grouping tests of seminal stains on a bedsheet showed that they could have come from Sinclair or Nilsen. Flesh from a bloodstained board was found to be human in origin and gave reactions for a blood group common to Nilsen and the unknown 'third person'.

Anne Davies' preliminary testing of nine items taken from beneath the floorboards at Melrose Avenue indicated that seven were bloodstained but the age of the staining made it impossible to confirm these reactions. Eight of the items contained puparia (the final larval skin of the maggot) from Ophyra flies, which lay their eggs on decaying flesh.

Inch-by-inch examination and sieving of the soil in the Melrose Avenue garden located some 3,000 fragments of bone which, assembled by an expert anatomist, were found to constitute components of at least eight bodies. Patient detective work led to the identification of seven of Nilsen's victims. The others remain unknown.

Charged with, and convicted of, six murders, Nilsen was found to be sane and was sentenced to life imprisonment.

Asked for his opinion as to the motives for the killings, Detective Chief Superintendent Chambers said that, although Nilsen had never vouchsafed any information on the subject, he had formed the conclusion that loneliness had been a root cause. 'He would kill people ... and leave them sitting in chairs for two or three days while he went to work ... He just did not want them to go.' It seemed to be a combination of rock music and alcohol that had triggered off the murders, Chambers added. He 'tended to the feeling' that Nilsen was asexual rather than homosexual, despite the fact that he had told women at his workplace that he was 'gay'. He had, Chambers believed, said this 'to keep the women at bay'.

Chambers also asserted that Nilsen had always denied that there was anything homosexual in his killings.

Another experienced policeman involved in the case, 41-year-old dark-bearded Detective Sergeant Ronald Stocks, told me that writings found under the floorboards at Melrose Avenue had shown that Nilsen had at one time belonged to 'gay' organizations and had experimented as an active homosexual but had found that it was not to his liking. Stocks offered the theory that this aversion had led to Nilsen developing 'a down' on practising homosexuals and so to the murders. It was also his view that Nilsen had been 'fascinated by death'.

It was known, Stocks told me, that Nilsen had had his first homosexual encounter during service with the army in Germany. There, he had received some training as a butcher. There, too, his heavy drinking had begun.

From well-authenticated accounts of incidents since the start of his incarceration, it is evident that this seemingly unfeeling killer is not without a sense of humour. Asked by a prison governor whether he was interested in sport, Nilsen is reported to have replied that he was – and added that, in his present circumstances, the sport that was of greatest interest to him was pole-vaulting! At the opening of an interview with a police officer, he asked what he should do with the remains of a cigarette he had been smoking. When told 'Put it down the toilet', he is said to have responded 'The last time I put anything down the toilet I got into trouble.' Hearing that a film company was considering making a movie on his activities, he wrote to Chambers asking him to use his influence with the producer, to ensure that the list of credits showed the cast in order of disappearance rather than appearance!

CHAPTER 14

Poisoned pellets

THE YEARS THAT HAVE PASSED since the death of Georgi Ivanov Markov have done little to diminish interest in the bizarre manner of his demise. Nor has that period produced any firm information about the persons responsible for his killing.

To a populace fascinated by the intrigues of international espionage and assassination but at that time unaccustomed to political murder on its streets, the Markov story read like imaginative fiction. The facts that some aspects of the case are not generally known and that there have been elements of misreporting and misunderstanding persuade me that the affair deserves inclusion here.

Well known as a successful novelist and playwright in his native Bulgaria, 49-year-old Markov was an open rebel against the Communist regime in his country. Taking refuge in Britain in 1971, he obtained an appointment with the Bulgarian service of the British Broadcasting Corporation. He broadcast on political and cultural affairs to his homeland from the BBC, from the Deutsche Welle radio station in Frankfurt and from the CIA-supported Radio Free Europe in Munich.

Markov had met Todor Zhivkov, the head of the Bulgarian Communist Party, and other major political figures and had, for a time, been a regular visitor to the exclusive suburb of Sofia where those dignitaries had their villas. While complying with Radio Free Europe's policy against naming individuals, Markov used his broadcasts from that station to expose the corrupt lifestyles and shabby deceits of those holding power in Bulgaria.

Unknown sources made numerous attempts to jam the transmissions of Markov's exposés, but these exertions were only partially successful. A 'secret' joke circulating in Sofia said that members of the politburo never watched television on Thursday nights because they were too busy listening to Georgi Markov on Radio Free Europe.

But there was nothing humorous about a message received by Markov's brother Nikola, a stamp dealer in Bologna, Italy, in 1977. Via clandestine channels he was informed that the Bulgarian authorities had decided that the time had come for Georgi to be 'eliminated'.

While staying with friends during one of his visits to West Germany – for his personal safety he always avoided using hotels – Markov told them that, three months earlier, an unidentified man had telephoned him threatening him with 'a refined execution, something out of the ordinary' if he did not stop working for Radio Free Europe.

A month later, in the early afternoon of Thursday September 7 1978, Markov drove his Simca car into the temporary parking lot he customarily used, on a cleared building site on the south-eastern side of Waterloo Bridge, where the National Theatre now stands.

Not being a lover of walking, it was his habit to catch a bus across the bridge to his office in Bush House, Aldwych. While standing at the bus stop he suddenly felt a stinging blow on the back of his right thigh. Swinging round, he saw a man bending down to pick up an umbrella.

After apologizing in a halting, foreign accent, the man hailed a taxi that was passing. The driver seemed to have some difficulty in understanding the instructions given by his passenger, but the cab moved away and disappeared into the traffic.

After arriving at his office, Markov told a friend, Teo Lirkoff, of what had happened on the bridge and said that he was in pain. There was blood on his jeans. Lirkoff saw 'an angry red spot, like a pimple' on the back of his thigh. When Markov reached his Clapham, south London, home that evening he told his wife Annabel, whom he had married three years earlier, of the incident and said that he was feeling weak. Next day he developed a high temperature, began vomiting, and found difficulty in speaking. Admitted to St James' Hospital, Balham, and seen by Dr Bernard Riley, he was found to have a rapid pulse and swollen lymph glands. There was a small area of hardening around the puncture mark on his thigh. The thigh was x-rayed from two angles but no abnormality was detected.

The following day, Saturday, there was a dramatic collapse of his blood pressure, his pulse rose to 160 a minute and his temperature fell, leaving him cold, sweating and dizzy. Thought to be suffering from shock due to septicaemia, he was transferred to intensive care. He then stopped passing urine, indicating kidney damage. Blood was appearing in his vomit and his white cell blood count had risen alarmingly. This continued to rise, reaching three times the normal level.

An electrocardiogram early on Sunday September 11 showed a blockage of the conduction system of the heart and it was decided that an electrical pacemaker might have to be employed. Before that could be done Markov became confused and agitated and began pulling out his intravenous therapy tubes. His heart stopped at 9.45am and attempts at resuscitation were abandoned at 10.40am.

On September 12 an autopsy was conducted by pathologist Rufus Crompton, a senior lecturer in forensic medicine at St George's Hospital Medical School. He later reported 'an air of scepticism' in the *post mortem* room, where it was felt that Markov's description of the Waterloo Bridge attack as an assassination attempt might have been 'largely due to the wholly understandable paranoia of a political defector'. From the effects observed in the lungs, liver, small intestines, lymph glands, testicles and pancreas and haemorrhages in the tissues, it was concluded that death was due to blood poisoning.

Crompton cut away a block of flesh surrounding the mark on the right thigh and a corresponding piece from the left. Sealed in separate plastic bags, these were sent to the Metropolitan Police Forensic Science Laboratory. An investigation was launched by Scotland Yard's Anti-Terrorist Squad, led by Commander James Nevill.

Because of the 'cloak and dagger' background, it was decided to send the excised tissue for examination at the Government's Chemical Defence Establishment at Porton Down, Wiltshire. There, drawing on their expert knowledge of poisons, pathologist David Gall and his colleague Dennis Swanson were asked to determine what had killed Markov.

Informing a London meeting of the Medico-Legal Society of what followed, Gall said that, scrutinizing the flesh from the right thigh, he had 'seen that Rufus had put in a pin to keep his orientation on a piece of loose tissue and had pushed it to the hilt, obviously to give him some kind of mark. Idly, as one does, I just tipped this with my gloved finger to make sure that that was what it was. To my alarm this pinhead moved an inch across the tissue; it was a loose piece of metal. It was really very lucky that it did not roll off the *post mortem* table onto the floor, under the cupboard and down the drain.'

At first Gall thought it was 'the sort of metallic bead that you sew onto a woman's handbag', but on examining it more closely he saw that the pellet had been drilled with two holes at right angles to one another. 'Through one I could see daylight, through the other I could see nothing as there was clearly a lot of congealed tissue inside.' He reckoned that the pellet measured about a millimetre and a half in diameter and could have contained about half a milligram (500 micrograms) of material.

Despite best endeavours, no poison was found in the body tissue and the blood cultures were negative. By a process of deduction from the symptoms shown during Markov's final days, Gall and Swanson eliminated bacterial and viral infections and diphtheria and tetanus toxins. Endotoxin, a known cause of fever and increased white blood cells, was also dismissed because of the quantity that would have been needed to cause death. Of the chemical poisons, only dioxin was considered to be a possibility but, again, Markov's death had not been characteristic.

Lastly, the investigators turned to natural toxins, the products of the plant and animal kingdoms. Most, like snake venom, would have produced a different clinical reaction, such as swift death with convulsions. There was, however, knowledge of two seemingly admissible plant toxins, ricin and abrin. The most likely, it was decided, was ricin, a derivative of the castor oil plant. The director of Porton Down's Medical Division, Dr Frank Beswick, had had dealings with work on it some years earlier and recalled that it gave a clinical picture like that of Markov's – a slow onset with fever, a high white blood cell count, shock, damage to lymph nodes, widespread haemorrhages and a slow death.

Although experiments with the substance had been carried out on small animals – mice, rats and guinea pigs – little had been done with larger creatures. It was, the Porton Down experts decided, necessary to do a test with an animal of about the same weight as a man. An unfortunate pig was chosen for the purpose and an appropriate injection administered. Six hours later the pig began to show signs of illness, its temperature and white cell count rising. It did not vomit but was clearly off its food. Next morning it was very subdued and unwilling to eat. The white cell count was still going up but there was difficulty in obtaining blood samples, possibly a sign of circulatory failure. An electrocardiograph showed an extremely abnormal rhythm of the heart. The animal died just over 24 hours after receiving the injection. A *post mortem* examination showed that it had suffered multiple haemorrhages to internal organs in similar fashion to the injuries inflicted on Markov.

Four years later there was some direct clinical evidence of the effects of human ingestion of ricin. This came from Wayne Snodgrass, director of the Mid America Poison Centre, in Kansas City. Dr Snodgrass reported the receipt of an irate telephone call from a suicidal 32-year-old man who, having gained information about ricin at a public library, had swallowed 50 or more castor bean seeds – between ten and 50 times the reported lethal dose. He telephoned to complain that he was still alive. He was kept talking long enough for his call to be traced and an ambulance despatched to collect him.

Initial treatment retrieved a number of whole and partly-chewed beans from his stomach and he was given activated charcoal as a binding agent. Some seven hours after swallowing the beans he developed severe throat, abdominal, and kidney pain, with a marked decrease in urine output. His pulse rate increased and blood pressure dropped. After receiving large volumes of intravenous fluids his condition improved. There was then a setback, with breathing problems for which he required four days of respiratory ventilator assistance.

Attributing the man's recovery to the swift attention he had received, Snodgrass ended his report 'The general public should be made more aware of the toxicity of castor bean seeds.'

The pellet found at Porton Down was sent to the Metropolitan Police Forensic Science Laboratory, where it was received by Robin Keeley, a physicist and head of the Electron Microscopy Group. His first task was to acertain what the pinhead-sized bead, resembling the decorative silver balls sometimes seen in cake-icing, was made of. The scanning electron microscope enabled it to be chemically analysed and revealed that it was composed of about 90 per cent platinum and ten per cent iridium, a commercially-available alloy harder than steel and resistant to corrosion. Being biologically inert, this material would be unlikely to provoke rejection by human body tissues. X-ray spectra gave more technical information. In an effort to trace a possible source of the pellet, the laboratory staff contacted every known manufacturer of ballpoint-pen tips in Europe. The results were surprising rather than helpful. It emerged that some ballpoints contain between eight and ten different metals. Nothing similar to the Markov pellet, which measured 1.53 millimetres in diameter, came to light from these sources.

Discussing the case with the slender, youthful-looking Keeley at the laboratory in January 1988, I asked whether he had any views as to how the neat holes had been made in the tiny ball. He told me that, apart from his professional work, he was 'something of a model engineer and instrument maker'. From a workshop manual he had found that mechanical drills were available with which holes of the size of those in the pellet – 0.35 of a millimetre – could be achieved.

Nevertheless, he was of the opinion that the holes had most probably been made by spark erosion, a process in which the object being worked on is placed in a bath of electrolyte and a strong current of electricity applied through a tool, causing sparking which erodes the workpiece as required. No high-tech facilities would be needed to produce the ball or the holes, Keeley said; the equipment employed in a good craftsman jeweller's workroom would suffice.

Considering the properties required to accomplish the purpose for which the pellet had evidently been made, Keeley began with hardness because of the need to avoid the distortion that can be caused to missiles when striking their targets, even when passing through clothing. Too much damage to the pellet might result in part, or even the whole, of its contents being lost. Having hit the target, the next necessity would be for the pellet not to draw attention to itself by causing irritation or inflammation and so creating the feeling that there was something beneath the small puncture in the skin. Hence the choice of the inert alloy. It was, however, a fact that the metal was one of the most radio-opaque materials known. When the x-rays of Markov's thigh were re-examined, the embedded ball was visible in the shadow of the femur, about one centimetre under the skin. It had, Keeley thought, probably been mistaken for a speck of dirt, a common phenomenon on hastily-produced hospital x-rays.

The dose that could be carried by the pellet was estimated as about 0.2 of a milligram. Thus, experts concluded, ricin 'came into the frame right away' as the probable toxin. Their reasoning was explained on the basis that, for a person of 70 kilograms body weight, some 100 milligrams of arsenic or cyanide, 'the man-in-the-street's idea of deadly poison', would be needed for a fatal dose. Similarly, at least ten milligrams of the organic poisons nicotine, methyl-mercury, or fluoro-acetates would be required to cause death. In the field of nerve gases, such as Tabun and Sarin, milligram rather than sub-milligram doses were needed to kill. Of the bio-toxins, lethal amounts of snake venom or diphtheria, tetanus or botulinum bacilli would be within the capacity of the pellet but were eliminated because of Markov's inappropriate clinical symptoms. Intensely toxic radioactive isotopes like plutonium 239 and radium 226 were also quantitatively admissible, but the high neutron capture cross section of iridium meant that significant radioactivity would have been detectable in the pellet. Only a normal background level was found.

Giving his theories as to the device used to propel the pellet, Keeley pointed out that there was no substantive evidence that the umbrella Markov said he had seen his supposed assailant picking up had necessarily played any part in the attack. The close-range use of a firearm, even one fitted with a silencer, would almost certainly have left traceable scorching or powder marks on Markov's jeans, but no such signs had been found. Indeed it had, said Keeley, been quite difficult to detect the place where the pellet had gone through the jeans. Nor, because of the wide bore of needle that would have been needed, did he think that the pellet could have been injected. In his view the propelling weapon had been some form of gas or airgun.

Admitting that some of his colleagues were of the opinion that something other than ricin might have been used, he said that, in 1978, there had been little knowledge of the substance. Each effort to produce antibodies had resulted in the death of the animal experimented with.

The news of Markov's death added anxiety to sadness for his 26-year-old friend, Bulgarian fellow-writer and defector Vladimir Kostov, who was working in Paris. A short time earlier he had received a letter from Markov warning him of 'serious reasons for anxiety' and urging him to be on his guard. On August 26 1978 – just 12 days before the attack on Markov – he and his wife Natalia had been on a Métro escalator going up to the Champs Elysées when he had felt 'a sharp blow in the back just above the belt, accompanied by a muffled report'. Turning, he had seen a man carrying a small bag. The couple had noticed him earlier because he had seemed eager to stand near them on the train. On reaching the street the man had disappeared into the crowd.

Later that afternoon, the pain in his back being no better, Kostov had consulted a doctor and been told that the tiny puncture was probably a wasp sting. Kostov's suggestion that there might have been an attempt on his life was received with disbelief.

The following day, finding that he was suffering from a high fever and painful swelling, Kostov had gone to a hospital. The doctor who saw him there acknowledged that he had suffered something more serious than an insect bite but said he could not be more specific unless Kostov checked in for tests. Receiving an assurance that he was in no grave danger, Kostov had decided to see whether the condition would improve. Three days later the fever and swelling had begun to subside.

When he learned of Markov's death, Kostov told the police he believed he had been similarly attacked. They gave him immediate protection and informed Scotland Yard. Information about the pellet found in Markov was flashed back to Paris. An x-ray showed that Kostov had a tiny metallic object beneath the skin where he had been struck. Carried out under local anaesthetic, the operation for its removal had to be done with particular care because of the possibility that injudicious movement might release further poison. Embedded in a piece of excised flesh, the foreign body was taken to London by an officer from Scotland Yard. When examined at the laboratory, it was seen to be a pellet almost identical to the one removed from Markov, the sole difference being that it was 0.01 of a millimetre smaller in diameter. (Readers who are unfamiliar with such measurements may find it helpful, for purposes of comparison, to know that the average thickness of human skin is between one and two millimetres.)

I asked Robin Keeley about his views as to the origins of the pellets. Was it known whether the expertise for their manufacture and the knowledge of subtle toxicology existed in Bulgaria? He answered that, judging from the revelations made at international scientific conferences, it was possible but not probable. The USSR was, he said, known to be the world's major supplier of the platinum/iridium alloy. My next questions were why had Kostov survived while Markov died and why had the former been hit in the back and the latter in the leg? Keeley gave the opinion that Kostov might have survived because he was larger, younger and probably fitter than Markov. As to the point of impact, Kostov had been wearing only a shirt and trousers in the summer heat of Paris, while Markov had worn a coat in the approaching autumn of London. There was, Keeley agreed, also the possibility that there might have been an error of dosage or some other miscarriage with the Kostov attempt which had been rectified with Markov.

In a *Reader's Digest* article published in December 1979, Kostov claimed that, as the former Paris bureau chief of Bulgarian radio and television, he had had access to confidential proceedings when Bulgaria had been host to a conference of Soviet-bloc nations. Russia was then having trouble with dissidents within its own territory as well as with Poland and Czechoslovakia. At the conference, stress had been laid on the suppression of internal dissent. His homeland, a nation of less than nine million people, had 30,000 agents in its intelligence apparatus, all under Soviet control and administered by KGB advisers who reported to Moscow, Kostov wrote. Following his defection in 1977, he had learned from well-informed friends in Bulgaria that the Party chief Zhivkov had discussed him and Markov with General Dimiter Stoyanov, the minister of internal affairs who had control of the secret police. This discussion had ended with a decision that, as both Markov and Kostov were regular broadcasters to Bulgaria on Radio Free Europe, silencing them would be a way to discourage the growing dissident activity within the country. Kostov's article added that a former colonel in the Bulgarian secret police, Stefan Sverdlev, had testified on a BBC *Panorama* television programme that Russian approval would have been essential for the murder of Markov.

The public outcry over Markov had, for the moment, seemingly given him immunity from open attack, Kostov believed. While continuing his broadcasts to Bulgaria, he was nevertheless bearing in mind a chilling remark made by Stoyanov on Bulgarian television four days after Markov died: 'Our enemies cannot evade our action anywhere. For us, borders do not exist.'

An unsigned article published in the London *Times* in April

1984 stated that ricin had been the subject of intensive research in Hungary. The item also asserted that a G A Balint of Szeged University had received a doctorate on the effects of ricin poisoning when working as a visiting lecturer at Makerere University in the Uganda of Idi Amin.

Less than a month after Markov's death another Bulgarian employed by the BBC was found dead in strange circumstances. He was 30-year-old Vladimir Simeonov, a translator and news reader who lived alone in Plaistow, east London. Like most of his colleagues, he had been a frightened man after the Markov affair. Comforting himself with the thought that he was no important enough to warrant the attention of the Bulgarian secret police, he nonetheless revealed that he had received a threat of death from a Bulgarian seaman who had met him in the foyer of the BBC. Traced and interviewed by Commander Nevill, the sailor was exonerated from implication in Simeonov's death.

Simeonov died from inhaling blood after apparently falling down stairs at his home. His injuries included a broken nose, cut upper lip and bruising of the chest, left eye and throat. A pathologist said he thought the throat to be an unusual site for an injury due to a fall. The body contained no alcohol, drugs or pellets. A small aneurysm found in the heart was considered to be a possible cause of episodes of dizziness. The inquest returned a verdict of accidental death.

The Metropolitan Police Forensic Science Laboratory has not closed its file on Georgi Ivanov Markov. The Lilliputian pellet that conveyed the minuscule cargo that killed him is being kept in safe custody at New Scotland Yard.

CHAPTER 15
Loathsome landlord

A CARDINAL REQUIREMENT OF FORENSIC scientists is that their knowledge and skills must be applied dispassionately, free of emotional entanglement and unbiased by the apparent rights and wrongs of the situations they encounter. The sciential regimen is their greatest aid to the attainment of these ends. Lesser mortals, lacking the discipline of tutelage within a system of immutable laws and principles, would experience some difficulty in always maintaining an attitude of unwavering academic impartiality. They would face particular problems in cases like that of Mohan Gulrajani.

The son of a Karachi magistrate, Gulrajani was a wily schemer and an insatiable sexual pervert. He took up residence in Britain in 1956, when he was 26. Using a combination of cunning and persistence, he gradually acquired property in west London. He also gained a criminal conviction for gross indecency. By 1979 he owned or had a financial holding in 14 houses. These were let out in rooms, mostly to young male foreigners. A few of them received board and lodging in exchange for menial work.

As most of his tenants were either illegal immigrants, unauthorized overstayers in Britain or criminals, Gulrajani exercised total power over their lives. At the least sign of rebellion, he would threaten any 'difficult' individual with exposure to the authorities. He took possession of passports and worked his 'employees' brutally hard while keeping them in squalid conditions. He also forced them to gratify his homosexual penchants. Anyone who fell behind with the

payment of rent was punished by having his personal
belongings confiscated. Cupboards were filled with the
proceeds of these seizures.

On Sunday August 26 1979, a day of West Indian carnival
in nearby Notting Hill, the police were called to one of
Gulrajani's houses – 89 Earls Court Road. When they entered
the room he occupied there, they saw that it had been
ransacked. The contents of wardrobes and drawers were
strewn about and the bed was piled high with clothing.
Removal of this apparel revealed the dead body of Gulrajani,
clad only in a vest which was rolled up above the waist. The
bed was saturated with blood from a wound in his neck.
Scrawled in blood on the wall above the corpse were the letters
'Rob'. There was a pool of blood on the floor near the door and
written with a ballpoint pen on another wall was the message
'You call me a mother fucker/nigger. You must die you stupid
bastard. My name is …'

The case was referred to the Metropolitan Police Forensic
Science Laboratory, initially for drug screening, blood group
testing and the examination of oral, penile and anal swabs
taken from the body.

Some of the first police inquiries, directed by Detective
Superintendent John Pole, were centred on the message
written in blood, with the theory that this might have been the
dying man's attempt to identify his killer. The room below
Gulrajani's had been occupied by a young Uruguayan named
Robert Fearne, who had departed the day before discovery of
the murder. The police were told that Gulrajani had made
sexual advances to Fearne, who had responded by holding a
knife to his throat and threatening to kill him if he persisted
with his unwelcome attentions. Fearne, an illegal overstayer,
was traced to a flat in Earls Court, where he was found hiding
in a wardrobe.

But the widening investigation led elsewhere. Among the
people who were questioned, three other young men were of
notable interest to the detectives. One, a 24-year-old from
Singapore, gave the name Suresh Nair. Having arrived in
London only a few weeks previously, he said he had seen one
of Gulrajani's advertisements and, on contacting him, had

been engaged as a kind of houseboy at 89 Earls Court Road. Gulrajani had not given him a room and he had had to sleep on a couch in the living quarters. It was later discovered that this individual's true name was Duarkh son of Hardayal, that he was known in Singapore as Ashok Kumar and that his girlfriend there called him Steve Ashok. He had come to London using a passport belonging to a lookalike acquaintance, a fact that had become known to Gulrajani, who had, as usual, taken charge of his employee's official documentation. 'Nair' said that he had no knowledge of the killing.

Andrew McDonagh, another resident in the house, said that he had been anxious to see Gulrajani about a grievance. He had seen 'Nair' sitting in their landlord's small office the previous day. 'Nair' had told him that Gulrajani was not in. The occupants of rooms were under instructions to leave their keys on a plate in the hallway and, when 'Nair' had become engaged in conversation with another caller, McDonagh had taken several keys and gone upstairs. Finding that one key opened Gulrajani's door, he had looked in and seen the disorder. At that moment 'Nair' had arrived and said 'You can't go in there.'

The following morning, the Sunday, 'Nair' had again been busy with numerous callers at Gulrajani's office. Declaring himself 'fed up' with the situation, one, a forceful young New Zealander named Gary Ogle, announced his intention of kicking the landlord's door in, to check on the report that he was away. Accompanied by 'Nair' and another lodger named John Grayden, he had gone to Gulrajani's room and carried out his threat. Astounded by the disarray within, Ogle had pulled some of the clothes from the bed and all three men had seen the body. The police had then been summoned.

'Right from the start I had a feeling that "Nair" was not telling the truth,' former Detective Chief Superintendent John Pole told me during a conversation about the affair in February 1988. 'I wrote "Suspect" in red at the top of his statement.' Still affirming his ignorance of the crime, 'Nair' was arrested on suspicion of murder and because he was found to be in possession of a holdall containing jewellery and other items that were believed to have belonged to Gulrajani. Embroiled in the case, Pole had to cancel his eagerly-awaited annual holiday in North Wales but was given permission to take a day's leave to drive his wife and children to their booked destination. On his return to London he found that 'Nair' and the property had had to be released. More evidence was needed.

It was then, nearly three weeks after the murder, that the police asked the laboratory to carry out an additional scrutiny at the scene of the crime, to see whether any further indications could be discovered. Dr Ann Priston, a biologist whose gentle manner, petite build and dark good looks disguise an incisive mind and resolute will, tackled the task on September 14.

The difficulties she faced were profound. 'During those weeks the room had been examined many times by many people,' she said during a talk with me at the laboratory in January 1988. 'The furniture had been moved and the floor well walked on. Part of the wall with the writing in blood had been taken away and plaster had been ground into the floor. However, during my examination I noticed some scuffed remains of what looked like a shoe mark in blood by the side of the bed.

'The entire square of lino was removed at my request and brought to the laboratory, where the mark was grouped and shown to be in the blood of the dead man. My colleague Dr Clive Candy examined the mark with a view to identifying the wearer and matched up, like a fingerprint, 16 points of comparison with the right shoe of "Suresh Nair".

'Interpreting the shoe mark in the context of the scene led to four observations. First, the mark was made while the blood was still wet. Second, the wet blood covered the entire underside of the shoe – therefore it could not have been made by a dry shoe stepping into a drop of blood. Third, the print pointed towards the bed. Fourth, there were no shoe prints leading from the only other source of blood in the room – that by the door.

'The only explanation was that the mark was made by the wearer stepping backwards off the bed onto the floor. Since the only way the shoe could have become wetted with blood was by being on the bed before the body was covered over, it followed that the maker of the shoe mark was present at the time of the killing.'

Pole again interviewed 'Nair'. Though still proclaiming his innocence, the Singaporean began to embellish his version of events. Three West Indians had killed Gulrajani after forcing their way into the house and had threatened him with a similar death if he betrayed them, he averred. The intruders had also taken his return ticket home, he went on. But Pole's team established that the ticket had been cashed by 'Nair's' brother in Singapore, soon after 'Nair' had arrived in London. 'Nair' was rearrested, on a charge of murder.

His legal representatives intimated the intention of entering a defence against that charge, but this resolution weakened when they learned of the damning testimony of the shoe print. It was then decided that 'Nair' would plead guilty to manslaughter, with provocation. Provocation had been defined in this connection by Lord Devlin, for four years a Lord Justice of Appeal, as 'Some act or series of acts done by the dead man to the accused, which would cause in any reasonable person and actually causes in the accused a sudden and temporary loss of self-control, rendering the accused so subject to passion as to make him for a moment not master of his mind.'

It thus became a matter for Pole to decide whether to proceed with the charge of murder, which, being contested, would have entailed some significant cost to public funds. Representatives of the Director of Public Prosecutions advised that the claim of provocation would probably succeed with the jury. The charge was therefore reduced to one of manslaughter.

'Nair's' final story was that, on the morning of the murder, he had taken four pills to gain the courage to approach Gulrajani about getting 'his' passport back. He had gone to Gulrajani's room, taking him his customary cup of tea. Gulrajani had promised he would discuss the passport if 'Nair' masturbated him, which he had done. But the man had still refused to give him the document and an argument had followed, with 'Nair' standing by the bed and Gulrajani sitting up on it.

In his exasperation he had picked up a fruit knife from the bedside table and held it at Gulrajani's throat, 'Nair' continued. Gulrajani had slid down the bed and 'Nair' had jumped onto it, kneeling astride his tormentor with the knife still held against his throat. Gulrajani had a large Alsatian dog called Top, which slept in his room. Gulrajani had shouted the animal's name and it had jumped up at 'Nair's' back, knocking him forward. In consequence, the knife had gone into Gulrajani's throat. After partly withdrawing it, he had pushed it in hard, 'Nair' confessed.

With Gulrajani bleeding profusely, 'Nair' had again asked about 'his' passport, whereupon Gulrajani had pointed at the floor then dipped his finger in the blood and written 'Rob' on the wall. Asked whether he meant Robert Fearne, Gulrajani had nodded affirmatively.

Dashing downstairs, he had searched Fearne's room but had not found the passport, 'Nair's' recital went on. On returning to Gulrajani's room, he had found the man holding a pillow to his throat and moving towards the telephone. After snatching and throwing the pillow towards the door, 'Nair' said, he had pushed Gulrajani back onto the bed, where he had died. Still seeking 'his' passport, he had twice searched the room without success. Finally he had left, locking the door behind him.

The trial, at the Old Bailey on May 6 1980, lasted less than half an hour. Defended by Kenneth Machin QC, 'Nair' was sentenced to five years' imprisonment. A deportation order was served on him, to take effect on his discharge from gaol.

Pole left the police force in June 1986, to become head of security in the gargantuan, many-tentacled empire of multi-millionaire publisher Robert Maxwell. Dark haired, strongly built and immaculately dressed, he paid tribute, during our talk, to Ann Priston's vital discovery of the bloody shoe print. 'But "Nair" was a frightened little man who lied all the way through,' he told me. 'I'm sure the tale about the dog was not true because it was a big, dopey animal that wouldn't have gone leaping around.' Sadly, he thought the inoffensive creature had probably been put down. Nor, in his view, had Gulrajani been trying to involve Fearne by beginning to write his name on the wall. 'With blood gushing over his fingers from a wound that had severed his larynx and made it impossible for him to speak, I am sure he was simply trying to get "Nair" out of the room.'

I asked why 'Nair' had not fled after release from his first period of detention by the police. Pole said that he thought this was because the killer had become convinced that, had he done so, he would certainly have been recaptured. He was also still without 'his' passport. It was legally correct that he had been convicted in his falsely-assumed name, Pole added: 'If you call yourself Mickey Mouse, you'll be charged as Mickey Mouse!'

When we discussed the importance of avoiding emotional involvement in forensic casework, 45-year-old Dr Priston commented that, although she did not find detachment difficult, 'It would be a sad day when we are not affected.' With 17½ years of experience at the laboratory, she acknowledged that the work 'could be depressing'. Married to a civil servant and the mother of a 14½-year-old son and eight-year-old daughter, she said she complemented her scientific duties by taking a close interest in the law.

CHAPTER 16
Homosexual horror

FEW HOMICIDES ARE EXECUTED WITH more frenzied ferocity than those that occur in the jealously spiteful, shadowy world of male homosexuals. The death of well-known actor Peter Arne was no exception. His final exit was made under a rain of blows inflicted with a log snatched from the fireplace of his bijou ground floor bedsitter flat at 54 Hans Place, Knightsbridge, and with a heavy stool, the latter being smashed into his head with such violence that the seat was distorted from its joints with the legs. As well as administering these massive injuries, the murderer also cut the 63-year-old's throat with a razor-sharp kitchen knife, severing both a carotid artery and a jugular vein.

Arne's struggle for life was evidenced by the bloodstains that extended into the communal hallway of the building and by the crimson streaks that were left on floorcoverings when his slayer dragged him back into his own quarters.

The killing occurred early in the sultry afternoon of Monday August 1 1983. A bizarre aspect was uncovered by the later revelation that passers-by in the stylish thoroughfare had heard sounds of noisy conflict transmitted over Arne's entryphone, the internal handset of which had been knocked from its holder during the fracas. But no one paid attention; the British tradition of 'It's not my concern' is deeply entrenched, especially in the modish environs of London SW1.

The alarm was raised by Miss Eva Bravo, a Philippino nursemaid employed by a family living above Arne. She was startled to find bloodstains, a blood-covered log, a wallet and other items scattered about the communal hallway of the house.

The police inquiries were directed by Detective Chief Inspector Stephan Landeryou, who was assisted by Detective Sergeant Roy Grover, a liaison officer at the Metropolitan Police Forensic Science Laboratory. Also on the scene on the day of the murder was a scientist from the laboratory, biologist Dr Christopher Price.

Price found little sign of disturbance and only a small amount of bloodstaining in the principal room of Arne's home. There were two coffee mugs on a trolley, two cigarette ends in an ashtray and a partly-consumed jar of honey on the floor. But near the door were a rolled-up sleeping bag and an open rucksack, both of which bore smears of blood. A shirt and towel in the rucksack were bloodstained. The shirt was in a position in which blood could have fallen onto it, but the towel, being lower in the rucksack, could not have received its bloodstains in that way. A pair of soiled underpants, a pair of trousers, a torn shirt and a pair of size 10½ boots lay around the rucksack. All were heavily bloodstained. The toecaps of both boots, which were of a size that is taken by only three per cent of the British population, were strangely distorted in the area of the middle toes.

In the hall of the flat, where Arne's body was lying, there was heavy bloodstaining, in the form of spots, smears, splashes and runs on the floor, walls, ceiling and inner side of a door. Blood splashes in the bathroom appeared to have been projected from the hall. In the communal hallway there were extensive, heavy smears, splashes and spots of blood along both walls, on the ceiling and on the inside face of the front door. Impressions of hair in blood smears on a wall near the floor indicated that a head had been in contact there.

The upper part of Arne's body, which was lying face downwards, extended from the hall of his flat into the tiny kitchen. Long streaks of blood on the carpet showed that he had been dragged into that position. Heavy bloodstaining on the lower parts of the kitchen walls radiated out from his head. On the kitchen floor were a knife and a wooden stool, both

heavily bloodstained. The kitchen sink contained diluted
blood and there were diluted bloodstains on the sink surround
and a dishcloth.

Price's tests showed that none of the blood from which
reactions were obtainable was of a group different from
Arne's. This suggested that his assailant had suffered no
significant injury during his onslaught. The results of tests
carried out on dried saliva from the coffee mugs showed that
one had been used by someone other than Arne. Spermatozoa
were found on a rectal swab taken from the body. Reactions
obtained from semen stains inside the underpants found near
the rucksack established that they were of a group different
from Arne's.

From these pointers, Price gave the opinion that Arne was
first attacked in his living-cum-bedroom, sustaining a
relatively minor injury that bled and so caused some slight
bloodstaining on the bed-settee. It seemed likely that he had
then left the room, followed by his assailant, who was wielding
the log taken from the fireplace. The assault had probably
continued as Arne passed through the hall of his flat into the
communal hallway, right up to the front door. After this he
had apparently been brought back into the flat, being finally
dragged into the position in which he was found. The absence
of blood distribution consistent with arterial spurting
suggested that his throat had been cut as he lay prone on the
floor or after his death.

The first task confronting the police was to ascertain
whether the attacker had been a burglar who had gained entry
through the open window, an intruder who had started his
assault at the front door and continued it into the flat, or
someone with whom Arne had been acquainted, who had been
admitted as an accepted social visitor. It soon became clear
that someone known to Arne had been responsible for his
death.

Among the people questioned were 24-year-old Thomas
Jackson, an unemployed northerner who had been living with
Arne while approaching various London modelling agencies in
search of work, and 44-year-old John Joseph Ryan, a friend of
Arne's, who lived nearby. Both men were cleared of any

1

2

3

4

1 Michael Hart, the man who brutally murdered Angela Wooliscroft during a raid on Barclay's Bank at Ham, Surrey (see Prologue).

2 Mrs Susan Barber, who murdered her husband by lacing his food with paraquat, pictured with one of her lovers (see Chapter 23).

3 Kingsley Rotardier, killer of Dr David Napier Hamilton, his former lover (see Chapter 24).

4 Henry 'Big H' MacKenny, found guilty of four contract killings (see Chapter 12).

The 'Stockwell Strangler', Kenneth Erskine, convicted of murdering seven elderly people (see Chapter 30). (Press Association Photos).

Dr John Baksh and his first wife Ruby, also a doctor, whom he murdered. His second wife, Madhu, survived after he cut her throat (see Chapter 25). (Press Association Photos).

John Francis Duffy, the 'railway' rapist/murderer (see Chapter 27).

Scenes of crime: Doria Schroder's maisonette in Walton Street, Knightsbridge (see Chapter 19).

Part of the living room in Doria Schroder's maisonette showing the fan heater, the cord of which was thought to have been used to strangle her.

18 Denmark Place: the front door and the letterbox through which John Thompson poured petrol before setting fire to the building killing 37 people (see Chapter 20).

Inside the front door: the stair way which burst into flames when the petrol was ignited.

Rear view of the burnt-out building.

The lorry overturned by reckless driver Mark Mellor. Cyclist Christopher Stafford was crushed to death beneath it (see Chapter 34).

1 Dr Ann Priston (see Chapters 15, 18 and 19).

2 Mrs Anne Davies (see Chapters 13, 27 and 30).

3 Dr Elizabeth Wilson (see Chapters 12 and 26).

4 Brian Arnold (see Chapters 12 and 38).

5 Robin Keeley (see Chapter 14).

6 Andrew Clatworthy (see Chapter 23).

7 Dr Christopher Davies (see Chapter 24).

1

2

3

4

5

6

© METROPOLITAN POLICE

7

1 Dr John Taylor (see Chapter 25).

2 David Halliday (see Chapter 31).

3 Dr Brian Gibbins (see Chapter 32).

4 Douglas Stoten (see Chapters 33 and 35).

5 Dr Brian Connett (see Chapter 37).

6 Former Detective Chief Inspector Peter Jay
(see Chapter 13).

7 Detective Sergeant Richard Cain (see Chapter 17).

1 Detective Sergeant Roy Grover (see Chapter 18).

2 Detective Chief Inspector Hugh Parker
(see Chapter 22).

3 Detective Sergeant Derek Hancock
(see Chapter 25).

4 Former Detective Chief Superintendent David Little
(see Chapter 26).

5 Detective Chief Superintendent Vincent McFadden
(see Chapter 27).

6 Commander Brian Jackson (see Chapter 30).

7 Sergeant (formerly Constable) Stuart Anderson
(see Chapter 32).

The building housing the Metropolitan Police Forensic Science Laboratory. The Laboratory occupies the upper floors of the block at the rear.

Dr James Davidson, the first director of the Laboratory (see Chapter 6).

One of the scanning electron microscopes in action (see Chapter 11).

1 Dr Roger Berrett using Autocad – a computer-aided device for the production of diagrams depicting the scenes of fires (see Chapter 11).

2 A greatly-enlarged view of the pellet used to kill Georgi Markov. (Note: μ signifies microns. One micron is equivalent to .0000393 of an inch. See Chapter 14).

3 & 4 The paper fragments recovered from the stomach of William McPhee (see Chapter 28).

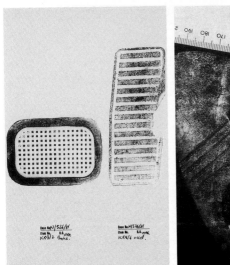

'Autocide' that killed another: the sole of Jobling's right shoe shows a clear imprint of the accelerator, proving that he was still urging his car forward at the moment of impact (see Chapter 33).

Jobling escaped with minor injuries, but 42-year-old Anthony Victor Gladen, driving the van on the right, was killed.

The car driven by Jobling (see Chapter 33).

Gladen's van.

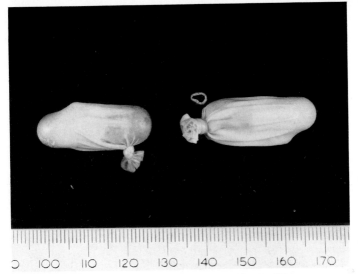

Drugs found in the internal organs of Ian Fuller (see Chapter 37).

Plastic bags containing parts of some of his victims' bodies found at the North London home of Dennis Nilsen (see Chapter 13).

Mohan Gulrajani's disordered bedroom (see Chapter 15).

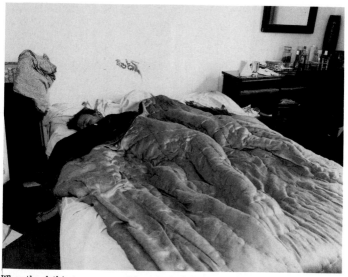

When the clothing was removed from the bed, Gulrajani's body was revealed. Note the message 'Rob...' written on the wall in his own blood by Gulrajani as he was dying.

Michelle Sadler and Robert Vaughan (see Chapter 17).

David Carty, their murderer.

The dumper truck containing the bodies of Michelle Sadler and Robert Vaughan.

Above: The entrance to 164 Union Street, scene of the murders of Michelle Sadler and Robert Vaughan.

Left: The trolley on which David Carty wheeled the bodies of his victims through the streets of Southwark in the early hours.

Below: The basement workshop at 164 Union Street.

involvement in the crime, but Ryan described a recent occasion when Arne had told him he was going to take some sandwiches to a man 'down on his luck' in Hyde Park. Ryan said he had accompanied Arne on this mission and had seen that the recipient of the food was a tall, strongly built, bearded individual, who spoke no English. Arne had said that the man was Italian. As Arne spoke no Italian, the two had conversed in French.

The detectives learned that, on the morning of the murder, Arne had been to the BBC Television Centre to be fitted with his costume for a part in the children's science fiction serial *Dr Who*. He had returned to Hans Place at about midday. Inquiries in the area revealed that some people had seen a large man with a beard and a rucksack eating from a jar of honey outside number 54. An artist's impression was produced from their descriptions and prepared for public distribution.

But at 11am on Thursday August 4, only three days after the murder, a river police patrol found the rapidly-decomposing body of a tall, strongly-built, bearded man floating in the Thames at Wandsworth. An observant officer noticed that the corpse resembled the sketch of the man seen in Hans Place. The body was nude save for a scarf tied to one ankle. On both feet the middle toes were deformed, being raised sharply above the others. The state of undress was linked with the discovery of a set of muddy but neatly-folded clothing in the riverbank 'security' area of a Shell depot near the confluence of the rivers Thames and Wandle at Putney, barely a mile from the place of discovery of the body.

The clothing consisted of a pair of size 10½ boots, blue underpants, a green, zip-fastened leather jacket and a tracksuit. The toecaps of the boots were misshapen in the same way as was the footwear found in Arne's flat. Plaster casts of both pairs of boots were taken by chemist David Castle. They matched the feet of the corpse. The boots, the tracksuit and the lining of the jacket were all bloodstained and gave reactions showing that the blood could have come from Arne. With the clothing was a passport containing a photograph of the dead man, whose identity was given as Giuseppe Perusi, a 32-year-old Italian schoolteacher.

During his examination of the tracksuit, Price found large and small bloodspots spattered over the front of the jacket and on the backs of the legs of the trousers. He reported that this distribution would have arisen if the wearer of the garments had had the trousers on back to front and the jacket done up and had been hit by a 'head on' spray of blood. A fingerprint on the honeypot found in Arne's flat tallied with one taken from the corpse.

From the clues provided by the two sets of clothing, Price postulated that, after bludgeoning and dragging Arne back into the hall of the flat, Perusi had undressed, leaving his heavily bloodstained garments on the floor. After washing the blood from his hands and face in the kitchen sink, he had, Price thought, put on the second pair of boots and the tracksuit. Then, for some reason, he had resumed his attack on Arne, possibly, at that stage, using the stool and knife. This second assault might, Price conceded, have been provoked because Arne had shown signs of continuing life. It seemed that, finally satisfied that the object of his hatred was dead, Perusi had donned the leather jacket, the lining of which had absorbed some of the blood that had been newly spattered on the tracksuit.

Presented with this accumulation of interwoven forensic evidence, the inquest on Arne produced a verdict that he had been unlawfully killed by Perusi. The Italian's death was recorded as suicide while the balance of his mind was disturbed. Perusi's family contended that he had never been violent or homosexual, pointing out that the scarf found tied to his ankle had been a gift from his girlfriend.

With both parties to the squabble dead, the motive for the killing, carried out as ferociously as any of its kind, is unlikely ever to come to light. Only conjecture remains. Some who have considered the matter take the view that Perusi, who, on a year's leave from his job, had been 'sleeping rough', may have been upset by Arne refusing to accommodate him while, at the same time, he was providing the younger man Jackson with a roof. Others, drawing on the investigators' discoveries that Arne had been in the habit of picking up youths at London railway stations and had, during the weekend preceding the murder, housed a 15-year-old he had met at Charing Cross, are of the opinion that Perusi may have been infuriated by the sight of the boy leaving Arne's flat while he waited outside on that fateful Monday. Whichever, or whatever other, explanation may be the truth, Perusi exacted a terrible revenge for his injured feelings.

During a talk with me at the laboratory in 1988, Price suggested an alternative explanation of Perusi's death. Bearing in mind that the Italian had been living a tramp-like life, that the weather was oppresively warm, that he had taken the trouble to undress and neatly fold his clothing and that he left no note to friends or relatives, it was, Price maintained, possible that the man had simply decided to take a swim and had then accidentally drowned.

Like the reason for his lethal battering of Arne, the purpose Perusi had in mind when he stepped into the grimy water of London's river will almost certainly remain an enigma.

CHAPTER 17

Dead in a dumper

ENJOYING THE RAPID PHYSICAL development that has become the norm for the young in well-nourished Britain, 17-year-old sweethearts Robert Vaughan and Michelle Sadler had announced their intention to marry. Dark haired, five feet six inches tall, slimly built and youthfully handsome, Robert, a packer at the Union Street, Southwark, workshop of Courier Display Systems Ltd, lived with his parents in Cherry Gardens Street, Rotherhithe. A tall, slender, attractive blonde, Michelle, still a schoolgirl, lived with her 49-year-old mother in Chudleigh Street, Stepney.

Early in the morning of Sunday February 5 1984, a woman walking her dog on a grassed-over open space at the junction of Southwark Bridge and Marshalsea Roads, adjacent to Union Street, caught sight of a strange whiteness in a small dumper truck that was parked near the centre of the area. A closer inspection sent her reeling back with shocked disbelief. The whiteness was the body of a slim young woman, lying face upwards and naked except for a pulled-up jumper. Her flung-back head exposed a livid ligature mark around her neck. Beside her, face downwards deeper in the truck, was the body of a young man clad in a jumper and heavily-bloodstained jeans. His corpse was almost floating in blood-reddened water.

Police inquiries were opened by Detective Sergeant Richard Cain and soon established that the bodies were those of Robert and Michelle. His throat had been cut with a sharp instrument and she had been sexually assaulted and strangled. A gag of paper was found in her mouth. Neither of the youngsters had returned home after leaving the previous morning, causing such anxiety that the police had been notified of their absence.

Robert's employers were contacted and explained that he had asked for and been given permission to work overtime on Saturday February 4, to help in preparing material to meet an urgent order from Germany. A conscientious and responsible employee who was popular with his fellows, he had been saving hard for his anticipated wedding. He had been authorized to take Michelle to assist him at the workshop.

The police were also told that another Courier Display Systems employee, an 18-year-old West Indian named David Carty, was thought to have been at the workshop that Saturday. A muscular six-footer living with his mother, two brothers and a sister in Linsey Street, Rotherhithe, he was immediately interviewed by the detectives and held in custody as a suspect. At first he denied all knowledge of the deaths, responding to questions with jaunty cockiness. But as inquiries progressed, his attitude and story changed.

Adrian Emes, a biologist with 16 years of experience at the Metropolitan Police Forensic Science Laboratory, was called to the workshop, in the basement of 164 Union Street, on February 6 and made two subsequent visits for continued examinations. He found that the premises consisted of a room measuring some 60 by 20 feet, reached via an eight feet wide corridor of similar length. Near the entrance to the corridor was a men's toilet equipped with three washbasins and three cubicles, two of the latter containing 'sit down' arrangements and one a double urinal.

Emes discovered that the drain in the urinal was blocked with bloodstained paper. Dilute blood from the drain was of the same groups as a sample taken from Vaughan. Although obvious efforts had been made to wash the urinal, he detected blood on many apparently clean tiles and on the grouting between them. Much of the blood was on the left wall and above the urinal fittings. Blood was also present on parts of the walls above the level of the tiling, where attempts had been made to scrape away the surface paint. Several small spots of blood were found on the back of the door to the urinal, in a position that would have been overlooked by someone engaged in the hasty removal of the signs of crime. From the position of the bloodstains in the urinal area, Emes formed the opinion that Vaughan had been attacked from behind as he stood using the left urinal. This view also served to explain why, when his body was found, Vaughan's jeans were unzipped and his penis exposed.

On the floor of a narrow passageway near the toilet, Emes found a small spot of blood of the same groups as Vaughan's. Careful scrutiny under special lighting of the red-painted floor of the main corridor to the workshop revealed eight evenly-spaced prints made by the partly-bloodstained sole of a left shoe. Attempts to group the blood from some of the prints were unsuccessful, but one produced results showing that the mark had been made with blood of the same groups as Vaughan's.

Similarly identified blood spots and smears were located on the floor of the workshop, along with two smeared stains which, when tested, were found to consist of semen mixed with blood. These stains gave reactions for the same blood group as Carty's. One also gave reactions for the same group as Michelle's and Carty's, a result which Emes attributed to the blood element in the stain. A screwed-up paper tissue found in a rubbish box in the workshop had apparently been used to wipe up blood and semen. The reactions obtained from it suggested that the blood and/or semen could have come from Carty.

The handle of an Olfa knife, an implement normally fitted with extremely sharp, disposable blades, was found in the workshop minus its cutter. Although it had been wiped clean, blood of the same groups as Vaughan's was present in several crevices. The combinations of groups obtained from this blood occur in about one in 1,200,000 of the British population. Another Olfa knife, with blade, was smeared with blood which could not be grouped.

In an area leading to a loading bay were drag-marks beginning with bloodstains which gave reactions for the same groups as Vaughan's. More bloodstains were found on a raised platform in the loading bay, but these could not be grouped.

Although vaginal swabs taken from Michelle revealed the presence of semen, efforts to gain grouping reactions were unsuccessful. A penile swab taken from Vaughan disclosed no semen or vaginal material. Both of his trainer-type shoes were extensively and heavily bloodstained.

Traces of semen but no blood or vaginal material were found on penile swabs taken from Carty some 35 hours after the murders. A small bloodstain, which could not be grouped, was present on the upper part of the left sleeve of his blue tracksuit. His tracksuit trousers gave the appearance of having been washed or wiped over, but several smears of blood were present on both legs and a heavier stain just below the waistband gave reaction for the same groups as Vaughan's. Reactions for the same group as his own were obtained from stains of blood mixed with semen on Carty's underpants.

Still in police custody and markedly less confident, Carty began to acknowledge that he knew more about the murders than he had at first admitted. When he was told that the sole of his left shoe matched the bloodstained prints found in the workshop corridor, he said that he had been there with Robert and Michelle on the Saturday morning but, after a while, had left to go shopping in the West End. On his return to Union Street he had found that the couple had been murdered, he claimed. Frightened by the thought that he would be accused of the crimes, he had decided to clean the place up and remove the bodies. During the early hours of the Sunday, he had wrapped the corpses in transparent plastic sheeting, loaded them onto a four-wheeled trolley belonging to the workshop and had then trundled it, unnoticed, through the streets to the small open space nearby, where he had unwrapped and pushed the bodies into the dumper truck.

He added that he had gathered up the items of Michelle's clothing which he had found scattered about the workshop premises and stuffed them into a plastic bag. This he had thrown onto the roof of a wooden shed used as a tea bar in Surrey Row, close to Union Street. Recovered from that place, the articles were sent to Emes for examination in the laboratory.

A few small spots of blood, one of which gave reactions for

the same groups as Vaughan's, and some smears were found on Michelle's green corduroy trousers. On the inside of the left upper front area of the garment there was staining consisting of blood mixed with semen and some cellular material which could have been vaginal in origin. The reactions obtained were thought to be due to the semen present and were of the same groups as Carty and Vaughan.

Michelle's tights were found to have a large hole and several small ladders in the upper front of the left leg. The right foot was almost completely torn off and the left heel was torn. A few light smears of blood were present but could not be grouped.

Her brassiere was undamaged but on the front of the right cup were two small stains of blood mixed with semen. One of the stains gave reactions for the same group as Carty's. Two large areas of staining were found on the outside back of her knickers, each consisting of blood, semen and cellular material which could have come from her vagina. Slightly different reactions were obtained from each of these stains, one being of the same groups as Carty's and Vaughan's. The other result was thought to be due to the vaginal material. There was no urine staining, suggesting that she had not been wearing the knickers when she died.

The 'trainer' type shoes worn by Carty on the day of the murders were also carefully examined by Emes and his colleagues. To the unaided eye their dark blue suede appeared to be clean, but when examined microscopically it was seen to be covered with soaked-in bloodstains. In places there were reactions for blood even though no blood became visible under magnification. Not unexpectedly, Carty claimed that these stains had been collected whilst he was cleaning up the traces of the killings.

While recognizing that some of the marks were consistent with the wearer having walked on and cleaned up a bloodstained floor, Emes gave it as his opinion that many, particularly those on the tongue and left side of the left shoe, were most likely to have resulted from the wearer being close to the origin of the blood at the moment when it was shed. These had, he said, probably been caused by blood splashing directly onto the shoe and by the spray created from blood dropping onto the floor nearby. 'These stains are in such a position that they are unlikely to have arisen whilst the wearer was cleaning up the bloodstained walls and floor of the gents' toilet,' his report affirmed.

To prove his point, Emes enlisted the aid of colleagues to re-enact the murder of Vaughan as he believed it had been carried out. His contention, from the evidence he had gathered, was that either after, or more likely before, assaulting and strangling Michelle, Carty had crept up behind Vaughan as he stood urinating in the toilet, had put his right arm over Vaughan's right shoulder and drawn the Olfa knife across his throat, severing the carotid artery. This would have produced instant, massive and fatal spurting of blood forward and to the left of Vaughan, from which, standing behind him, the killer's body would have been largely protected. But his shoes, particularly the one on his left foot, would have been more vulnerable to the flying blood.

Emes provided the police with a detailed report and photographs describing and illustrating his experiments. They showed how blood had been dropped from neck height onto a floor in front of two people, one standing behind the other. This was repeated, with the two people changing places. The two pairs of shoes worn by the persons standing at the rear had collected numerous spots of blood over their fronts and sides.

'Wearing a third pair of shoes, I walked and stamped on the bloodstained floor, and while still wearing the shoes I washed the blood from the floor with paper towels and water,' his statement added. 'Stamping in the blood produced a large number of spots along the inner aspect of the other shoe. As the shoes became damp many of these spots became diffuse or disappeared. The shoes were deliberately splashed during the cleaning up and many dilute bloodstains were visible ...' Stamping on a bloodstained floor approximately four inches away from a tiled wall produced a few minute spots of blood along the side of the shoe nearest the wall, much as Carty's left shoe had been marked. All of the shoes used in the experiments were, with Carty's own footwear, offered as evidence.

Carty's trial opened at the Old Bailey on November 26 1984, nearly ten months after the killings. He pleaded not guilty to both charges of murder. His defence counsel, Miss Helena Kennedy, described the case as having 'a horrible, Hitchcock quality'. The prosecution was conducted by Allan Green, a senior prosecuting counsel at the Central Criminal Court since 1979. He became Director of Public Prosecutions in 1987. He said that Carty's bloody footprints had led the police to the killer. Summing up on December 4, Mr Justice Kenneth Jones said that there were many unanswered questions in the case, the most outstanding being why Carty should have killed the couple. Virtually no light had been thrown upon that question, he stated. Found guilty on both counts, Carty was sentenced to youth custody for life, a penalty which meant that, on reaching 21, he would be transferred to adult imprisonment for the remainder of his term.

Leaving the court, Vaughan's parents were seen to be in tears. His father was quoted by a newspaper as saying of Carty 'I am not glad he has gone down. He was only a boy at the time.'

Commenting on the question of motive when we discussed the case in June 1988, stockily-built, grey-haired Detective Sergeant Cain, the police officer who dealt with crucial aspects of the investigation, told me that, apart from the sexual attack on a desirable young girl, several items of her gold jewellery had disappeared. So had some £30 or £40 Vaughan was known to have had with him following the payment of his wages the previous day. Carty had received pay of £50, had given his mother about £20 and had then bought a bicycle for £55.

After experience in ten murder cases during his 19 years with the Metropolitan Police, he had given some thought to the 'why?' of Carty's brutality, Cain said. In his estimation, the first factor that needed to be noted was that, as a boy, Carty had been sent to schools, in Guildford and Grimsby, for maladjusted youngsters with emotional and behavioural disorders. His IQ had been assessed as 109. His attacks on the young couple had, in Cain's opinion, stemmed in part from a quarrel with Vaughan, who had criticized him for keeping a cross-bred Alsatian dog at his home – a flat without a garden. The squabble between the two had been overheard by another employee at the Union Street workshop. Vaughan had threatened to report Carty to the RSPCA. Ill with canine distemper, the dog had been put down at an animal centre on February 2 – the day before Carty's 18th birthday and two days before the murders.

The occupants of flats near the workshop had told of hearing screams at about 1.30 pm on February 4, Cain went on. But nothing untoward being visible in the street, the sounds had been attributed to squealing cats. Cain described experiments that were carried out with the co-operation of a female colleague. Screaming at the top of her voice in the basement premises, she had been able to make herself heard in the street only from a position near a fire-escape door. This door had required considerable strength to open and, because of the drag-marks found there, he believed it was the spot at which Michelle had fought for her life against Carty's onslaught.

Cain paid particular tribute to the help he received from Woman Police Constable Susan Brooks, an officer who, at that time, had had no experience of such cases. Like Adrian Emes, she received a commendation on her work from the then Commissioner of Police for the Metropolis, Sir Kenneth Newman. The police had had to pay £340 for hire of the dumper truck during their investigation, Cain added.

Speaking of his numerous findings of blood mixed with semen, Emes said that this was probably due to Carty having a condition called haematospermia, in which there is leakage of blood into the genito-urinary tract.

Six blood grouping systems had been used in the tests, he explained. 'The groups AK, EAP and Hp can only be detected in blood, ABO and PGM are detected in blood, semen and vaginal secretions, and the secretor status is only in body fluids other than blood, such as semen and vaginal secretion. The stains found in this case were subjected to the appropriate tests in attempts to determine their origin.

'Another complication arose because Carty and Vaughan were both group AB secretor, a group which occurs in only two per cent of the population,' Emes said. 'The probability of picking any two people at random from the population and finding them both to be AB secretor is about one in 2,500, and yet here was a case in which both men had this group. This meant that, wherever semen was found, additional grouping was necessary to determine its origin. Sometimes this additional grouping failed. For example, on Michelle's trousers there was staining of blood and semen which gave reactions for AB secretor; further grouping failed and therefore the staining was reported as being of the same group as Carty and Vaughan.'

CHAPTER 18

Fatal holiday

NO ONE WHO RECEIVED A FAREWELL from 36-year-old Roy Porjes before he left his Belsize Park, north London, home on May 3 1983 imagined that the leave-taking would be his last. Still less could they have dreamed that the journey he was about to undertake would convey him to obliteration.

A former dealer in antiques, Porjes was a successful businessman who had much to look forward to. He was engaged to be married. When he announced his plan to go, alone, on a prolonged motoring holiday on the Continent, it was assumed by those who knew him that the trip was to be a final self-indulgence before his wedding.

With the intention of driving to Greece via France, Italy and Yugoslavia, Porjes bought and fitted out a Volkswagen 'Caravanette'. Holding Access and Barclays credit cards and a Williams and Glyns cheque book, he arranged that a friend, David Tieder, would pay the monthly amounts that would be due on his accounts.

He made frequent telephone calls to his fiancée, Jacqueline Sheridan, as he progressed in leisurely fashion across Europe. On June 27 they discussed an idea that they should meet in Greece. It was their final conversation.

Increasingly worried by the silence that followed, Miss Sheridan contained her anxiety until July 31, when she told the police that she believed something was wrong. Her report was dealt with by Detective Inspector Leopold Pickersgill, whose first inquiries disclosed that some £5,000 worth of goods had been bought with Porjes' credit cards – conduct entirely unlike his previous use of the facilities. The articles purchased included jewellery, clothing and other items for which he would have had no need. So clearly uncharacteristic was this behaviour that Tieder refused to pay the accounts.

With his continuing investigation aided by a quota of good fortune, Pickersgill learned that a man using Porjes' name had sold his Volkswagen to a garage in Bognor Regis, Sussex. There, Pickersgill was told that the vendor had been accompanied by another man and a young woman. The female was identified as 21-year-old Stephanie Belcher, who was thought to be a hotel employee. In November she was traced to the Shore Road, East Wittering, Sussex, address where she was living with 32-year-old Alan John McQueen, an unemployed painter and decorator with a criminal record for violence and dishonesty. Both were arrested and charged with the theft of a motor vehicle and conspiracy to defraud the London clearing banks.

While interviewing the pair, Pickersgill learned that McQueen had had a male companion during some travels on the Continent. The man was reported to have gone abroad again soon after their return to Britain. Because of the manner of Porjes' disappearance, a more senior officer, Detective Chief Superintendent John Peel, then took over the direction of police activity in the affair.

According to Belcher, she had met McQueen and his friend while she had been working on a boat in the south of France. McQueen had then been driving a hired Ford Fiesta car. The trio had travelled to Pisa, in northern Italy, where they had hired a Ford Camper van which they had driven back into France. The Fiesta's number plates had been transferred to the van and the car abandoned. The three had then decided to go to Greece and arrived in Athens on June 23. They had met Porjes in a car park there on June 30. After a conversation, he had left them at nine pm.

The next day, Belcher said, she had gone to see a man known to her as 'Mohammed' to borrow some money, because she and her companions were short of cash. On her return, she had found McQueen cleaning out the van. He had then told her not to worry any further about money as they now had some. He had, she claimed, answered her questions with the statement that Porjes had been mugged of his bag, credit cards and money. The three of them had, she said, driven away in the two vans, the Ford Camper and Porjes' Volkswagen.

Belcher alleged that McQueen had been reluctant to talk about what had happened to Porjes, telling her to mind her own business. The Ford Camper had been abandoned in Yugoslavia and the three had travelled on in the Volkswagen, going to Graz, in Austria, where they had had a spending spree. En route they had obtained petrol by siphoning it from other vehicles. Their journey had continued into Germany and Belcher said she had returned to England from Frankfurt on July 11. She had next seen the two men, still driving Porjes' Volkswagen, on July 17. By this time she knew she had become pregnant by McQueen. She had questioned him persistently about Porjes and had finally been told that he had been hit on the head, 'hurting him quite badly'. After making this admission, McQueen had persuaded her to promise she would say that they had never met Porjes in Greece, she declared.

Belcher's statements were of little value without corroborative evidence. Inquiries had to be made in France, Italy, Yugoslavia, Austria, Germany and Greece. The route Porjes had taken was traced through his valid credit card transactions, but the tasks of the British detectives were not eased by the limited co-operation they received from police officials in Italy, Yugoslavia and Greece.

The Ford Camper had been returned to its owner, a formidable Italian grandam, who had subsequently sold it to a family in Florence. By comparison with the information provided by the signora, the scanty aid afforded by the police of three nations seemed positively helpful. She maintained that, on the relevant dates, the Ford had been hired by an Italian businessman. She permitted an examination of her books, but they revealed no sign of any hiring by McQueen or his companion. The books appeared to confirm the hiring to the businessman, but he had reported the Camper stolen. It became apparent that, for accountancy purposes, the lady's business records were receiving certain adjustments. Later inquiries showed that McQueen had been in possession of the vehicle, in Austria, at the time of the alleged hiring to the businessman.

Permission to carry out forensic tests on the vehicle having finally been granted by the new owners and the Italian authorities, Detective Sergeant Roy Grover, a liaison officer at the Metropolitan Police Forensic Science Laboratory, was given access to examine it at a police station near Florence. By this time some 14 months had passed since Porjes' disappearance.

Grover's first cursory check verified Belcher's statement that the interior had been cleaned up, but traces of blood were found in places unreached by perfunctory examination. Dr Ann Priston, a scientist whose work has been mentioned in an earlier chapter, was then asked to complete the inspection. She devoted long hours to the assignment on September 14 and 15. Assisted by Grover and working against the clock to meet a date on which the vehicle, fully reassembled, was wanted by the owner, to go on holiday with his family, she carefully dismantled parts of the interior fittings. Behind skirting boards and fascia panels, inside screwholes, on pipework, on fabric from a wall panel and on foam from a cushion filling, she found smears, splashes, stains and flakes of dried human blood. A 10 by 14-inch area of upholstery fabric had been abraded by scrubbing. It too gave a chemical reaction for blood. Some puzzlement was caused by the fact that, in places where the traces of blood were found on upright sections which joined the floor, the floor itself was entirely unmarked. This was explained when she was told that a new floor had been fitted since the time of the McQueen hiring.

Dr Priston's report spoke of her finding 'a fairly large area of bloodstaining which had been wetted and scrubbed' and of blood distribution which 'suggests to me a considerable quantity of blood either in the form of a pool or a bleeding body being on the floor towards the rear of this part of the vehicle.' Disappointingly, she was unable to gain more specific data from the blood marks, which had become ungroupable because of dilution, the lapse of time and the heat generated inside the van by the Italian climate.

But another complication then arose. It was thought that the defence might claim that the vehicle which had been examined was not the one McQueen had hired. The prosecution case appeared to be in danger – until one of the investigators, Detective Inspector Kenneth Clark, remembered that a photograph Belcher had handed to the police had shown the two men leaning against the front of the Ford Camper, on the bonnet of which was a large, coloured decoration depicting a girl's head and the word 'England'. No such embellishment had been visible on the vehicle when it was scrutinized by Priston and Grover.

To solve the problem, Grover returned to Italy in May 1985, under instructions to negotiate with the Camper's new owners (the vehicle having again changed hands) for the purchase of its bonnet. The deal was accomplished and the bonnet duly arrived at the laboratory. There, under ultra-violet lighting and using a new laser technique, the imprint left by the decoration was clearly shown. The identification was reinforced by the revelation of slight misalignments which had occurred in positioning the individually-affixed letters spelling the word 'England'. Comparison of the laboratory finding with the photograph established beyond question that the vehicle examined was the one Belcher and the men had used.

McQueen's trial opened at the Old Bailey on June 3 1985. He pleaded not guilty to a charge of murder but admitted conspiracy to defraud the London clearing banks and four counts of obtaining property by deception. Presenting the prosecution case, Michael Worsley QC said that there could be no doubt that Porjes had died after being attacked and robbed in Athens. Belcher became a key witness against the father of her child.

The judge, the Recorder of London, Sir James Miskin QC, said that Porjes had died after being robbed 'far away from home and country'. The attack had been followed by 'skilful and totally successful concealment of the body'. Directing the jury that a verdict of murder would not be applicable, he added that he had to proceed on the basis that the killing resulted from a blow which had not been expected to be fatal.

He told McQueen that the crime had been followed on his part by months of lies in an attempt to save his own skin. Those untruths had led to enormous expenditure of time and money by the police in Britain and abroad. They had also caused 'appalling worries' to Porjes' mother, Mrs Valerie Goodman, his step-father, Mr Samuel Goodman, and his fiancée and friends.

On June 14 1985, nearly two years after Porjes' disappearance, McQueen was convicted of manslaughter and the conspiracy and deception charges. He was sentenced to seven years' imprisonment for the killing and three years' for the conspiracy, those sentences to run consecutively, and to 12 months' imprisonment on each of the deception charges, those terms to run concurrently.

When we talked of the case at the laboratory in February 1988, Grover, elated at having just become a grandfather, told me that the 'purely speculative' theory reached by the police as to the fate of Porjes' body was that it had either been weighted and dumped in the Aegean off Piraeus or hidden in lonely countryside near Athens. No report had been received from the Greek authorities of the recovery of any human remains likely to be those of the unfortunate holidaymaker.

Two months later a surprising development suggested that the police might be correct in one of their suppositions regarding the manner of disposal of the body. In a letter dated April 9 1988, addressed to Valerie Goodman and written from his cell in E Wing at Blundeston Prison, near Lowestoft, Suffolk, McQueen declared 'For days I've been trying to word this letter to you in my mind. There seems to be no end to the terrible thing I did in Greece and the pain and suffering it's caused you. I can't live a lie any longer and I know that I must put your mind at rest if that's at all possible.

'I have written to His Honour Judge James Miskin QC, to set the record straight and that I am guilty of taking your son's life. I know this will not mean much to you, but I am deeply ashamed and sorry for what I have done ... I know you will never be able to forgive me. I'll never forgive myself.

'It is me alone that is guilty. The prosecution's case was quite aquerate (please excuse spelling) – that this crime took place in the car park in Greece. I'm afraid I was in a state of shock and dazed afterwards and we drove aimlessly into the hills until we found a place that was isolated and quiet.

'I can't remember what area this place was called. I know that you will wish for detail of the location and I have to give you all the information you require. I don't know if I can pinpoint it if I have a good map. I remember the general direction we went in ...

'I am sorry with all my heart. I wish to God I could put the clock back. But all I have the power to do is to stop the lie and give you some rest. No words can make up for what I have done. No amount of prison can alter or change or even punish what happened. Words are just so useless.

'21.4.88. I've just studied this map. It's not really much help to you and I can't give an aqurate point from it. I've cross marked two areas from my memory that's the best I can do ... It was a fairly decent roade going through hilly country.

'The actual place was in on a bend with an area/hard shoulder where a couple of cars could park off the road. This area was obviously used by local people as a dumping area. I don't remember seeing any buildings from the spot. There was some trees which gave the area seclusion.

'We placed the body under a double mattress and placed some rocks on top of that. Yours sincerely, Alan John McQueen.'

Beneath the signature the letter included a crude sketch depicting a curving, tree-lined road, with the cross marks McQueen had mentioned.

According to an account in the *Daily Telegraph* of July 20 1988, McQueen's confession had followed months of effort made by Samuel Goodman, who was said to be a survivor of the Auschwitz concentration camp. In his search for information regarding the whereabouts of his stepson's remains, Goodman claimed, he had talked and given gifts to prisoners working in a yard near the gaol. By this means he had finally made contact with a man who said he was McQueen's best friend. The prisoners had, Goodman said, declared that 'McQueen would be a fool not to tell the truth. He had nothing to lose since no one could be tried for the same crime twice.'

The *Telegraph* also quoted Goodman's reason for his endeavours: 'I was driven by the one burning purpose to find out where our son's body is and bring it back home for our sake and for the sake of his two daughters.'

A 'news roundup' paragraph published by the *Times* the following day reported that Goodman had said he wanted Scotland Yard to intercede with the Greek authorities to trace the body before he and his wife died. The *Times* item added that Scotland Yard had said that it would 'look sympathetically' at any request for such help.

CHAPTER 19

Liberal lady

IT IS GENERALLY ACKNOWLEDGED THAT the laws of England are administered with what 18th-century Whig politician Edmund Burke described as 'the cold neutrality of an impartial judge'. The learned legal dignitaries who preside over courts hearing charges of serious crime are uninfluenced by the knowledge that those who stand accused are brought to trial only after rigorous investigation has been carried out by the police, after significant evidence has been assembled, after all the known facts have been carefully examined by experts representing the Director of Public Prosecutions and often after at least one preliminary hearing, in a lower court, has established that there is a case to answer. The presence of a jury, whose sole task is to decide whether the accused is guilty or innocent, provides no help or support to the individual who is expected to be unfailingly correct in decisions that only he can make.

It cannot be surprising that the human beings who carry such awesome responsibilities occasionally issue rulings which astonish those of lesser standing in the field of court craft. Recent years have seen few examples of such surprises to rival the case of 45-year-old barman David Jones, who was arraigned at the Old Bailey on a charge of murdering 57-year-old 'gay divorcée' Doria Kate Schroder.

Mrs Schroder (*née* Hall) was born in Hugglescote, Leicestershire, in September 1921. Her mother died when she was five. Two years later her father emigrated to Canada, leaving her and her younger brother in an orphanage. Both children were adopted by an uncle when she was 14. After studying dressmaking in Leicester, she joined the Women's Royal Air Force. In 1942 she married Robert Mordan. A son was born in 1946 and a daughter in 1947. In 1956 she went to the USA and was divorced two years later. In 1962 she married Hans Schroder, an American hairdresser. A separation order was made in 1968 and the marriage was dissolved in 1973, when she returned to Britain. The following year, after answering an advertisement in the *Times*, she was engaged for a month as temporary resident cook by a 65-year-old widower, a retired stockbroker, at his home in Berkshire.

Although the relationship which developed did not involve sex, her employer enjoyed her company. In July 1975 he bought her a first and second floor maisonette in Walton Street, near London's fashionable Knightsbridge, and paid for its expensive furnishing. He also made her an allowance of £100 a week, which he paid quarterly. In return, she stayed at his home for two weekends each month and lunched with him at the *Savoy* Hotel during his occasional visits to London. She did not disguise the fact that she found these obligations tedious and commented to acquaintances that his promise to bequeath £50,000 to her on his death was disappointing because she had expected £100,000.

In 1977, after she had attempted suicide by swallowing aspirin tablets, she was seen by a consultant psychiatrist, who described her as 'A vital, active, enterprising person although probably temperamental and prone to anxiety with occasional panic attacks; bored, with symptoms of neurotic depression.'

She made no secret of her eager sexual appetite, informing several women friends, her niece and even her son's sister-in-law of her amorous adventures. A vivacious artificial blonde whose physical attractions were marred only by some post-menopausal chubbiness, she granted her favours to a wide range of male acquaintances, including sundry tradesmen and minicab drivers. Indulging a particular penchant for partners of Greek or Arabic origin, she often visited a Westbourne Grove, North Kensington, club that was frequented by men of those races.

In March 1978 she began a more constant sexual

relationship with her dentist. The strength of her attachment to him was mirrored by remarks she made to friends, to the effect that she was disenchanted with life in Britain and was inclined to return to the USA where, after marrying her lover, she would seek a suitable practice in which he could continue his dentistry.

To maintain her yearly renewable right of entry into that country and to deal with the disposal of the contents of an apartment she had occupied in New York, she spent 17 days in the USA from Thursday September 21 1978. During her absence the Walton Street apartment was occupied by her son, with his wife and their two-year-old daughter. A research scientist, he travelled daily to his work in nearby South Kensington. Although originally scheduled to return on Thursday October 12, Mrs Schroder brought the arrangement forward and arrived back in Walton Street at 11 am on Monday October 9. Her son, daughter-in-law and grandchild left at six pm. According to a statement he made later, the dentist spent the night of October 9/10 with her, having sexual intercourse three times before leaving at 6.30 am. She spoke with him on the telephone at 9.30 am and again when he called her at 10.30 pm. She also talked with her son by telephone at 11 am, when they arranged to lunch together at the apartment the following day.

But there was no response when he rang her doorbell at 12.45 pm on October 11. Seeing that her curtains were closed, he assumed that she was sleeping late. Deciding not to disturb her, he left. Similarly, there was no reply when the dentist telephoned her at 6.30 pm. After three more unsuccessful calls, at 12.15, 8.45 and 9.15 am on October 12, he became anxious and contacted her son, who went to Walton Street at 10.15 am but again received no answer to his ringing on the doorbell. Returning home, he collected a set of keys to the maisonette. There, at 1.20 pm, he found his mother lying dead on the sitting room floor. She was naked except for a flimsy and disarranged yellow housecoat. There was a ligature mark across the front of her neck. The position of the housecoat suggested that she had been dragged to the place where she lay. Spread across the sofa in the room was a large, satin-lined fur wrap. Doria Schroder's hectic love-life was over. But who had ended it so brutally?

Police inquiries began at once. There were no other signs of violence or forced entry into the property, indicating that the killer had been known to the victim and so had been freely admitted. Her son said his mother was 'security conscious' and would not have opened her door to a stranger. Exceptionally, it seemed that she had received a guest without applying the cosmetics she always wore when expecting visitors.

Interviews with some of the former stockbroker's relatives, friends and servants revealed that several of them considered her to have behaved rudely towards him and to have mixed uneasily in other company he kept. Some of those questioned said that they had formed an impression that the relationship was coming to an end, but this was denied by the lady's kindly benefactor, who had become partially incapacitated following a stroke. He offered a reward of £1,000 for capture of the killer. The forensic scientist called in was Dr Ann Priston, some of whose accomplishments have already been described. She found spermatozoa on a swab taken from the dead woman's vagina, but the blood grouping of their originator could not be ascertained. It was assumed that they were a consequence of the dentist's intercourse with her on the night of October 9/10. There were also large areas of seminal and urine staining on the inside back of the housecoat and in a coinciding position on the lining of the wrap. The seminal stains gave reactions for group A secretor, PGM (1+), GLO 2-1, a category found in only some six per cent of the British population. The relative locations of these stains, coupled with the fact that urine is often emitted during strangulation, indicated that the woman had been killed while lying on the sofa, where the liquids had soaked swiftly through the housecoat onto the lining of the wrap. It appeared probable that the flex of a nearby electric fan heater had been applied as a ligature to her neck.

Forensic examination of the housecoat produced three head and one pubic hair that were not from the victim, also 19 polyester and viscose fibres in shades of blue and brown which had not come from any fabric on the premises. Two of the head hairs and the pubic hair were common dark brown, but the other head hair was totally black and unusual. Another pubic hair which had not come from Mrs Schroder was found adhering to jam on a table knife which had fallen to the floor.

A *post mortem* examination was carried out by pathologist Professor Hugh Johnson, who reported that the victim had been healthy and had died in consequence of 'crush injury to the larynx'.

Detectives set about the time-consuming task of tracking down and interviewing the dead woman's numerous male acquaintances and making the customary local house-to-house inquiries. On Friday October 13, one of the investigators, Detective Constable Victor Bulaitis, visited the nearby *Enterprise* public house, in Walton Street, as part of this duty. Among the people he questioned there was David Jones, an employee who lived on the premises. Asked whether he had ever served the murder victim in the bar, Jones answered 'Yes, I think she used to come in here lunchtimes,' but added that he could not remember the most recent of such occasions. Later that evening, Detective Sergeant Geoffrey Cullingham also visited the *Enterprise* and, showing photographs of Mrs Schroder, continued the inquiries there. Jones looked at the pictures in the presence of the licensee's wife. When she asked him whether he was sure he was unable to recognize the woman, he said he might have seen her passing in Walton Street when he had been sitting on a bench outside the bar.

First suspicions as to his truthfulness were aroused when it was noticed that Doria Schroder's will, found among her papers, had been witnessed and signed 'D. Jones, 35 Walton Street, London SW3. Bar manager.' Taken for an interview at Kensington police station, Jones told Detective Constable Terence Wreford and Detective Sergeant Noel Conway that he had forgotten about signing the will and knew the woman only as a customer in the bar on about two occasions. After allowing police surgeon Dr John Shanahan to take samples of his blood, saliva and head and pubic hair, he was driven back to the *Enterprise*. A policeman in the car noticed that he had difficulty in getting his legs to support him when he alighted from the vehicle. In common with action being taken in respect of several men, the officers took possession of clothing Jones said he had been wearing during the period under investigation. This included a pair of trousers.

Some of the men mentioned in the murdered woman's diaries were no longer in Britain, but blood, saliva and hair samples were taken from a total of 54 individuals, including the dentist and a 40-year-old domestic appliance service engineer whose only known connection with the case was Mrs Schroder's announced intention of having her faulty dishwasher repaired. Fifty-two of the men were eliminated from the investigation because their blood groupings differed from the data gained from the semen stains. The two who were left were Jones and the engineer, but the latter was cleared because of his fair hair. The samples of Jones' head and pubic hair matched those found at the scene of the crime.

Given this information, the police again questioned him on Thursday and Friday, December 7 and 8. He was interviewed by Detective Superintendent Simon Crawshaw, Detective Inspector John Bunn and Detective Sergeant Barry Thorne. Still vehemently protesting his innocence, he was released pending further inquiries.

Meanwhile, Ann Priston was concentrating her expert attention on the fibres found on the housecoat. They were subjected to a range of sophisticated laboratory tests, including cross sectioning and micro-spectrophotometry. They matched exactly in fibre type, dye composition and chemical behaviour the material of the trousers belonging to Jones. It then became necessary to check on the possibility that similar trousers had been worn by someone else at the murder scene. It was established that Jones had purchased his trousers through a colleague in the bar, who had obtained them from Janet Frazer Mail Order Ltd, of Sunderland. Contact was made with that company, with the trouser manufacturers, S. Morris and Son (Hindley) Ltd,and with the makers of the fabric, A.S. Orr Ltd. It was learned that only 3,410 pairs of trousers had been made from the same batch of material and a representative of Janet Frazer Ltd estimated that only some seven per cent of their goods were sold in the London area.

Having received a full forensic report, the police arrested Jones on February 7 1979 and charged him with the murder. He continued to deny that he had ever visited the Walton Street maisonette. The regular drinkers at the *Enterprise*, who knew Jones as 'Bill', showed their liking for him by opening a fund for his defence. His 45-year-old employer, a tenant licensee, praised his work in the tavern. One of his former colleagues, who was then serving a prison sentence for stealing money from the *Enterprise*, said that Jones was 'Rather shy towards women but this would disappear after a few drinks.' Five people, including one of his previous employers, gave information about his drunken behaviour in the presence of women.

Jones described himself as a heavy drinker. When the police asked him what his usual daily consumption of alcohol was, he told them 'About four to five lagers and then 10 to 11 scotches.'

He was less honest about his background. When asked whether he had been in previous trouble with the law, he said he had not. This was disproved when it was learned that in 1967 he had been sentenced to 12 months' imprisonment for desertion from the army in 1961. He had signed on for 22 years' service in 1953. In 1960 he had attempted suicide by swallowing aspirins in a London park. Asked about his sexual activities, he told the police officers that the last time he had had intercourse was two years earlier, with a Paddington prostitute named Jane Bond. Efforts were made to trace her but were unsuccessful. Admitting a tendency to premature ejaculation and a liking for what he called 'kinky' habits, Jones said he preferred to be 'passive' during intercourse, with the female taking the more active role on top of him. An extract from his army record, written in 1960 by a captain with experience in psychiatry, stated 'In the last six years, after several unsuccessful courtings, he gave up all interest in women, feeling himself to be genetically inferior and impotent. In the last two years this has narrowed his interest to pub life.' Police notes made after several interviews with the prisoner included the comment 'Jones sees himself as being sexually inadequate because of what he considers to be the comparatively small size of his penis. This has created a long-standing inhibition in his relationship with women.'

Despite police opposition, Jones was granted bail, his employer standing surety in the sum of £5,000. The terms imposed included a curfew requiring Jones to be indoors between the hours of 11 pm and 8 am.

After a preliminary hearing before three justices at Horseferry Road Magistrates Court, Westminster, on June 7 1979, Jones was committed for trial at the Old Bailey. The case opened there on Monday February 25 1980, before Bernard Gillis QC, an Additional Judge. The prosecution was conducted by David Jeffreys, senior prosecuting counsel to the crown. Barry Chedlow QC appeared for the defence. The presentation of police and pathological evidence and the testimonies of prosecution witnesses occupied the entire week. It was noticed that, as he sat in the dock, Jones, apparently unconcerned, occupied himself with newspaper crossword puzzles. On Monday March 3 the defence made a submission to the judge that the case was founded on 'forensic conjecture' and that the quality and quantity of the scientific evidence was unsatisfactory. The following morning the judge announced that he agreed with this view. After smiling and waving to the gallery, Jones walked from the court a free man.

Two years and two weeks later, on Thursday March 18 1982, he threw himself under a train at South Kensington underground station. He left no note or other indication of his intention. The inquest verdict was 'Suicide'.

I discussed the course of events with Detective Chief Inspector Bunn (he was promoted in 1984) in March 1988. He told me he had felt confident of obtaining a conviction because of factors additional to the forensic evidence, vital though that was. 'For example, Jones denied having any knowledge of Doria Schroder, yet he had signed her will in July 1978 – only three months before she was killed,' he said.

He handed me a copy of the document, bearing Jones' somewhat crabbed signature. The testament contained no bequest to Jones. The beneficiaries were her children and other family connections, with a provision in favour of an anti-cancer fund-raising charity in the event of those persons predeceasing her. She also requested that her body 'should be used for therapeutic purposes'.

'We established that Jones was in the habit of leaving the pub and walking around the area – "to get a bit of fresh air," according to him,' Bunn went on. 'This would give him the opportunity. There is no doubt whatever that he left the pub that evening. He was always the one who locked up last thing. Doria Schroder would never admit anyone she did not know and always looked out of her window to see who was calling when anyone rang the bell. We know that Jones had this tendency to premature ejaculation, that he had an inferiority complex with women and that he could become very short tempered after he had been drinking. If he had attempted intercourse and she had been scornful about his sexual parts or performance, that could have been enough to put him into a rage. We thought that, over and above the forensic, there was a lot there.'

As to Jones' suicide, Bunn said that, after his discharge from court, he seemed to have gradually fallen out of favour with his former friends among the regular customers at the public house. About a year after the trial he was sacked from his employment there.

When I asked whether it was possible to estimate the cost of the police time spent on the case, Bunn paused from examining the 14-inch thick dossier of papers that had been accumulated concerning the affair. 'At 1980 values, about £250,000,' he said. That sum did not include the forensic work or the legal aid provided to Jones from the public purse.

CHAPTER 20

Furious flames

THIRTY-SEVEN PEOPLE WERE ASPHYXIATED or burnt to death because 42-year-old John ('Gypsy') Thompson thought he had been overcharged for a rum and coke.

Living in Elvin House, Morning Lane, Hackney, east London, Thompson, self-described as 'a general dealer', was a habitué of the sleazy clubs proliferating in Soho and the surrounding area. In the early hours of Saturday, August 16 1980, clad in a white safari suit, he was in the second floor premises of the *Spanish Club*, also known as *Victor's*, an illegal drinking den in a small, elderly, three-storey building at 18 Denmark Place, a seedy alleyway overshadowed by the soaring Centrepoint building at the junction of Charing Cross Road and Oxford Street. The ground floor of the property was used to store street traders' barrows. A separate entrance door gave access to a steep and narrow stairway leading to the first floor, the home of a similarly unlicensed enterprise known as the *Colombian Club* and patronized mainly by people of South American origin. The second, top, floor was reached via an iron staircase outside the rear of the building. This stairway had been boxed in with timber and hardboard, to afford its users some protection from the weather. Most of the front windows of the building had been boarded up, but one on each floor was used to throw the door key down to acceptable callers.

Having been served with his drink, Thompson, who was already intoxicated, tendered a five pound note. When no change was forthcoming, he began to voice loud protests. The manager of the club told him that £5 was the price of a rum and coke there. Furious, Thompson raged out of the building. Taking a taxi from an adjacent minicab office to a garage near King's Cross, he bought a gallon of petrol, which was provided to him in an emptied battery acid container made of white plastic. He then took the cab back to Denmark Place. There, mistakenly believing himself to be unobserved, he poured the petrol through the letterbox of number 18 and threw in lighted matches.

In the confined space of the stairway, the petroleum vapour reacted with enormous force, sending a concentrated fireball roaring upwards. Within seconds the entire interior of the building was engulfed in flames. People sitting at the bar on the first floor fell dead still clutching their drinks and the fire ate away at their clothing and bodies. Upstairs, some of the customers of the *Spanish Club* had fleeting moments' warning of their impending doom. Rushing into a tiny kitchen at the rear, a tightly-packed group tried to escape through a two feet square window. A few succeeded, sliding down a sloping roof below, but the majority were trapped and overwhelmed by the inferno, their entangled, piled-up bodies being reduced to a charred heap. It was 3.30 am. After the fire brigade had succeeded in extinguishing the flames, it was found that 13 people had perished in the *Colombian Club* and 24 in the *Spanish Club*. The building was gutted and part of the slated roof had collapsed.

The gruesome task of obtaining identifications of the bodies was directed by Detective Inspector James Rapley. Astonishingly, bearing in mind that some of the dead were illegal immigrants, every one was, at length, identified. The police were helped by the fact that some foreign passports carry the fingerprints of their holders. Nevertheless, 'It was a hell of a job,' former Detective Chief Superintendent Geoffrey Chambers, the investigator who took charge of the case, told me during a conversation in May 1988. Having retired after serving for 32 years with the Metropolitan Police, a career during which he dealt with more than 100 murder cases, he recalled the scene on his arrival in the Denmark Place property as 'Absolutely terrible. There were bodies piled up everywhere. You cannot imagine what that place was like.'

He regarded the solution of the crime as 'one of our best achievements and a classic example of good, old fashioned police work'. The first problem had been to look for the motive – 'was it terrorism, was it a protection racket, or what?'

During his briefing of his team of detectives, Chambers said, he had told them to keep in close contact with all the clubs in the district, instructing their proprietors to notify the police immediately there was any sign of a man fitting the description of one who had been seen running away after a fire had been started against the door of a bookmaker's shop in Denmark Place a short while earlier.

'It turned up trumps,' Chambers chuckled to me between his smoker's coughs. 'He turned up in a club just off Tottenham Court Road one night. The owner rang us. We went round and grabbed him, got him into the police station at Tottenham Court Road and had a chat with him and eventually he put his hands up.' (Admitted committing the crime.) The detainee was Thompson, the possessor of a reputation as a petty thief and drug addict.

Affectionately known by some of his colleagues as 'Fag ash and confusion,' chain cigarette smoker Chambers had simplified his account of the task of catching the killer. Another Thompson, Detective Chief Superintendent Kenneth Thompson, who, as a detective chief inspector, acted as one of Chambers' aides in the case, gave me additional details. 'We had three other suspects who were taken into custody,' he said. 'But we were able to eliminate them from our inquiries.'

The evidence against Thompson, who was arrested nine days after the fire, strengthened as the police gathered information. The minicab driver was traced. He remembered driving Thompson to and from the garage. Fourteen-year-old Mark Delaney, whose mother operated a street vendor's barrow near the clubs' entrance, told of seeing a man wearing a light-coloured safari suit standing with his back to the wall in an attempt to hide in the alleyway. The boy said he later saw the man kneeling outside the door to the clubs, with a white plastic container at his side. Shortly afterwards, just before the building burst into flames, the lad said, he had seen liquid coming from under the door of number 18 and had smelt petrol.

At the outset of his inquiries, Chambers initiated the gathering of substantive forensic evidence on such matters as the origin of the fire and the levels of carbon monoxide and alcohol in the blood of the dead. Thirty-four-year-old Adair Lewis, a chemist and physicist with 13 years' experience as a fire investigator based at the Metropolitan Police Forensic Science Laboratory, was summoned from his Welling, Kent, home at five am. Arriving at the burnt building just before seven, he saw at once that the fire had started just inside the door and noted that unused extinguishers showed that the victims had had no time to attempt to fight the blaze. Fifty yards up the alleyway, he found a plastic container labelled 'battery acid'. It still held a small amount of petrol. There were also some pieces of rag and a length of bent metal which could have been used as a funnel. He discovered traces of petrol in the debris behind the door and on the stairway. It was clear that, no doubt because of the warm summer night, internal doors had been wedged open on both floors. Had they been closed, many lives might have been saved. Using established guidelines, Lewis was able to judge the intensity and duration of the fire from the degree of burning of the bodies.

After being placed in bags, the corpses had to be lowered through the windows. 'The press would have had a field day with that if it had not been in an alleyway to which they were not able to gain access,' Lewis commented during a talk with me in 1988. 'One of the effects of burning causes the muscles to contract, putting the body into a sort of pugilistic position. It is not until muscle tissue has been burnt away, exposing the bones, that the body starts to disintegrate.'

The position of the corpses in the kitchen showed that people had tried to climb over one another in their fight to escape, Lewis said. 'There certainly wouldn't have been room for them all to have stood normally in that small space. Wherever we went initially, we bumped into more bodies. We started labelling them alphabetically but began to run out of the alphabet. So we went from letters to numbers.' He did not think that the presence of stocks of bottled spirits would have caused any significant worsening of the conflagration, because those items would have been counterbalanced by such things as beer and 'soft' drinks.

Within two hours of beginning his examination, Lewis was able to confirm to Chambers that it had been a case of arson, thus enabling the CID investigation to proceed without delay.

Lewis left the Metropolitan Police laboratory in 1987 to become head of technical services at the Fire Protection Association, an organization financed by the Association of British Insurers and Lloyds for the purpose of giving guidance on fire protection to commerce and industry.

Thompson's trial opened at the Old Bailey on April 30 1981. He was charged with the murder of Archibald Campbell, one of the victims of the fire; with unlawfully killing Campbell and also with committing arson at a flat at Exbury House, Hackney, where he was alleged to have poured petrol through the letterbox because he felt he had been slighted by the occupants. Happily, they had been out when the fire started, but their home had been destroyed. Thompson denied all the charges, claiming that his confession at Tottenham Court Road police station had been made because he had been threatened with violence by the police and had 'had the horrors' while 'coming down' after taking drugs. 'I was under the impression that, if I didn't make the statement, I would be kicked to hell. It was self-preservation,' said the man who showed no sign of remorse over his cruel execution of 37 fellow-beings.

Defending him, Gilbert Gray QC declared that an offer of £5,000 had been made by 'protection racketeers' for the purpose of getting his client convicted. This accusation was based on the fact that the minicab driver, Raji Dawar, had not come forward with some items of evidence until the week of the trial, whereas the fire had happened eight months earlier. Affirming that he knew nothing of any such offer, Dawar said that he had been on holiday in America and, while there, had remembered things he had not mentioned in two earlier statements to the police. One of these details was that Thompson, who was known to him as 'Punch', had hooked his thumb in the direction of the *Spanish Club* and muttered that he was 'going to fix them bastards'.

A German, 20-year-old Andreas Baumann, one of the fortunate ones who had escaped through the kitchen window, said that the first anyone had known of anything being wrong was a bang 'like a plane going through the sound barrier'. He and a friend had been standing near the door on the second floor when smoke had suddenly begun filling the place 'and panic broke out. The lights went out and then flames came up the stairs.'

The trial ended on May 7. Thompson was found not guilty of the Hackney arson but was convicted of murdering Campbell. He was sentenced to imprisonment for life.

CHAPTER 21

Persistent poisoner

ONE OF THE THINGS THAT impressed his colleagues most about the newly-recruited, £24-a-week assistant storeman at the factory was his eagerness to collect their mugs of tea from the trolley that was pushed twice daily through the premises. In other respects they found the pale, lean-faced, black-haired fellow less engaging. A kind of absent-mindedness suggested that he was not greatly interested in his job, although it was understood that he had received tuition in storekeeping techniques at a government training centre. Much of his conversation baffled them. He seemed to know a great deal about medical matters and, in his remarks on those subjects, used words they did not understand. He was also inconsistent in his behaviour, one day joining in the light-hearted banter that was customary among the happy workforce and the next withdrawing within himself and hardly speaking to anyone. It was talk about chemistry or politics that really brought him to life. He declared himself an admirer of Adolf Hitler and Nazi Germany – they had had the right ideas about many things, he said.

No one at the works, from the chairman downwards, knew, then, that, for nine of his 23 years, the new employee had been locked away in Broadmoor, the hospital for the criminally insane, after pleading guilty to charges of maliciously administering poison to his father, his sister and a school friend. The judge at his trial, Mr Justice Melford Stevenson, had ordered that he should not be released, without the consent of the Home Secretary, for at least 15 years. Quantities of antimony, thallium, digitalis, ionine, atropine and barium chloride, with a handbook on poisons and books entitled *Poisoner in the dock* and *Sixty famous trials*, were found in the 14-year-old's room. Despite considerable suffering, all three of his victims had survived their experience. But then unknown to anyone other than the boy himself was the fact that he had also administered poisonous substances to his stepmother, who had died in agony a short time previously. Her death was attributed to the prolapse of a bone at the top of her spinal column, following an accident. There was no *post mortem* and no inquest.

On Thursday June 3 1971, less than a month after the young man, Graham Frederick Young, had joined the firm, John Hadland Ltd, manufacturers of high-speed optical and photographic instruments, at Bovingdon, near Hemel Hempstead, Hertfordshire, his boss in the storeroom, 59-year-old Robert Egle, a military veteran of Dunkirk, was taken ill with severe diarrhoea. After being laid up in bed for three days, he returned to work on June 7. Next day, 49-year-old Ronald Hewitt, a storeman-cum-driver who had given notice of his intention to leave the company and whose duties Young had been engaged to take over, was stricken by sharp stomach pains, with vomiting and diarrhoea. He was away from work for a week, his doctor attributing the trouble to a chill or food poisoning. For three weeks he suffered similar bouts, being forced to take days away from work. Fortunately for him, his period of notice then expired and he left the factory.

On Tuesday June 29, a day after he had returned to work following a week's holiday with his wife at Great Yarmouth, Norfolk, Egle was again taken ill and went home. He told his wife that the ends of his fingers had gone numb. He was unable to walk without staggering. After he had a spent a sleepless night, his doctor decided that he was suffering from peripheral neuritis. He was admitted, in great pain, to West Hertfordshire Hospital. The next day his condition grew worse and he was transferred to the intensive care unit at St Albans Hospital. Paralysis spread through his body. He lost the power of speech. His heart stopped twice but was restarted by emergency treatment. After eight days of intense torment, he died.

At the factory each day during Egle's stay in hospital, Young went upstairs to the managing director's secretary, Mrs Mary Berrow, and, showing great concern, asked how the sufferer was getting on.

The managing director of Hadland's, Godfrey Foster, decided that the man he had in mind as Egle's successor in charge of the stores – Young – should accompany him, representing the staff, to the funeral. They drove in Foster's car to the cremation service at Amersham, Buckinghamshire. As they left Bovingdon, one of Young's first remarks was a question as to the cause of Egle's death. Foster answered that the death certificate specified polyneuritis. That was only a generalization, meaning that the nervous system had been affected, Young responded. Surely there was more detail? Yes, Foster remembered, there was a French-sounding term. 'It sounds like the Guillain-Barré syndrome,' said Young. Somewhat astonished at this display of knowledge, Foster told him he was right. 'It's a relatively new discovery,' Young exclaimed with enthusiasm. 'It has only recently been isolated. Various treatments are being tried.' On the return journey, he told Foster that polyneuritis would have caused broncho-pneumonia, which would have killed Egle. How sad it was that a man who had survived the horrors of Dunkirk should have succumbed to a strange virus, he added.

Two months passed. Then, early in September, 60-year-old Frederick Biggs, head of a department responsible for issuing parts for assembly, began to vomit and suffer violent stomach pains. He recovered during a touring holiday with his wife. On the day of his return, on September 20, the head of another department, Peter Buck, the firm's import/export manager, developed similar symptoms shortly after drinking a cup of tea with Young and another worker, David Tilson. Buck recovered the next day, but three weeks later Tilson began to experience 'pins and needles' in his feet. When his legs began to go numb, he went to his doctor. He was told to rest.

One Friday evening Young was working late with 39-year-old Jethro Batt, a colleague who often gave him a lift home to his £5-a-week bedsitter lodging at 29 Maynards Road, a pebble-dashed semi-detached house in Hemel Hempstead. Young turned the conversation to the subject of poisoning, telling Batt how easy it was to kill a person but make the death appear to be due to natural causes. When Batt returned from a visit to the lavatory, Young gave him a cup of coffee. It tasted bitter and Batt took only a mouthful, pouring the remainder away. Jokingly, Young asked 'Do you think I'm trying to poison you?' Both men laughed.

During the weekend, Batt felt severe pain in both his legs. At the same time, Tilson was suffering with pains in his chest and stomach and having problems with his breathing. On the Monday morning, both men went to their doctors. Tilson was admitted to St Albans City Hospital. His hair had started to fall out. Still at home in bed, Batt was also beginning to lose his hair. In growing agony, he suffered terrifying hallucinations and told his wife he wanted to die. A few days later, he was unable to move. Three weeks after his troubles began, he was admitted to the West Hertfordshire Hospital. His head was completely bald and he was suicidal. Tilson returned home but was far from well. On November 1, he was readmitted to hospital. Most of his head, face and body hair had gone. Both men had become impotent.

Meanwhile, at the factory it was stocktaking time. With Egle's post still vacant and Tilson and Batt away ill, Young was the only full-time member of the storeroom staff remaining at work. He agreed to put in overtime hours on a Saturday and was assisted by Biggs and his wife. Having obtained the key to the refreshments cupboard, Young made tea for them. When Foster visited them in the afternoon to see how things were getting on, Young offered to make tea for him too. Foster accepted but after Young had left the room to prepare it, Biggs said that the essential work was virtually finished. Calling Young back, Foster told him not to trouble about the tea; they could all go home.

Next day, Sunday, Biggs felt unwell. Too ill to go to work on the Monday, he consulted his doctor, who prescribed some pills. On Tuesday he developed severe pains in his chest and feet and had difficulty in walking. On Thursday November 4 he was admitted to West Hertfordshire Hospital.

By this time the mysterious illness that appeared to strike employees at the Hadland works had become known as 'the Bovingdon Bug'. But some people were openly expressing suspicions about Young. One, Mrs Diana Smart, who occasionally helped out in the storeroom and had had a bout of sickness, stomach and leg pains after taking a cup of coffee with him, said she thought he was carrying some form of infectious disease. Soon after this remark became known to Young, she suffered another severe attack at the factory and was forced to go home. As her illness developed, her husband complained that she had begun to smell offensively. The situation caused such friction that he left home for a week.

Great efforts were made to discover the cause of Biggs' illness. During his six-day stay in West Hertfordshire Hospital he was examined by seven doctors. Their conclusion was that he had been stricken by some severe nervous debility. His condition worsened and on Thursday November 11 he was transferred to the Whittington Hospital in Highgate, north London. Racked with increasing pain, he lost the power of speech. He was then transferred to the National Hospital for Nervous Diseases in Queen's Square, London. Early in the morning of Friday November 19, after 20 days of suffering, he died. When the news reached the factory, Young paced up and down in agitation. 'Poor old Fred,' he remarked to Mrs Smart. 'I wonder what went wrong. He shouldn't have died. I was very fond of him.'

In an attempt to stem the frightening rumours that were spreading through the workforce, Foster called in the Medical Officer of Health for the Hemel Hempstead area, Dr Robert Hynd. With an investigating team, Hynd examined the conditions at the factory, paying particular attention to suppositions such as contamination of the water supply and radioactivity from a nearby, disused, government airfield. Nothing of significance was found. All the staff were interviewed. Like his colleagues, Young said he was absolutely bewildered by the mystery. The Hynd investigators retired defeated.

With alarm rising daily among his employees, John

Hadland, the chairman of the company, asked the firm's medical officer, a local general practitioner named Iain Anderson, to give them a talk. Anderson told the workers, assembled in the canteen, that three possible explanations had been examined: radiation, heavy metal poisoning and some unidentified virus. There was no possibility of radioactive contamination, he assured them. When it came to the question of heavy metal, special attention had been paid to thallium, a substance sometimes used in the making of lenses like those produced at Hadland's. But no thallium was kept or used on the premises. Only 'the Bovingdon Bug' remained, Anderson declared, and he felt sure it would soon be identified.

A momentary silence followed his asking whether anyone wished to raise any queries. Then he faced a positive barrage of questions from a young man at the back of the room. Why had heavy metal poisoning been ruled out? Weren't the sufferers' symptoms indicative of that cause? Were the symptoms of those who had been taken ill any different from those of the two who had died? What about the alopecia? Was he suggesting that such hair loss could be of psychosomatic origin? The questioner was Young. Exchanging glances with Hadland, Anderson did his best to reply effectively. When the meeting closed, he went to talk to Young in the storeroom. Flatteringly congratulating him on his evident knowledge of such matters, he led the conversation into realms of greater complexity. Shortly afterwards he was able to tell Hadland that Young appeared to have considerable understanding of heavy metal poisoning but no great grasp of other medical subjects.

Realizing that every avenue had to be explored, Hadland made inquiries which revealed that, in his pre-engagement interview with Foster, Young had said that he had suffered a nervous breakdown following the death of his mother, but was 'now completely recovered'. After consulting his solicitor, Hadland decided to confide his growing suspicions to the police. Telephoning Hemel Hempstead police station, he spoke to Detective Chief Inspector John Kirkpatrick. After examining the company's employment register, Kirkpatrick wired certain employees' names, including Young's, to

Scotland Yard, to see whether they appeared in the files at the Criminal Record Office. After at first returning a blank, the CRO rechecked and came back with the news that, six months earlier, Young had been released after spending nine years in Broadmoor for poisoning his father, sister and schoolfriend.

A police officer was sent immediately to Young's lodgings. The owner of the house, Mohammed Saddiq, a Pakistani who spoke little English, said that Young was away for the weekend, he knew not where. The background information about Young included a note that his sister, Mrs Winifred Shannon, lived with her husband at Leverstock Green, Hemel Hempstead. Writing Christmas cards when police officers arrived, she told them that her brother was visiting their father, Frederick Young, who was living with their aunt, Mrs John Jouvenat, and her husband, in Alma Road, Sheerness, Kent.

Briefed by the officers at Hemel Hempstead, the Kent police moved swiftly. Warned that Young might attempt to escape, they first surrounded the house. Then two officers rang the doorbell. Fred Young answered it. When the police asked for Graham Young, he stood aside and pointed towards the kitchen, where his son was engaged in making himself an egg sandwich. Never having forgiven his offspring for the suffering caused to himself and his daughter, Young senior had also nursed a deep-rooted suspicion that the boy had had something to do with the death of his second wife, Molly. It was Graham's ceaseless nagging on the subject that had persuaded him to have her body cremated rather than buried.

Young was handcuffed and taken to Sheerness police station, where he was searched and his clothing removed for forensic examination. Wearing two blankets, he was collected by Kirkpatrick and Detective Sergeant John Livingstone and told that he was being taken back to Hemel Hempstead for questioning on suspicion of murder. During the journey, Young repeatedly questioned Kirkpatrick about the accusations against him, starting with the query 'Did you say murders, plural?' Later, his audacity coming to the fore, he informed his captors that the onus of proof of his guilt lay with them. He had, he said, committed the perfect crime in murdering his stepmother in 1962. Her death had been certified as being due to natural causes, her body had been cremated and the ashes buried.

Kirkpatrick steered the conversation towards the happenings at Hadlands, reminding Young that two of his colleagues were seriously ill, possibly dying. Would he not reveal the poison he had used, so that appropriate treatment could be given? Young answered that he would tell them what antidote should be used – dimercaprol and potassium ferric cyanoferrate.

Before Young's arrest at Sheerness, Livingstone and two colleagues, Detective Inspector John Ratcliffe and Detective Constable Michael Grinstead, had examined his room at Maynard's Road. They found its walls decorated with pictures of Hitler and other Nazis. There were crude drawings of graves, tombstones, spidery men clutching their throats, and wielding containers marked 'Poison'. Many were bald and some were shown with their hair falling out. The window ledge, tables and chairs were lined with bottles, phials and tubes containing various substances. The wardrobe drawer was full of bottles, many carrying the labels of a well-known pharmacy, John Bell and Croyden. A phial containing white powder was found in the breast pocket of a brown corduroy jacket. Young said later that this was his 'exit dose'. There was a pile of books on medical and chemical subjects. Under the bed they found a loose-leaf exercise book full of closely-handwritten pages. Its contents showed it to be the meticulously-kept log of a systematic poisoner. The handwriting was Young's.

When Detective Chief Superintendent Ronald Harvey, the head of Hertfordshire CID, confronted him with this damning diary, Young answered that it was merely a collection of memoranda for a novel he was planning to write. Harvey pointed out that initials used on some of the pages tallied with the names of people employed at Hadland's. At first Young denied that there was any connection, but when Harvey resumed his questioning the following day, there was a change of heart. Young agreed to confirm or deny the correctness of Harvey's interpretations. In this way it was agreed that B meant Bob Egle, D David Tilson, Di Diana Smart, F Fred Biggs, and P Peter Buck.

Turning to questions about the now-identified contents of the chemical containers found in his room, Harvey asked what use he had made of ether, of sodium tartrate mixed with antimony salt, of antimony potassium tartrate and of thallium. He had inhaled the ether, Young replied, but was not addicted to it. He had used the sodium tartrate and antimony on Diana Smart, the thallium on Egle, Biggs, Batt and Tilson and the antimony potassium tartrate on Smart, Buck and Hewitt and on Trevor Sparkes, a 34-year-old fellow-trainee at the Slough, Buckinghamshire, centre where he had received his training in storekeeping.

Deliberately flattering Young by congratulating him on his knowledge of poisons, Harvey asked why he had chosen thallium for some of his victims and antimony for others. Antimony was less toxic and more rapidly excreted, Young answered. He was not willing to say how he had decided who should receive which of the substances. When Harvey accepted his offer of a description of the effects of thallium, Young obliged with a recital of clinical detail. No longer used as a rodenticide, it was sometimes employed in the manufacture of highly refractory optical glass, he told the listening policemen. After taking a fatal dose, death would be unavoidable unless an emetic was swallowed within half an hour. Without that, vomiting would follow and there would be diarrhoea and pain, then a loss of sensation in toes and fingers, spreading throughout the limbs, caused by the destruction of nerve tissues. Thallium was an accumulative poison, Young said. It would cause death if small, non-fatal doses were administered over a period. After detailing the effects on the brain, the respiratory system and the eyes, he described the progressive symptoms, including loss of hair, scaliness of the skin, internal pains, degeneration of the nerve fibres, loss of control of the limbs, hallucinations, suicidal delirium and paralysis. Antimony also caused vomiting and stomach pains but was rarely fatal, Young pointed out. It was sometimes used as an emetic. There were, however, few doctors in Britain who could identify thallium poisoning.

Aware that the police notetaking had stopped, Young then remarked 'You must feel revulsion for me.' Harvey answered by asking whether he realized what the things he had described meant in human terms. 'Not completely. I have never seen death,' Young replied.

At one point, thinking that Young was beginning to show signs of remorse, Harvey commented on it to Kirpatrick, who was in the room. Young stifled the idea, remarking 'No, that would be hypocritical. What I feel is the emptiness of my soul.' He laughed when Harvey asked whether he was willing to make a written statement confirming all he had said. 'I'll let you know,' he promised. 'If I did, I could always say it was taken under duress.' He was returned to his cell.

The following afternoon Harvey attended the *post mortem* on Biggs. It was conducted by Professor Hugh Molesworth-Johnson, senior lecturer in forensic medicine at St Thomas' Hospital Medical School. He had spent the previous weekend on some concentrated research concerning thallium, following an urgent telephone call from Harvey. Professor John Cavanagh, neuropathologist at the London Institute of Pathology, attended the examination at Molesworth-Johnson's request. Also present was Nigel Fuller, a chemist serving at the Metropolitan Police Forensic Science Laboratory.

Several of the known symptoms of thallium poisoning were noted as dissection of the corpse proceeded. There was scaling, discoloration and breaking away of the skin around nose and scrotum, the hair could be pulled out with ease and reddening of the air passages showed the onset of pneumonia. From a microscopical examination of the internal organs, Molesworth-Johnson concluded that Biggs had been healthy before his final illness. Cavanagh examined sections of the brain, spinal cord and other nerves. But neither expert was able to find any trace of thallium in Biggs' remains.

Finally, organs were handed to Fuller for more detailed scrutiny at the laboratory. He also received the ashes of Egle, which had been exhumed, at Harvey's request, from their place of burial at Gillingham, Norfolk, Egle's birthplace. It was Fuller, 'going back to basic chemistry', who had identified the chemicals found in Young's room.

Among the checks that were made were inquiries at the crematorium where Egle's remains had been incinerated,

Fuller told me during a conversation about the case in June 1988. It was established that Egle's had been the only cremation on that particular day, 'so we were pretty confident that the ashes were his.' Although far from confident as to the outcome of his tests, thinking that all traces of the poison might have disappeared in the 1,300 degrees Centigrade temperature of the cremation process, Fuller nevertheless found nine milligrams of thallium in the 1,780 grams of ash. Calculations indicated that this would have been equivalent to some five micrograms per gram before cremation. Knowing that tiny quantities of thallium may be ingested from the atmosphere during a normal lifetime, Fuller also tested the ashes of another body which had been dealt with at the crematorium – the remains of a man said to have died of a heart attack. No thallium was revealed. Meticulously thorough in his methods, Fuller also tested a kidney which, because of the unusual circumstances of his death, had been removed from Egle's body and preserved at St Albans City Hospital. After allowing for a tenfold quantity reduction caused by mounting the organ, Fuller identified 2.5 micrograms of thallium per gram. It was ,therefore, evident that the cause of Egle's death had been incorrectly diagnosed and certified. Legal history was made when Young was charged with his murder – it was the first time that such a charge had followed from the exhumation of cremated human remains.

From his tests of the organs taken from Biggs, Fuller found 120 micrograms of thallium per gram in the gut, 20 micrograms per gram in the left kidney, five in muscle tissue, five in bone marrow and 10 in a section of the brain. The urine contained six micrograms of thallium per millilitre. Blackness found in the roots of head and pubic hair was also symptomatic of thallium poisoning. It was clear that the quantities of thallium found were the residues of a much larger initial intake – more than sufficient to cause death. 'Young didn't have a balance,' Fuller told me. 'His method was to use tubes, measuring against aspirin tablets, which are half a gram, to compare in volume terms. But thallium, being heavy, doesn't compare that way.' Tasteless and colourless, it was easily administered.

In Brixton prison awaiting his trial, Young wrote to a female cousin assuring her of his innocence – 'antecedents notwithstanding' – and expressing the view that he stood a good chance of acquittal.

At the opening of his trial, at St Albans Crown Court on Monday June 19 1972, Young pleaded not guilty to 10 charges, two of them alternatives. He was accused of the murders of Robert Egle and Frederick Biggs, the attempted murders of David Tilson and Jethro Batt, and the malicious administration of poison with intent to cause grievous bodily harm to Trevor Sparkes, Ronald Hewitt, Peter Buck and Diana Smart. 'Malicious administration' charges were also brought, as alternatives to those of attempted murder, in respect of Tilson and Batt. The judge was Mr Justice Eveleigh, John Leonard QC conducted the prosecution and Sir Arthur Irvine QC MP was the leading counsel for the defence.

The macabre evidence included readings, by Leonard, from Young's loose-leaf notebook, dubbed by the popular press his 'diary of death'. One entry declared 'In a way it seems a shame to condemn such a likeable man to such a horrible end. But I have made my decision and therefore he is doomed to premature decease'. Another extract read 'News from other fronts ... F is now seriously ill. He is unconscious and it is likely he will decline in the next few days. It will be a merciful release for him as, if he should survive, he will be permanently impaired. It is better that he should die. It will remove one more casualty from the crowded field of battle.' A later entry announced 'It is still extremely annoying. F is surviving far too long for my peace of mind.' In another note the record observed 'Di irritated me intensely yesterday so I packed her off home with an attack of sickness. I only gave her something to shake her up. I now regret I didn't give her a larger dose, capable of laying her up for a few days.'

'You may well have come to the conclusion that this young man had a desire to establish his power over other people and that this is the real motive for what has happened,' Leonard told the jury. 'I suppose that a possible motive is that the defendant might have had a scientific, experimental approach to the whole problem. Perhaps he had a tendency to treat human beings as guinea pigs.' But the victims had died 'in circumstances which could be described politely as being unpleasant'. Death had eventually come to them when they became unable to breathe.

The all-male jury reached their unanimous verdicts, after an hour and 38 minutes of deliberation, on Thursday June 29. Young was found guilty of murdering Egle and Biggs; guilty of attempting to murder Tilson and Batt; not guilty of administering poison with intent to inflict grievous bodily harm to Sparkes, Hewitt, Buck and Smart; not guilty of a reduced charge, of administering poison with intent to injure Sparkes and Buck, but guilty of that offence in respect of Hewitt and Smart.

Addressing the judge before the penalties were imposed, Irvine said 'In considering sentence, I submit, your lordship, you may bear in mind one matter which I mention with the greatest reluctance. I refer to it as part of my duty. It was only possible for Graham Young to commit these offences because he had been released on licence. This release may appear, in the light of events, to have been a serious error of judgment. The authorities had a duty to protect Young from himself as well as a duty to protect the public. If you are balancing the desirability of a custodial sentence with a hospital order, I think it is right that I should say to you that Graham Young himself thinks a prison sentence would be better for his condition than a return to Broadmoor. The Broadmoor experience thus far has had tragic consequences of which we have learnt at this trial.'

Young was then sentenced to life imprisonment on each of the murder and attempted murder convictions and to five years for each of the offences against Hewitt and Smart, those terms to run concurrently with the life sentences. He received the verdicts and sentences without visible sign of emotion. He was, in fact, being held discreetly by four officers, having told court officials of his intention to commit suicide by smashing his head and the back of his neck against the dock.

The revelation, after the convictions, of Young's earlier history created a new storm in the press. 'Why was this fiend let out from behind bars?' demanded the *Sun*. Revealing that his release from Broadmoor had been arranged by the medical superintendent, Dr Patrick McGrath, and South African psychiatrist Edgar Udwin, the paper reported that both had refused to comment, saying that they were forbidden to do so under the Official Secrets Act. A front page headline asked 'Did he kill his mother as well?'

Under another front page headline: 'Broadmoor: big shake-up', the *Daily Mail* declared that the verdict on Young was an indictment of the Home Secretary, Reginald Maudling, who signed the release papers; of the police, for not keeping track of Young's movements, and of the after-care service, for not checking up on him. 'Checks have been ordered on all 331 people released from Broadmoor over the past 12 years, in case another maniac is at large', the report stated.

The *Daily Mirror* topped its front page story with the headline 'Scandal of the "cured" killer.' Each of the tabloids illustrated their articles with a thin-mouthed, staring-eyed picture which Young was said to have taken of himself in a photobooth.

A *Times* story by their Home Affairs Correspondent Peter Evans reported Maudling's statement in the House of Commons that Lord Butler of Saffron Walden was to chair 'a fundamental review of the provisions of the criminal law relating to mentally abnormal offenders and the facilities for their treatment'. A leader in the same issue of the paper declared that, although the public would rightly demand stricter safeguards, it was important that the government 'should not over-react in the anxiety of the moment ... Psychiatry is not such a precise science that all risk can be eliminated.'

A *Guardian* leader commented 'While disclosure of past criminal activity to employers ought not to be done without telling the individual concerned, a distinction must be drawn between a person with a criminal record and a person with a record of serious psychopathic disorder. If the employer had been aware of Young's background, a tragedy could have been averted.'

The *Daily Telegraph* opined 'Doubtless those concerned

[with Young's release from Broadmoor] acted in good faith. But they must be anxiously wondering, and not for the first time, whether the present state of psychiatric science enables anyone to pronounce with confidence who is mentally ill and who is not, who is cured and who is not, who is safe, who not.'

In the London *Evening News*, under the title 'Why Broadmoor needs stronger locks', lawyer/criminologist/writer/broadcaster Edgar Lustgarten pointed out that, although he had been sent to prison, Young's case could later be dealt with by a commission of medical men whose findings could result in a switch of penalty – sending him back to Broadmoor. That institution might, he wrote, 'conceivably and usefully ... be locked up a little more tightly'.

Under the headline 'Where did he get poisons?' the London *Evening Standard* put a finger on a pivotal aspect of the affair, with the announcement that an investigation had been ordered into how Young had managed to obtain dangerous poisons. 'The fact is that practically every poison is available over the chemist's counter,' the paper alleged. 'Arsenic, cyanide and the poisons used by Young on his victims – thallium and antimony – can be bought by members of the public from their local chemist. But there is a three-point safeguard which, in theory at least, ensures they don't fall into the wrong hands. A qualified pharmacist can sell a poison to a person if he knows the customer personally and is satisfied he is "a fit and proper person" to handle it. If the customer is not known to the chemist he may be given a form to be filled in and signed by a householder and by the local police.'

During the trial, Young said that he had purchased the thallium and antimony from the Wigmore Street, London, premises of John Bell and Croyden, using the name 'M E Evans' as a 'short cut' around the restrictions governing the sale of poisons. This action had been 'irresponsible but hardly felonious', he claimed. A pharmacist, Alfred Kearne, employed by John Bell and Croyden, said that he had sold poisons to a 'scholarly looking' young man aged about 25. This same young man had asked for 25 grams of antimony potassium tartrate on a previous occasion, but had been refused as he had no certificate of authorization permitting him to make the purchase. But a week later the young man produced a bill heading with writing on it authorizing him to obtain the poison. He signed the poisons book with the name M E Evans. Although it was customary for pharmacists to retain such authorizations on their records, searches had failed to find the document that had been provided.

A book, *Obsessive Poisoner*, said to have been written by Young's sister Winifred but carrying a copyright mark in the names of Max Caulfield and European Press Enterprises, published by Robert Hale and Company in 1973, included the comment 'The Pharmaceutical Society, for its part, began an investigation into exactly how Graham managed to obtain his poisons. Theoretically, there are safeguards against poisons falling into the wrong hands, but as Mr Desmond Lewis, the society's secretary, said "No system could be good enough to prevent this extraordinary young man, who was so determined, from obtaining poisons." The difficulty is that it is impossible to ban the sale of all poisons because of the variety of uses, useful uses, that there are for them.'

Another book, *The St Albans Poisoner*, by Anthony Holden, published by Hodder and Stoughton in 1974, alleged that, during his time in Broadmoor, Young had made some efforts to seek employment which he could take up on his release. A letter he wrote applying for a job with the Metropolitan Police Forensic Science Laboratory had, it was said, produced a prompt refusal. A curt reply to his request for details of the Pharmaceutical Society's training scheme and terms of membership had 'alienated him further'. It was tempting to wonder whether a more sympathetic response might have changed the boy's future, Holden reflected. He added that, several months after Young's trial, the two firms of chemists where Young had bought his poisons – Freeman Grieve, of St Albans, and John Bell and Croyden – were fined for failing to comply with the Pharmacy and Poisons Act of 1933, which provided controls for the sale of poison. The St Albans firm had also been censured by the Pharmaceutical Society, Holden wrote.

In June 1988 I contacted Desmond Lewis, the three-years-retired former secretary and registrar of the Pharmaceutical

Society of Great Britain, at his Twickenham, south-west London, home and asked for his recollections of the case, with particular reference to the manner in which the society's Statutory [disciplinary] Committee had dealt with the pharmacists involved and his memory of the letter he was said to have received from Young.

He recalled these matters with clarity and supplied me with copies of documents from the society's records. 'As far as I knew, Young had none of the academic requirements for registration as a student – three plus A-levels in chemistry, physics and biology,' he told me. 'He had been in detention since he was 14 years of age. Then, with three plus A-levels, he would have had to undertake a three-year full time course and obtain a degree in pharmacy. After graduation he would have had to complete a year of pre-registration practical training, to the satisfaction of his training pharmacist. Then he would have had to apply to the registrar (me!) for statutory registration. Before I could accept the application, I would have had to refer it to the Statutory Committee, as he had a criminal conviction in his past. All this I would have told Young. Maybe he thought my reply was curt, perhaps it was. It was the only inquiry I ever had about a career in pharmacy from someone incarcerated in Broadmoor! To my amazement, he ended by referring to "an indiscretion in my youth" and said he hoped it would not impede his ambition!'

As to the disciplinary processes, Freeman Grieve had been 'told off in no uncertain manner', Lewis said. 'He was distraught at the time. He thought he had found a genius. I don't think he ever recovered from it all.' Regarding Kearne, Lewis provided me with a transcript of comments made by the chairman of the society's Statutory Committee, Sir Gordon Willmer, a former Lord Justice of Appeal. After declaring that the committee had decided, from the evidence it had heard, that Kearne had supplied Young with poison on two occasions, he added that the pharmacist had been 'taken in by a plausible rogue, on the basis of a document which he says was produced by Young purporting to come from some department of the University of London and purporting to be signed by a professor ... Unhappily, if such a document ever existed, apart from existing in the brain of Mr Kearne, it has been lost.'

Willmer pointed out that the section of the Pharmacy and Poisons Act 1933 which governed transactions of the kind carried out by Kearne made it unlawful to sell any poison included in Part I of the Poisons List to any person unless that person was (i) certified in writing in the manner prescribed by rules and by a person authorized by rules to give a certificate, or (ii) known by the seller or by some registered pharmacist in the employment of the seller at the premises where the sale is effected, to be a person to whom the poison may properly be sold. Kearne and his employers were reprimanded, Kearne being cautioned against 'any repetition of such behaviour.'

It was, Lewis commented to me, 'interesting' that Young had gone to John Bell and Croyden – 'probably the only pharmacy in Great Britain that had thallium in stock, and God knows why. The sale to Young was probably the only sale ever made of the stuff in any pharmacy in Great Britain.'

The beginning of Young's deadly games with poisons, when he administered doses to his father, sister and a schoolfriend, had followed from his pestering a pharmacist with questions, Lewis added. Impressed by the boy's intelligence and eagerness to learn, the pharmacist had loaned him books and his college lecture notes. When Young told him he wanted to do an alkaloidal assay and needed some belladonna for the purpose, the pharmacist remembered that he had an unopened jar of belladonna leaf in his cellar. He gave it to Young, who promptly used it for his nefarious purposes. Although foolish, the pharmacist had not broken the law, because the Pharmacy and Poisons Act of 1933 applied only to the *sale* of medicines and the belladonna had been a gift, said Lewis, a holder of qualifications as a barrister as well as a pharmacist. As a member of the Poisons Board (a committee advising the Home Secretary) from 1967 until his retirement in 1985, he considered that that body's recommendation of the tighter control of thallium was 'the least that could be done, and shown to be done, to satisfy the public'.

The 1933 Pharmacy and Poisons Act has been replaced by legislation providing better safeguards against any would-be imitators of Graham Young.

CHAPTER 22

Collegians in conflict

THE 36-INCH × 20-INCH × 20-INCH SILVER-COLOURED, metal-clad wooden trunk was heavy. It was no easy burden for 54-year-old company secretary/accountant Ronald Richens and his athletic 17-year-old public schoolboy son Andrew as they manoeuvred it downstairs from the second-floor flat in Ashdown Way, Upper Tooting Park, south-west London, and loaded it into Richens' car. Its delivery upstairs in Park Mansions, in stylish Knightsbridge, was less of a struggle, that destination being reached via a lift. This was an apartment in use by a 51-year-old senior management executive employed by the Rothmans tobacco organization. He was also the guardian in London of Sabrina Ngiau, Andrew's 17-year-old Malaysian girlfriend.

Pleased when the task was completed, Richens senior thought he had been helpful in acceding to his son's request for aid in moving a quantity of Sabrina's books. But Andrew knew that the trunk contained no books. Just the body of a 17-year-old former fellow-pupil.

The corpse was that of Wai Lim (William) Choi, son of a psychiatric hospital nurse in Hong Kong. Like Richens and Ngiau, he had been a student at Dover College, Dover, Kent (motto: 'Do not shirk hard work'). Members of Choi's family had clubbed together to pay the £6,000-a-year fees for him to attend the college as a boarder. Choi was last seen there on December 1 1986, when he departed to attend an acceptance interview at Brunel University and to keep subsequent similar appointments in Bristol and Sheffield. When he failed to return to Dover as scheduled, he was reported missing on December 9.

Police inquiries ascertained that, when visiting or passing through London, he had the use of the Ashdown Way flat. It was learned that, on occasion, he had invited schoolfriends to parties there. When Detective Constable Richard Bell checked the place, signs of wiped bloodstains were seen.

Dr Christopher Price, a biologist at the Metropolitan Police Forensic Science Laboratory, was summoned to the premises on Christmas eve. (His college librarian wife, Susan, was 'not amused' by his consequently delayed arrival, at two am on Christmas day, at their leisure-time home in a Gloucestershire cottage.) Price found spots and smears of blood in the hallway, in the bedroom and in the bathroom. The upper surface of the carpet between the bedroom and the hall was discoloured and gave reactions indicating the presence of blood. The underside of the carpet and the underlay in this region bore heavy stains of blood. This had a diluted appearance, apparently as a result of washing the surface of the carpet.

More bloodstaining was disclosed when walls were sprayed with leuco-malachite green, a sensitive reagent which reveals the presence of blood even though it has been diluted several thousand times. Attempts to blood group the stains were successful only with those found on the bedroom carpet and on the doorframe of an airing cupboard. Price formed the opinion that the distribution of bloodstaining was consistent with a violent assault, followed by extensive efforts to remove the traces by washing and wiping. These conclusions were included in his later report as an expert witness.

Directed by Detective Superintendent Christopher Bird, who was assisted by Detective Inspector Hugh Parker, the police investigation continued through the Christmas period. On December 30, Andrew Richens was arrested. After two days of interviews, on the first day of 1987, he confessed that he had killed Choi at the flat at about 10 pm on December 1, stabbing him a number of times, starting in the bedroom and finally cutting his throat in the bathroom. Richens said that he and Ngiau had then cleaned the place up and put the body in the trunk, which they bought from a nearby store. Later, with the assistance of her guardian's chauffeur, who was unaware of its contents, the trunk had been driven from Knightsbridge to Ightham, near Sevenoaks, Kent. There, again aided by Ngiau, Richens said, he had buried the corpse in a field behind his father's home, a detached, three-bedroomed house in Borough Green Road. They had then set fire to a collection of the dead boy's personal effects in the trunk, on an adjacent rubbish tip.

Choi's death had, it seemed, followed an allegation by Ngiau that he had raped her. Although she had not reported the assault to the police, she had been to hospital saying she had been 'torn apart' in the attack. After the killing, she had returned to her parents' home near Kuala Lumpur.

Following Richens' description of the place where the body had been buried, Detective Sergeant Roy Grover, serving at the Metropolitan Police Forensic Science Laboratory, was sent the same day to recover it. Assisted by colleagues, he disinterred Choi's remains, finishing the gruesome job under emergency floodlighting. 'Considering that a month had passed since the murder, the body was quite well preserved,' he told me during a conversation in May 1988. 'At the deepest point it had been buried about three feet six inches down in cold, wet clay.'

A *post mortem* examination carried out by pathologist Michael Crompton confirmed that Choi had suffered multiple stab wounds to the chest and back and had died of haemorrhage following a fatal wound to the throat, severing a carotid artery. An inquest conducted by Dr Paul Knapman returned a verdict that the boy had been unlawfully killed.

During questioning, the only sign of emotion that had been shown by Richens was his adverse reaction to a statement that the police proposed to go to Malaysia to arrest Ngiau, Detective Chief Inspector (he had received promotion) Parker recalled when we discussed the case in May 1988. He added 'Richens was heavily into transcendental meditation, Buddhism, yoga, karate and all that sort of thing. He was an expert on the martial arts. He was a very self-possessed young man.'

Choi had previously sexually assaulted a girl at a Lancaster Gate, Bayswater, London, flat where there had been some drinking and cannabis smoking, Parker asserted. 'Mr Bird and I went to a place near Kuala Lumpur to interview Ngiau and obtain a blood sample from her,' he said. 'She was legally represented at that meeting. She admitted being in the flat when Richens stabbed Choi but said she took no active part in the attack. She also admitted that she had assisted Richens in the disposal of the body.'

Continuing his forensic inquiries, Price ascertained that the bloodstains he had found on the carpet and airing cupboard doorframe at the Ashdown Way flat were of the same group as Choi's but were different from those of Richens and Ngiau. Price also examined a scout-type sheath knife which had been found at the Ightham house and identified by Richens as the weapon he had used to kill Choi. It had a blade $5\frac{3}{8}$ inches long and $1\frac{3}{16}$ inches wide. No bloodstaining was found on the sheath or the outer surfaces of the knife but, when he dismantled the handle, Price discovered two small stains of human blood on the metal inside. They were insufficient for grouping.

Richens' trial opened in court one at the Old Bailey on March 21 1988. He pleaded not guilty to the charge of murder, but admitted manslaughter. The judge was Mr Justice Pain. James Crespi QC conducted the prosecution. Gilbert Gray QC appeared for the defence. Four days later, on March 25, Richens was found guilty of murder and was sentenced to be detained during Her Majesty's pleasure.

Like other human tragedies of its kind, it was a drama affecting many lives in addition to those that were centrally involved. During a conversation in June 1988, Ronald Richens, clearly enduring immense anguish, told me 'I shall not be so quick to condemn other people in future.' Despite the confession his son had made to the police, the boy had assured him that he had not committed the crime, he said. Choi had, he alleged, been guilty of raping three girls, including Ngiau. As to the knife: 'I *know* that it never left the house. Only a few specks of blood were found on it and they were ungroupable.' He was hopeful that an appeal would produce an amended finding of manslaughter under provocation.

Another opinion was expressed to me a few days later by the

headmaster of Dover College, Jack Ind. 'Stories that William Choi had been molesting girls had no credence here at all,' he affirmed. 'He had been in this co-educational establishment for four years. If he had been interfering with girls we would have heard something of it. I protested to the press that his character had been blackened when he was not in a position to defend himself.'

Richens' parents had been asked to withdraw their son from the college after Andrew had told him that he and Sabrina had been smoking cannabis during a half-term holiday, Ind explained.

Sabrina had been at the college only since January 1986, he said. 'Academically, it did not go too well with her. Her father withdrew her from the college soon after Richens left.'

The affair had had serious effects on the college, he went on. 'Applications for admissions have sunk and sunk.' The local press had contributed to the damage, with unjustified headlines like 'Sex and drugs at Dover College', he claimed.

Richens had had a clerical job with the Law Society in London for a week before the murder, Parker told me. The boy was continuing his studies via the Open University and Ngiau had become an undergraduate at the University of Hawaii, he added. Although she was, technically, an accessary to the act of murder, the Crown Prosecution Service had decided not to seek her extradition to Britain to face charges.

CHAPTER 23

Paraquat pie

THE SEXUAL URGE, A PRIMEVAL instinct programmed into mankind, as into other creatures, to perpetuate procreation of the species, sometimes gives rise to equally primitive side-effects. In the male, it commonly prompts acts of direct, instant and overt aggression, even to the extreme of rape. In the female, the deviations usually take more subtle, covert and sustained forms. Like those evinced by Mrs Susan Barber, a mother of three children, who lived with her husband and family in a pre-war terraced house in Osborne Road, Westcliff-on-sea, Essex.

Married in 1970 aged 17, she was already the mother of a six-month-old daughter, the child of a previous boyfriend. Her husband, Michael, a 24-year-old unskilled worker who had held a variety of jobs, believed that the baby was his. Although locally regarded as friendly and industrious, he had been in trouble for stealing cars and for traffic offences. Two years after the marriage he faced more problems, for indecently assaulting his six-year-old niece.

Three doors from the newly-wed Barbers, 15-year-old Richard Collins lived with his parents and sister. Mrs Barber promptly initiated him into the mysteries of sexual intercourse. By 1980 the two were regular lovers, Richard entering the Barbers' bed after Michael had departed to his work as a packer in the Rothmans cigarette factory at Basildon, Essex, at five o'clock each morning.

On Saturday March 31 1981, Michael arose even earlier than usual and left his home at four am, to accompany a friend on a sea fishing trip. But strong winds had sprung up in the Thames estuary and the trip was cancelled. Michael arrived back home to find Richard naked in the bedroom, with Susan wearing only a hastily-donned housecoat. The outraged husband struck them both and Richard fled.

The following Tuesday the Barbers consulted their doctor about a painful bruise on Susan's ear, where Michael had hit her. When he learned the cause of the hurt, the doctor offered advice to the pair about their marital problems. Susan said she was willing to try to preserve the marriage and the couple returned home. But, secretly, Susan and Richard stayed in touch, through letters conveyed back and forth by an 'understanding' friend.

At the factory on Thursday June 4 1981, Michael developed a severe headache. He went to the works clinic, where the nurse gave him some tablets to relieve it. The same thing occurred the following day. Then he began to have stomach pains and feelings of nausea.

By Saturday June 13 his condition had worsened. With the headache persisting, he felt sick and had developed an inflamed throat. The doctor was called and prescribed an antibiotic. Two days later Michael was having difficulty in breathing. He was taken by ambulance to Southend General Hospital where the following day, gravely ill, he was admitted to the intensive care unit. On Wednesday June 17 he was transferred to Hammersmith Hospital, where specialized treatment was available for kidney malfunctions.

During his stay in Southend Hospital, Susan visited him twice. A registrar who told her that her husband had only a slim chance of survival was surprised by her calm acceptance of the news. She also visited Michael on two occasions at Hammersmith Hospital, once being accompanied by Richard, who waited outside while she was at her husband's bedside.

Barber continued to deteriorate, his symptoms baffling the doctors. At one stage Goodpastures Syndrome (a rare disorder of the nervous system) or Legionnaire's Disease were thought to be possible explanations of his condition, but these complaints were eliminated by tests. Lung and kidney problems were apparent but, because no specific infection could be identified, a registrar in respiratory medicine raised the question of possible poisoning by paraquat. This suggestion was conveyed to the consultant physician in renal medicine. He instructed junior ward staff to ensure that blood and urine samples were sent to the National Poisons Reference Centre for analysis. It was later understood that this had been done, producing a negative result.

Barber died on June 27. After receiving the news by telephone, his widow sent one of her children to fetch Collins. The two were soon engrossed in deep conversation. A death certificate was issued, giving the causes of 35-year-old Barber's demise as cardiac arrest, renal failure and bilateral pneumonia.

Professor David Evans supervised the *post mortem* examination, assisted by one of his pupils. Both were informed that tests had excluded the possibility of paraquat poisoning. The major organs were removed from the body and, following the taking of samples for processing into histology slides, were placed in a large bucket labelled with the deceased's name and *post mortem* number. The bucket was then filled with formalin, a preserving fluid, and placed in a mortuary anteroom. Both pathologists were of the opinion that the findings suggested paraquat poisoning but reserved their judgment until the histology slides became available.

Barber's body was cremated at Southend, Essex, on July 3. Members of his and Susan's families attended the service, as did Richard Collins. Collins was seen to be weeping. Following the ceremony, some of the mourners adjourned to Osborne Road, where Susan served food and drinks. The same night, Richard moved in to live with her.

Life looked good for Susan. Michael's employers agreed that she should be granted a maximum death benefit of £15,000, an £800 refund of her husband's pension contributions and £300 a year for each of her three children. She received these payments in October 1981. But by that time Richard had fallen from her favour and been replaced by another live-in lover.

Susan spent generously on drinks at the local public house, where Michael had captained the darts team, and on parties at her home. She also purchased a Citizens' Band radio and, using the call-sign 'Nympho', soon became something of a sexual celebrity in the area. Through that medium she made contact with a man who was known to the police through black magic rituals and drug offences. He became the next paramour to move into her home. Video and blue movie shows were held at the house and Susan was absorbed in a whirligig of sex and drink.

But, unknown to her, the mystery of her husband's death had not been put aside. Pieces of the jig-saw were, slowly, beginning to fall into place. In September 1981, Professor Evans examined the histology slides and came to the conclusion that they indicated an ingested toxin, probably paraquat. His report was sent to the renal unit, for the attention of the consultant who had been in overall charge of Barber's case. It caused some puzzlement because, as detailed earlier, that individual had already instructed that tests were to be made for paraquat poisoning and had been told that those checks had been carried out and had proved negative. Because of the strange combination of circumstances, it was arranged that a 'clinical conference' should take place at the beginning of the next medical term – in January 1982.

Preparing material for the conference that month, a doctor at Hammersmith Hospital noticed that, although paraquat was said to have been excluded, the file carried no note regarding samples having been examined by the National Poisons Unit. An inquiry made of the unit revealed that no samples taken from Michael Barber had ever been sent for analysis.

A bustle of activity followed. Serum samples were found and sent to the National Poisons Unit. Samples of tissue from the major organs – still, astonishingly, in the bucket at the mortuary some eight months after the death – were sent to Imperial Chemical Industries, the manufacturers of paraquat. The results of tests at both places came swiftly. Paraquat had been found in both serum and tissue. The situation was reported to the Hammersmith coroner, who informed the police.

A small team of detectives, directed by Detective Chief Inspector John Clark, began making inquiries in an endeavour to establish whether the death had been caused by accident or suicide or whether there was a more sinister explanation. Their work had to be conducted with great discretion, to avoid information about their activities leaking to the community. Particular problems arose from the facts that Collins' 28-year-old sister was a policewoman stationed at nearby Rayleigh and his mother had worked in a police canteen for several years and was acquainted with many locally-based officers.

During February and March 1982, interviews were arranged with every consultant, doctor and nurse at the two hospitals involved with Barber's illness. Various medical records were taken into police possession and a detailed history was compiled. ICI told the police that, following its discovery in 1955, paraquat had become one of the world's leading herbicides. Said to act only in sunlight on green foliage, it was claimed to affect only what it touched and, becoming inactive on contact with soil, caused no harm to seed germination. The product was, the police learned, available in liquid form for professional use under various trade names, including a strong version called Gramoxone. Its sale was restricted by law to professional farmers and others having a genuine need for it. Purchasers were required to sign the poisons registers kept by suppliers.

The manufacturers added that, in 1974, because of a number of accidents with the substance, they had introduced a 'stenching agent' and an emetic to all subsequent output of paraquat. The stenching material gave off an offensive smell and the emetic induced vomiting if the product was swallowed. Barber had worked for a firm of landscape gardeners in the early 1970s; friends and neighbours believed that he had kept a container of Gramoxone of that vintage in his garden shed.

Remembering the earlier errors and delays that had

occurred at Hammersmith Hospital, Clark decided that the police must have further supporting evidence from another, authoritative, source. More samples of Barber's blood were found at the hospital and these, together with samples of the organs in the bucket, were sent for analysis at the Metropolitan Police Forensic Science Laboratory. The items were dealt with there by Andrew Clatworthy, a pharmacologist whose rampant growth of hair and luxuriant, greying beard distinguish him from his more orthodoxly-trimmed colleagues. 'A good bit of work was required,' he said during a talk we had about the case in July 1988, 'because some of the poison had been leached out of the tissue by the long immersion in formalin. The formalin itself had also been changed. But there was no doubt whatever about it – there was paraquat in each of the samples.'

To make totally sure of the validity of the scientific findings, Clark asked Home Office pathologist Professor James Cameron to examine all the evidence the police had gathered. Cameron also gave the view that Michael Barber had died from paraquat poisoning.

'Amazement' would be a one-word understatement of the expression that is said to have appeared on Susan Barber's face when, on Monday April 5 1982 – nine months after her husband's funeral – police officers arrived at her home and told her she was being arrested on suspicion of having committed murder. Collins, then a warehouseman, was also taken into police custody the same day.

'There is no doubt that the two had lived for months in the belief that the perfect crime had been committed,' Clark recorded later in the *Police Review*. 'However, after a short time, both admitted the part they had played.

'The truth of the poisoning will never be known as Susan, well practised in the art of deception, gave, altogether, three different versions of her actions. One thing was certain: either just before or just after the assault on her by her husband, she had taken some paraquat from the garden shed into the kitchen of her house … One evening … she had put some in her husband's dinner and watched him eat his meal, which, she remembered, was steak and kidney pie. When nothing happened immediately, she followed this with a further dose administered by the same method. Whilst it could never positively be established, it was strongly believed by the investigators that she administered yet a third dose, this time in the medicine Michael had been prescribed for his sore throat, which was in fact the result of the first poisoning.

'Richard Collins proved to be the naive, inexperienced young man that those who knew him had described. He quickly admitted being told by Susan of her intentions and, whilst he had not taken an active part, he had agreed all along with her suggestions. He recalled a suggestion by her in early 1981 to cut the brake pipes on Michael's car. A suggestion which he had rejected. He had been present when the two of them had returned home from Hammersmith Hospital when Susan, having been asked by medical staff about poison, poured the contents of Michael's medicine bottle down the sink.

'Strangely enough, after being kicked out of the house by Susan ... he had told a number of people in Southend what Susan had done. However, those he told had thought he was just upset at the ending of the relationship and took the view that, "if it were true, the cause of death would have been discovered long ago".'

The trial, at Chelmsford Crown Court, opened on November 1 1982. Barber was accused of murdering her husband, of conspiring to murder him and of administering poison with intent to injure him Collins was charged with conspiracy to murder. Both pleaded not guilty. The judge was Mr Justice Woolf. The prosecution was conducted by Derek Spencer QC. Michael Beckman QC appeared for the defence.

Admitting that she had put the poison in her husband's food, Barber said she had done so only to make him ill, not to kill him. 'I gave it to him because I wanted to get away with my children. If he was ill he could not come after me,' she declared. She had administered the poison twice, in half-teaspoons on each occasion, she said. 'I got it from the shed, from a container. I gave it to him in his dinner, mixed with the gravy. I gave him the second lot because the first did not seem to work.'

She wept when she and Collins were found guilty on November 8. Sentencing her to life imprisonment, the judge said 'I cannot think of a more evil way of disposing of a human being.' The following day he sentenced Collins to two years' imprisonment, telling the 26-year-old 'While I fully accept that your role was a lesser one, I am satisfied that the only proper sentence is one of imprisonment.'

The press followed the case closely throughout the hearing, the headlines mirroring the heartlessness of the affair. 'Poison death was almost undetected, trial jury told', said the *Daily Telegraph* on November 2. 'Cheating wife who cooked poison pie', said the *Daily Mail* of the same date. 'Husband caught lover naked, murder trial told' and 'My affair, by the poison pie wife', said the *Daily Mirror* on November 4. 'Widow in black tells court: "I poured out the poison and mixed it with his gravy," ' it declared the next day, while the *Mail* topped its story with 'Runaway plan of poison pie wife' and the *Sun* underlined its heading 'Why I fed my husband poison pie meal'. The height (or depth?) of journalistic achievement was attained by two *Sun* reporters. The day after the verdicts, under the headline 'Poisoned pie killer's nine times a night sex', they quoted one of Barber's former lovers as saying 'She was like a bride on her honeymoon instead of a widow in mourning. When we went to bed I never worked so hard in my life – love-making turned into a marathon. Every muscle in my body would ache, but it was absolute heaven.'

The more soberly-inclined *Daily Telegraph* reported 'Cheating wife gets life for poison killing'. That paper's detailed summary of the murder and its outcome included the information: 'Paraquat causes chronic fibrosis of the lungs, turning them hard and leathery in a matter of days and making breathing almost impossible. It also attacks the kidneys and liver and burns the gullet.

'Dr Thomas Hart, medical adviser to ICI, says two teaspoon-fuls of Gramoxone taken together are enough to kill. A smaller dose could cause sickness for at least three weeks before resulting in death.

'The longest surviving victim was a man who lived for 104 days after taking the poison. The quickest death occurred in a victim who died two hours after swallowing a pint of the weedkiller.'

CHAPTER 24

Missives after murder

'IT LOOKED QUITE GOOD, BUT there was something funny about it. Things weren't quite right,' 33-year-old questioned documents examiner Dr Christopher Davies told me at the laboratory in June 1988. He was referring to a handwritten letter posted in Hanover and seemingly penned, on December 3 1985, by 55-year-old Dr David Napier Hamilton, Old Etonian, Fellow of Trinity College, Oxford, head of the chairman's office at the County Hall headquarters of the Greater London Council, friend of royal persons and 'secret' homosexual with a penchant for black men.

Addressed to Tony Banks, then chairman of the now defunct GLC, the 15-line letter read 'Dear Tony, I am truly sorry that I could not give proper notification of my absence from my duties at the office, but my life is suddenly a shambles. My good friend Kingsley Rotardier is looking after things for me, and is at my house. You may reach him there.

'I am having great difficulty writing, I cannot keep a steady hand. I am trying.

'Because of the state of my illness, I am forced to give you notice of my resignation.

'Please forgive me. David.'

The missive was one of a number of letters and postcards, some carrying an untidy script and others typed with only the shaky signature handwritten, that were addressed to Hamilton's friends. Some were sent from France, Germany and Malaysia. They all appeared to confirm what 44-year-old Kingsley Ignatius Rotardier, a West Indian who described himself as a male model, actor and dancer, said: that Hamilton had contracted Aids and had gone abroad to seek treatment or to die. But no one had any recollection of his appearing to be at all ill or distressed. The day before his disappearance he had seemed quite happy, helping to host a dinner with an education minister who was visiting London from the Gambia. On November 18 1985, the last day he was seen, he told colleagues that he was taking a week's leave to entertain a friend from Germany. He kept several appointments that day, including one with Archbishop Trevor Huddleston. He was also scheduled to attend a meeting of the Anglo-Ethiopean Society, of which he was chairman. After dinner that night he returned, alone, to his elegant home in the house he owned, at 164 Brixton Road, south London.

Rotardier next claimed to have received a letter from 'a doctor in Paris' saying that Hamilton had been given treatment for an illness which was so severe that he would never again be able to return to work at the GLC. Producing the document, Rotardier asked the GLC to pay to him the £17,000 redundancy payment due to Hamilton when the GLC was dissolved by government edict, followed by the £6,000 a year pension to which Hamilton was entitled. The request was refused.

As time passed with no clarification of Hamilton's whereabouts, suspicions increased. The police were informed and, at the outset, treated the matter as a 'missing person' case. A year after his disappearance, Scotland Yard issued a statement requesting anyone who had seen Hamilton since November 1985 to come forward. His brother, the Reverend Dr Peter Hamilton, vicar of Stonegate, Sussex, put an advertisement in the *Times* asking for information. There was no response to either appeal. When Hamilton was mourned at a memorial service at Southwark Cathedral, the black-bordered cards that were sent included one signed 'Kingsley'.

Following inquiries made by Detective Inspector John Scullion, Detective Superintendent Robert Chapman, Detective Sergeant David Cooper and other officers, Rotardier was faced with six charges of fraudulently using Hamilton's credit cards, by means of which he had obtained some £3,000. Allowed bail, he was required to surrender his passport. Pleading guilty to all the charges, he was sentenced on January 5 1987, at the Inner London Crown Court, to nine months' imprisonment, suspended, and ordered to pay £1,068 compensation. Grinning as he left the court, his expression changed abruptly when he was immediately arrested, charged with murder and taken into custody.

Scullion, Chapman and Cooper had unearthed a number of facts concerning Hamilton's conceited and treacherous live-in 'friend'. They discovered that, 10 years earlier, while living in New York, Rotardier had been charged with killing the mother of his 16-year-old male lover after she had ordered him out of their flat. He was accused of battering, strangling and drowning the woman in her bath. The case was dismissed on a legal technicality – the police had not had a valid search warrant when they found bloodstained clothes and other evidence at his home.

On November 19 1985, the day after Hamilton's disappearance, Rotardier had used one of Hamilton's credit cards to purchase a butcher's meat cleaver and bone-saw. A couple occupying a flat in Hamilton's house told of the unwholesome stench they had smelled from an incinerator which had been kept burning all night in the garden. Later, Hamilton's Diners' Club card was used to pay for several journeys abroad, including trips to Paris and the USA. Some of the excursions coincided with the dispatch of letters allegedly written by Hamilton and posted in the places that were visited.

It was learned that Trinidad-born Rotardier had first met Hamilton in Port of Spain when, as a 12-year-old, he had been introduced to the distinguished-looking Englishman who was then personal private secretary to the Governor of Trinidad and Tobago. The next contact that was known to have taken place between the two was on a rainy evening in the autumn of 1985 when Rotardier turned up on Hamilton's Brixton doorstep. Soon afterwards the pair were seen dancing the nights away in the *Stallion Club*, Charing Cross Road. In leaving New York, Rotardier had deserted his wife and small son.

For many years Hamilton had shared his house with his devoted 'daily help', Florence Wakelin, and his Irish wolfhound, Simba. When Rotardier moved in Hamilton's friends worried about the new liaison, which threatened the confidentiality of an elite circle of relationships. It was rumoured that Hamilton had been under consideration as a potential private secretary to Prince Charles.

The long-running police investigation included a thorough examination of Hamilton's house and surroundings, but no trace of blood or remnant of his body was found. The post-disappearance letters allegedly written by him therefore became a focal point of the inquiries.

Initially involved with the examination of documents relating to the charges of fraud brought against Rotardier, Christopher Davies was later concerned with the gathering of evidence in connection with the accusation of murder. Provided with some samples of Hamilton's known handwriting, he set about the task of comparing them with the communications that had been received since their alleged writer had vanished. The job occupied him for some three months. 'Having looked briefly at the first letter [the one dated December 3 1985, addressed to Banks] I said to the officer "It's either genuine but a little bit funny or it's a very good copy",' Davies told me. He admitted that some variance from their normal script might be expected from someone who had recently learned that they were suffering from a terminal illness like Aids, but pointed out that no one had, so far, carried out any research concerning the effects of Aids on handwriting. 'One of the things I had to bear in mind right the way through was whether the features I found that were different could be the result of illness or of having been a copy made by someone else,' he said. 'All I had for comparison at the first stage were some carbon copy writing in a duplicate book and an old letter, dated 1975. The problem with the letter was that handwriting, even an adult's, may change to some extent over that period of time. But ultimately I had samples of Hamilton's writing over a 10-year period, including memos he had written at the GLC, letters he had written to people a few days before his disappearance, and so on. These enabled me to see the range of his normal variations.

'In cases where there is a large number of letters, we often group them together and decide whether they have all been written by the same person and then compare them with the writing of the suspect,' he continued. 'But in a case like this, where there is a suspicion that they are copies, you can't do that because two different people copying the same writing may produce writing that is very similar, since they are trying to get the features of the writing being copied to come across. But the other point in this particular case was that, if any one of these documents proved to be genuine or more likely to be genuine than not, then clearly the whole case would fall to pieces. Because if one of the documents had been written by Hamilton in 1986, then clearly he couldn't have died in 1985. So each one had to be individually assessed.'

Following a committal hearing at Lambeth, Rotardier's trial opened at the Old Bailey on January 13 1988. He pleaded not guilty. Presenting the case for the prosecution, Julian Bevan said that Rotardier had killed Hamilton at his home in the early hours of November 19, had spent his money and had tried to convince the world that his victim was still alive. But Hamilton had been well educated and Rotardier had not. The letters received by Hamilton's friends were not written in his meticulous style, contained mistakes of spelling and grammar and included various Americanisms. After murdering Hamilton, Rotardier had bought the butcher's implements and cut the body up, probably doing the dismemberment in the bath so as to facilitate the disposal of blood. The sawn-up parts had probably first been put into a refrigerator and then burnt, piece by piece, in the garden incinerator, he went on.

The court was told that, in a tape recorded interview with the police, Rotardier had said that, on the evening of November 18 1985 (the day when numerous colleagues and business contacts had seen Hamilton and thought him to be perfectly well and cheerful) he had found him 'crying uncontrollably' in the kitchen of the flat they shared. 'I hugged him and asked what was wrong,' Rotardier claimed. 'I got very upset. He finally came out with it and said "You don't want to touch me because I have Aids." '

Having informed the jury of Rotardier's fradulent use of

Hamilton's credit cards and attempt to gain the payments from the GLC, Bevan declared that the motive for the murder had been money.

Davies gave detailed evidence about the outcome of his examinations of the documents, speaking from the witness box on January 21 and 22. He had scrutinized a total of 84 items, including a number of cheques and envelopes. Of the 26 letters that had been gathered from Hamilton's friends and colleagues, 12 had been handwritten and 14 typed, the latter carrying only a hand-inscribed signature. Davies gave the opinion that nothing written after November 18 1985 had been penned by Hamilton.

During our talk at the laboratory, Davies told me that Rotardier had persuaded an airline employee to post one of the letters in Malaysia.

On January 27, after a four-hour retirement, the jury found Rotardier guilty as charged. The judge, Sir James Miskin QC, the Recorder of London, sentenced him to life imprisonment with a recommended minimum term of 20 years. Hamilton had been a highly intelligent, hardworking and successful man 'who had the misfortune to be homosexual', Miskin said. As he was taken to the cells, Rotardier hissed an expletive at the jury.

In feature articles on the case published the following day, the *Guardian* and *Today* newspapers suggested, each differently, that finance had not been Rotardier's only motive for the killing. The *Guardian* piece, by Gareth Parry, referred to police evidence regarding a row between Hamilton and Rotardier 'about the latter's newly-formed friendship with a young black actor'. The *Today* version, by Kim Sengupta, declared 'The couple quarrelled when Hamilton, who had had a string of affairs with black boys, began to switch his affections to actor Carl Andrews, Mac the mechanic in the TV soap *Crossroads*. When Hamilton agreed to take nude photographs of Andrews, Rotardier snapped.'

Describing Hamilton as a relative of Princess Margaret's personal secretary, Lord Napier, Sengupta added that Baroness Phillips of Fulham had proposed him for the post with Prince Charles. The baroness was quoted as saying 'This has all come as a tremendous shock. I admired David very much. He was a delightful, tactful man, extremely charming and very good at his job at County Hall, where he would meet statesmen from all over the world. He mixed regularly with Royalty and got on well with them.'

CHAPTER 25
Deadly doctor

ALTHOUGH ENGAGED IN A PROFESSION whose primary aim is the relief of human suffering, Dr John Baksh's true dedication was to the swift and easy acquisition of money. He felt no qualms about taking life for that purpose. Greed led him to commit one 'successful' murder and then to attempt another. In both cases the victims were women who trusted him and believed he loved them – his wives. In both crimes he used his medical knowledge towards achievement of his ends. And yet, despite his possession of that expertise, he failed in his effort to kill his second spouse. It was a blunder that brought his existence to ruins.

The secret story of the grey-haired, black-eyebrowed, square-jowled, 52-year-old general practitioner began to be unfolded just after one am in the freezing cold morning of January 5 1986, when an amateur naturalist hoping to see badgers in the moonlight found instead a pretty, dark-haired, dusky-skinned woman lying on her back in the undergrowth at Keston Ponds, a well-known beauty spot much frequented by lovers, near Bromley, Kent.

Dressed in a blouse and skirt but wearing no overcoat, she was motionless. Her flung-back head revealed an appalling open gash across her throat. Her blouse was darkened by soaked-in blood. When help arrived, summoned from a nearby house where a dinner party was still in progress, it was found that she was, miraculously, still alive although deeply unconscious. The sub-zero temperature had slowed the haemorrhage from her massive wound and the position of her

259

head had enabled breathing to continue. Rushed to Bromley Hospital, she was taken into intensive care. Doctors said later that, had she not been found for a further 30 minutes, she would have died. It was thought that she had lain on the frozen ground for some hours before discovery.

It was obviously a case of attempted murder. Police inquiries were conducted by Detective Superintendent Norman Stockford and Detective Inspector Thomas Hamilton. Detective Sergeant Derek Hancock, stationed at the Metropolitan Police Forensic Science Laboratory, noted that a mental patient with a history of violence was known to have been in the area at the time. The man was taken into precautionary police custody. A hospital gown stained with a small area of blood was found among his clothing. It was taken to the laboratory for grouping tests. A number of couples were found in vehicles near the scene during an immediate search of the locality. Taken to the police station for questioning, some faced embarrassment at the disclosure of extra-marital love lives.

The victim was identified as Dr Madhu Baksh, 42-year-old wife of Dr John Baksh and, like her predecessor Dr Ruby Baksh, a partner in his two thriving practices in the south-east London suburbs of Mottingham and Chislehurst. With her husband hovering near, the alert and cautious detectives maintained an unbroken vigilance at her bedside.

While still on a life support machine, she was examined by divisional police surgeon Eileen Gorman who, although of the opinion that there had been no sexual assault, nevertheless took the customary vaginal swabs. These were delivered to Geoffrey Willott, a biologist at the Metropolitan Police laboratory, for examination. Questioned by the police, Baksh said that he had last had sexual intercourse with his wife four days earlier. In the evening of January 4 he had reported her as missing, saying that they had arranged to go out together that night.

Madhu regained some feeble consciousness after emergency surgery but was unable to speak because of damage to her vocal chords. Struggling to communicate, she managed to mutter a few indistinct words. The names of two drugs,

Omnopon and methadone, narcotic analgesics, were heard. Then, unmistakably, 'morphine'.

Dr John Taylor, a toxicologist at the Metropolitan Police laboratory, was asked to carry out immediate tests to ascertain whether morphine had been used. Given just the one tiny sample of pre-transfusion blood that had been taken from the near-dead woman – sufficient for only limited examination – Taylor asked whether the investigators were sure that that was what they wanted. They told him it was and urged him to hurry. 'Analysis and radioimmunoassay tests confirmed that there had been a massive dose of morphine,' Taylor told me during a talk at the laboratory in June 1988. Answering my questions, he explained that, for someone unaccustomed to taking the drug, five to 10 single-strength 15 milligram ampoules would probable be fatal – 'But if I wanted to be sure of killing someone I would give them 10 ampoules.'

Meanwhile, pursuing their inquiries, the detectives had discovered that, from the two doctors' joint income of £80,000 a year, some £1,000 a month was being spent on insurance premiums. Baksh held policies worth a total of £215,000 on the life of his wife, one of the arrangements being so recent that the documentation was not delivered to him until after his dying partner had been found.

Gradually regaining strength, Madhu succeeded in scrawling a message on a piece of paper. It sealed her murderous husband's fate. Faced with the evidence that was piling up against him, he admitted his guilt.

As the police pieced the story together it became clear that Baksh, the son of a clergyman, had schemed to make his wife's death appear to be murder following abduction. He began by driving her car to South Street, Bromley, and abandoning it there. Surreptitiously, probably in a drink, he then administered a soporific drug to her and, whilst she was drowsy, injected the morphine into the back of her thigh. It was no problem to throw her limp body into his car (a BMW, with the personalized number plate JB70), drive to Keston and, under cover of darkness, place her in the undergrowth. There, he also cut her throat. Although the dreadful wound went into her voice box, it did not sever the vital jugular vein or carotid arteries.

Uncovering more facts as their inquiries continued, the detectives learned that Baksh's previous wife, Ruby, had been found dead in bed whilst the couple had been holidaying together in southern Spain in 1983. Her demise had been certified as due to a heart attack, but there had been no *post mortem*. Baksh had insured her life for £90,000. In line with local custom, the body had been interred in a concrete vault.

Three years after her death, the Spanish authorities were asked to give permission for Ruby's corpse to be exhumed. When consent was received, pathologist Iain West went to Spain and collected some of her internal organs and some leg tissue. These items were delivered to John Taylor, for examination in the laboratory. Again his tests showed the presence of a large quantity of morphine. Although the overdose had produced symptoms similar to those of a heart attack, Dr Ruby Baksh had been murdered by her husband.

According to a *Times* report published on December 19 1986, Baksh enacted a bizarre 'wedding ceremony' with Madhu less than two weeks after killing his first wife. During the performance he slipped Ruby's wedding ring onto her finger. The mother of two children, Madhu had joined the Bakshs' medical practices in 1979, when she was separated from her husband.

The couple were officially married a year later, in 1984, buying a house in Bickley, Kent, with the help of Ruby's life insurance money. The *Times* report added that, during their honeymoon in Paris, Baksh had told his new wife 'I sacrificed Ruby for you. What I have done is the biggest sacrifice anyone could do for love.' Although sickened and horrified by his confession, she had kept his secret, not dreaming that she was to be his next victim.

When she was able to return home after discharge from hospital, Madhu found, in a drawer in her bedroom, an empty hypodermic syringe and a packet containing five used morphine sulphate ampoules. They were sent to the laboratory for tests. Baksh had evidently underestimated the quantity needed to kill her.

Charged with murder and attempted murder, he was tried at London's Old Bailey in December 1986. The court was told that, having drugged Madhu, he had cut her throat in a way that would cause a slow, lingering death, so affording him time to establish that he was elsewhere when she died.

The jury of nine men and three women were unanimous in finding him guilty on both counts. Pronouncing sentences of life and 14 years' imprisonment respectively, the judge, Sir James Miskin, Recorder of London, said that Baksh was 'demonstrably a danger to those close to him'. The sentences were accompanied by a recommendation that he should remain in prison for a minimum of 20 years.

Madhu was reported as intending to resume medical practice and to devote herself to the welfare of four children, the two from her previous marriage and two from Baksh's marriage to Ruby. She obtained a divorce from Baksh, on the ground of his 'unreasonable behaviour'.

CHAPTER 26

Child killer

FORTY-FOUR-YEAR-OLD LORRY driver Colin James Evans was a keen amateur photographer who developed and printed his own black-and-white films. But his pictures were not of the sort that could be displayed openly in an album or sent elsewhere for processing. Because Evans was a sexual deviant who liked to keep a pictorial record of the abuses he perpetrated on young children. It was his photography that contributed to his undoing – after his evil ways had extended to murder.

It was on Friday March 11 1983 that four-year-old Marie Denise Payne was reported missing from her home in a council-owned housing estate at Dagenham, Essex. It was the 39th birthday of her mother, Brenda Payne, who had left the child in the care of her other daughter, 12-year-old Julie Lavinia, while she went to keep an 11.15 am appointment to have her hair permed at a salon about a mile and a half away. When that had been done she visited the home of her 63-year-old parents, unemployed Walter Stanley Sullivan and his wife Louisa, in Porters Avenue, Dagenham. Later, she went shopping for clothing and groceries.

Having received his fortnightly social security cheque that morning, Marie's unemployed father, 38-year-old John Leonard Payne, left the house at noon. He said later that he instructed Julie to put the bolt on the front door after his departure, to prevent Marie from wandering outside. Having called at a local shop to buy something to eat and a newspaper, he went to a public house where he had a drink, played a slot machine and studied the day's horseracing form. Shortly before one pm he walked about a mile to a job centre and looked at the factory vacancy cards for about five minutes. He then went to a nearby betting shop and placed some bets, after which he walked to another, similar, establishment and placed further wagers. Having spent the entire afternoon between the two betting shops, he began to make his way home at about five pm. On the way he bought a large bottle of cider at an off licence.

Reaching his house at 5.15, he found nobody at home, but his wife's shopping was in the kitchen. She had, in fact, arrived some 15 minutes before him and then gone looking for Marie. The only son of the family, 11-year-old Colin, had been at school all day. Finding Julie playing with a 12-year-old girl friend and no sign of Marie when he returned home at 3.45, he had assumed that his younger sister was out with their mother. But when Brenda came back to the house soon after her husband had returned, she said that Marie was missing.

The child's absence was reported to the police by a 999 call from a neighbour's telephone at 5.37 pm and inquiries, directed by the duty officer, Inspector David Spackman, began. One of the first actions was to question members of the family. It appeared that Sullivan, Mrs Payne's father, had seen Marie playing with the family dog on a grass covered area across the road from the house when he called there at about 12.30 pm. He stayed for only 15 minutes, but gave Marie and Julie money to buy sweets, which they did forthwith at a local shop. Julie said that, having eaten her sweets at home, Marie screamed to be let out again with the dog, a demand to which her sister evidently acceded. Marie was described as 'a wilful child'.

The police officers also interviewed 28 local people, adults and children, who claimed to have seen Marie in the area that afternoon. The most reliable account appeared to come from 47-year-old Mrs Edith Bailey, a 'home help' and Sunday school teacher, who claimed to have seen the girl and the dog walking in Goresbrook Road at 4.20 pm. No one other than an 11-year-old girl and a 38-year-old milk roundsman reported seeing anything unusual. The milkman said that, just before delivering milk to a neighbouring house, he had seen Marie and the dog in the street. While talking to the customer he was serving, he heard a long scream which seemed to come from a small girl. After two more deliveries, he went to the Paynes' home, where Julie paid the milk bill. While giving her change, he saw a man in the corridor whom he took to be Mr Payne. Julie contradicted this story and had no recollection of paying the milk bill. The Paynes did not believe that they had left money for Julie to pay the bill and said they could not remember how or when it was paid. Having told the police that she had seen Marie being dragged screaming into a yellow Ford Cortina car, the girl later admitted that she had made the story up.

A description of the missing child – three feet six inches tall, slim build, fair complexion, fair shoulder-length hair, blue/green eyes, clad in a blue flowered dress, red tights, red and orange cardigan, red and white 'trainer' type shoes with the word 'shoot' printed on the sides – was prepared and teams of policemen, some with dogs, searched the area surrounding the Payne home and nearby parks and marshland. Traffic Division officers drove through the streets using their public address systems to broadcast appeals for news of the child. A police helicopter equipped with searchlight and, later, with a thermal imager (a device designed to detect and photograph local heat sources such as energy created by biological action in a decaying body) toured the district.

Local Citizens' Band radio clubs began relaying appeals for information about Marie and the police were soon inundated by volunteers who wished to help in the search. 'So many people offered their services that we literally didn't know what to do with them,' 48-year-old former Detective Chief Superintendent David Little told me during a talk about the case in September 1988. He had retired only two weeks before our meeting and looked back on 30 years with the Metropolitan Police, 28 of them in the CID. Having become involved with the Marie Payne affair soon after it began, he had kept detailed notes of its progress and regarded it as one of the most memorable of his career. Not wanting to turn away any source of aid, he had suggested that the eager helpers should form themselves into groups and search in Epping forest, some 15 miles from Dagenham, he said. Although this did not produce results, the suggestion was strangely intuitive, as will be revealed later.

Many difficulties confronted the police in their quest for the missing child, Little added. Among them was the fact that on Castle Green, near the Paynes' home, a multi-storey car park was in process of demolition. Although it had been searched visually and with dogs, the lower levels were full of huge lumps of concrete, laying in piles. It was thought possible that Marie might have crept into a crevice in one of the heaps and could have been knocked unconscious by falling debris. Contractors were dismantling the building bit by bit, crushing the concrete in situ to provide marketable hardcore, a process scheduled to occupy several weeks. At a cost of some £25,000, the police arranged for a fleet of lorries to remove the concrete with maximum speed. The job was done in 48 hours, but there was no sign of Marie.

The following day, Saturday March 12, the police carried out a systematic search of all buildings in the area to which access could be gained. These included three blocks of flats, a church, industrial premises, an oil storage depot, railway lines and sundry other places. The traffic cars cruised through shopping centres at Barking, Romford and Hornchurch, broadcasting details of the child's disappearance and appealing for information. The searching helicopter continued to overfly the district, making a special survey of river banks and open ground. An underwater unit examined boating lakes in Mayesbrook Park, a long section of the River Roding and other waterways, lakes and ponds. Underground sewer routes and drains were searched, along with tunnels carrying cables from Barking power station. An incident room was set up at Barking police station.

During the night of Sunday March 13 a poster bearing a photograph of Marie and appealing for witnesses was distributed to business premises throughout the area and to all police stations in the district. It was widely publicized in the press and on television news programmes. On Friday March

18 a mobile control van was set up at the scene of Marie's disappearance and during that afternoon all persons passing along the road were stopped and questioned.

No success having attended any of these efforts, it was decided to search, with the occupiers' consent, every house in the area. This formidable task was begun on Saturday March 19. At the end, over 1,700 houses had been examined, including unoccupied premises, which were entered with the assistance of the local authority. The goodwill of householders and the tact of the investigating officers were evidenced by the fact that not one complaint was lodged in consequence of the operation.

While the physical searches were proceeding, other investigatory work was being done, under Little's command, at Barking. The first steps taken were checks that confirmed each of the Payne family's statements as to their movements on March 11. The web then spread wider, taking in friends and acquaintances of the family and other people with whom individual members had been in contact. In consequence, a number of private and personal matters were revealed. But, as Little's later report recorded, the inquiries were 'hampered by a complete and utter lack of clues as to the manner of Marie's disappearance'.

The case was featured on national radio and television news bulletins. Then came the reports of sightings of children, some said to have been showing signs of distress, who were thought to fit the description of Marie. These responses originated from various parts of London and from Cornwall, East Anglia, Wales and the Midlands. They mentioned such improbable locations as Lambeth pier and a men's washroom at the Ford Motor Company's Dagenham factory. All were investigated, but produced no constructive result. One, from a woman who said she had seen a small girl wearing clothing very similar to Marie's and wandering apparently alone in a Hornchurch supermarket, prompted a full-scale police reconstruction of the sighting, in the hope that it would stir the memories of other shoppers. A four-year-old cousin of Marie's played the key role. The reconstruction was enacted three times and received local and national news coverage. It did not help.

During the weekend of May 14-15, door-to-door inquiries were made throughout each of the three blocks of flats adjacent to Castle Green. Carried out under the pretext of learning who had been at home on March 11, the real purpose was to discover anyone living there who, though unknown to the police, entertained a penchant for offences relating to children. This enterprise provided no new information, but a 63-year-old resident in one of the blocks, a man known locally as 'Dirty Ken', had earlier admitted numerous indecent assaults on young girls he had lured to his flat. Arrested, held in custody and pleading guilty to all the charges, he was later made the subject of a two-year probation order. Other individuals on the police list of suspects were interrogated and their homes subjected to searches by forensic experts, but no useful outcome was achieved. Some of those on the list were found to be mentally subnormal. One man confessed to a habit of engaging young girls in casual conversation and then going away to masturbate. A man found to be a Borstal escapee offered information in exchange for bail. His revelations, mainly about the exploits of a gipsy fraternity, did not help. A 25-year-old father who had smashed windows at the home of a lorry driver who had knocked down and killed his 3½-year-old daughter on a pedestrian crossing was interviewed because of a suspicion that he might have abducted Marie. He was found to have two other daughters of his own and to be innocent of any connection with the missing child. In a separate tragedy, a 29-year-old husband committed suicide after becoming obsessed by the conviction that he was under police surveillance in consequence of the fact that he had taken a day off work on the date Marie had disappeared and would not be able to account for his movements at that time. The police reached the conclusion that his mental disturbance had been triggered off because of a visit he had paid to a massage parlour, where he had had 'some sort of sexual adventure' which had become known to his wife.

In a report compiled at the conclusion of this phase of their inquiries, the investigators gave the view that the most likely fate to have overtaken Marie was that she had been abducted, murdered and her body disposed of. At that point, the report added, 378 statements had been taken, 801 messages recorded and 721 actions completed.

But then, on Saturday October 8 1983, two young couples who had been walking together in the Lodge Road area of Waltham Abbey, in Epping forest, went to Epping police station to report that they had seen what appeared to be a complete set of child's clothing in a hollow tree. They were asked to return to the place, where they were joined by a police constable. The clothing was found to consist of a red woollen cardigan, a pair of red tights, a dress, a grey vest and a pair of 'trainer'-type shoes with the word 'shoot' on the sides. Taken to the Paynes' home, the items were at once identified by Mrs Payne as the clothing worn by Marie on the day she disappeared, seven months earlier.

A new incident room was set up at Chingford police station and Little set about the task of establishing how long the clothing had been in the tree. Appeals for information were made via the national and local press and radio and television. A number of people volunteered information about their sightings of the articles. The earliest that could be traced came from a 35-year-old Italian-born greenhouse worker who said that he had seen them in the tree in mid-August. Little expressed no surprise during our talk that there had been no earlier report to the police of the discovery of clothing. 'Bits of clothing are always being found in the forest,' he said.

On Sunday October 9 another police search was begun, in the vicinity of the hollow tree. Lines of officers, working shoulder-to-shoulder, checked the area yard by yard. They were backed up by dogs trained to search for dead bodies and by mounted officers who, from horseback, were able to see a different perspective of the ground. The thermal-imager-carrying helicopter was also used again. As well as looking for any trace of the child, the searchers were also briefed to be on the lookout for her pants, the only item of her clothing that had not been recovered. Again, there was no result.

Forensic examination of the garments by Dr Elizabeth Wilson showed that they were extensively bloodstained but carried no traceable evidence of semen or saliva. The tiny vest had been cut from neck to bottom edge at the back and across both shoulder straps. The zip fastener on the dress was undone and the remainder of the material, from the zip base to the lower hem, had been cut or torn apart. These findings led to the conjecture that the garments might have been removed from the child when her body was in a state of *rigor mortis*. Leaf mould and other vegetable debris found on the articles was tested but gave no reactions indicating the presence of blood. Soil samples from the vicinity of the Payne household and others taken at random in the Dagenham/Barking area were also tested for comparison purposes.

Again the trail dried up. On October 24 the inquiry centre returned to the incident room at Barking. That day the hollow tree in Epping forest was burnt down. The remains of a firework were found in the debris.

Once more, Little and his team turned to inquiries into the activities of people known to have been involved in offences against children. Reference to a national index of persons convicted of indecent assaults disclosed that those records contained more than 8,000 names. For a number of reasons it was impracticable to search through such numbers. Other checks showed that, at the time of Marie's disappearance, 28 people who had been convicted of child murder were at large on licence, three more were at liberty on release after serious repeated rapes and nine others convicted of the murder or attempted murder of children had been discharged from mental institutions. With the help of police forces throughout the country, inquiries were made concerning the whereabouts, in March 1983, of each of these individuals, plus a further nine in east London and Essex who had come to attention in consequence of indecent assaults. All 49 were eventually eliminated from the Marie Payne investigation.

It was there that the police quest might have ended, but for three incidents that occurred nearly seven months later, on Sunday May 6 1984.

At 11.45 am that day, Edward Sudbury, a 54-year-old carpenter, was working on his car outside his home in South Street, Rainham, Essex, when he saw a man wearing a blond wig speak to two young children who were later identified by the police as seven-year-old Tracey Turner and her three-year-old brother Paul. When the man left, Sudbury asked the children what had happened. They told him the man had said 'You're not having much fun today. Why not come with me?'

At 1.45 pm Bonny and Harriett Branch, aged five and three respectively, were playing on waste ground adjoining allotments at the rear of their home in Staines Road, Ilford, a few miles from Rainham. Looking out of a window, their mother, 27-year-old Joyce Branch, saw the children being led away by a man who was holding their arms. Mrs Branch called out to her 27-year-old bricklayer husband Robert, who ran across the allotments, a distance of some 250 yards. As he ran he saw that the man with his children was trying to open the front passenger door of a yellow Hillman Avenger car that was parked in Loxford Lane.

When Branch had almost reached him, the man released the infants and moved away. Branch grabbed his daughters and took them back to his wife. Returning to Loxford lane, he saw the man drive away in the yellow Hillman. He memorized the index number as HJB 821N and wrote it on an envelope as soon as he returned to his home. The police were informed of the incident and Woman Police Constable Sally Parsall attended to take details.

Half an hour later six-year-old Josephine Brisley was playing in the courtyard of her home in Peabody Buildings, in John Fisher Street, Stepney, east London, when her mother, 36-year-old Mary Brisley, heard her screaming. Going into the courtyard, Mrs Brisley found her daughter crying. She said a man had taken her ball way and had hurt her wrist. The child's father, 43-year-old maintenance engineer Alan Brisley, then arrived home and found his wife and daughter upset. He went to the local police station and reported the incident to Constable Robert Judd.

Police inquiries located an excellent witness in the person of 26-year-old Susan Eales, a bank clerk living with her fiancé in Peabody Buildings. She said that, on looking out of her window at about 2.15 pm, she had seen a man wearing a blond wig walk across the forecourt to the flats. Some 10 minutes later she had heard screaming and, on again looking out of the window, had seen the man pulling a little girl towards the road. He was carrying a ball in one hand and had the girl by the wrist with the other. The child had suddenly broken free but was pursued by the man. The witness had then leaned out of her window and shouted to her fiancé to get the police. The man looked up, then strolled back to the road, where he dropped the ball and walked out of sight. When her fiancé joined her at the window they had both seen a yellow Avenger car drive along John Fisher Street and disappear.

A subsequent police report recorded that, in noting the make, colour and index number of the car in which the man who had attempted to abduct his children had driven away, Branch had provided them with the most vital clue. But the number he had given – HJB 821N – sent the investigators in a wrong direction. After a warning telex had been transmitted to all police forces in the UK, an Edinburgh detective working on two other child murders realized that witnesses' unknowing transposition of the final numbers in vehicle index marks was a common failing. When he searched the computer for HJB 812N instead of HJB 821N, he identified a yellow Hillman Avenger owned by Colin James Evans, of Russell Street, Reading, Berkshire. This information was telephoned to Ilford police station and Thames Valley police were requested to locate and arrest Evans. Although the police at Reading duly supplied information in respect of Evans' history of child abuse (four convictions for indecency with children and child-stealing) there was then no indication that he was connected with Marie Payne's disappearance. It was learned that his wife and daughter had left him soon after his first conviction.

Evans was arrested at his place of work at 3 pm on Wednesday May 9 1984 by Detective Sergeant Edward Ditum and Detective Constable Graham Jones. He was detained pending the arrival of Metropolitan officers, who were joined by policemen from Ilford and by Detective Sergeant Colin Taylor, from Dagenham.

That evening, a combined team of Metropolitan and Thames Valley detectives subjected Evans' flat to a meticulous search. When Taylor, acting on some instinct, removed the rear panel of a radiogram, he found a number of packages concealed under the turntable. These contained two wigs, a large number of indecent photographs of young children, a piece of dowel and a candle. Among these items were 11 black-and-white photographs of what appeared to be a child's dead body. Detective Sergeant Gary Fermor, from Ilford, took possession of a receipt for petrol which was to prove significant. A bag containing a large number of children's knickers was found, but when these were shown to Mrs Payne she was unable to identify any of them as Marie's. Evans said later that he had collected the items for a jumble sale, about which Little commented 'I very much doubt that that was his motive.'

Having been kept informed of developments, Little, who was then stationed at New Scotland Yard, travelled to Reading to interview Evans. To begin with he confined his questions to the Ilford incident concerning the Branch children. Evans denied all knowledge of it, claiming that he had been at home throughout that Sunday. But the receipt found by Fermor, which had been signed by Evans, showed that he had bought petrol at a service station in Green Lane, Ilford, on May 6. A part-time forecourt assistant there identified his own writing on the receipt and said that the station had been open for the sale of petrol only from 10.00 am until 1.30 pm that day.

Resuming his questioning in the late afternoon in the presence of Detective Sergeant Taylor and Inspector Geoffrey Chivers, of Reading, Little began to ask about Marie Payne. When the photographs of the dead child were shown to him, Evans refused to comment, saying that he wished to see his solicitor.

Just before 7 pm Little asked Taylor and Chivers to leave him alone with Evans. 'Under informal conditions I then remained with him for about an hour, discussing his background, domestic circumstances and details of his previous convictions,' Little wrote later. 'Having gained his confidence, I could sense he responded favourably to informal questioning rather than the note-taking/formal style of interview and it became fairly obvious he wanted to talk about the murder. When I asked him if he had a conscience about

Marie's body lying in an unmarked grave, he made his first direct admission, i.e., "Mr Little, you will never know just what's been going through my mind. Ever since that day I've thought about nothing else. When I woke up the next morning and realized what I'd done I could have killed myself. Can't you take me outside and hang me?" I then cautioned him and he went on to admit the body was in Epping forest and agreed to take me to her grave provided his solicitor approved. I made an immediate note of the conversation with Evans, in my pocket book.'

Evans was then allowed a private meeting with his solicitor, after which another formal interview was conducted. Evans signed each of his answers as recorded in the contemporaneous notes.

These amounted to his admission that he had abducted Marie at about 2 pm on March 11 1983 and had taken her to Epping forest, where he killed and buried her. Describing how he had begun to indecently assault the child after removing her tights and knickers, he said she had started screaming and running away. Claiming that he had panicked, he said he had hit her over the head with a heavy, fallen branch.

According to Evans, he had then dug a hole and stripped and abused the child, after which he had taken the photographs. 'It was obvious he was lying at this point,' Little's later report observed, 'as the photographs found in his radiogram clearly show the body had been buried.'

Evans subsequently admitted that he had photographed Marie in the forest whilst she was alive but that, because of a fault in his camera, the film had become 'fogged'. Having initially concealed the dead child under a mound of leaves and hidden her clothing under leaves in a tree stump, he had returned three days later, uncovered the corpse, taken the photographs that had been found and then buried her in a shallow grave. Asked about the negatives, Evans declared that he had burnt them on a bonfire.

With his solicitor, Timothy Hammick, Evans was taken to Epping forest and shown the spot where Marie's clothing had been found in the tree. (The burnt-out remains of the stump had been removed.) Leading the party of policemen, accompanied by Alan Parker, a Scotland Yard photographer who was to make a sound/video recording of events, some 250 yards into the forest, he pointed out the area where he thought he had buried the child's remains. Evans was then removed to Barking police station and the place he had indicated was cordoned off.

A large number of uniformed officers took part in the new, concentrated, search. Little was present when Constable David Minns, from Chigwell, exposed part of a badly decomposed body about eight feet from the place Evans had identified. It took several hours of careful excavation to totally expose the remains without causing further destruction. Detective Sergeants Sandy Sanderson and Peter Kent-Woolsey carried out the bulk of this unpleasant operation. Dr Peter Jerreat, a forensic pathologist and lecturer in forensic medicine at the London Hospital, was called to the scene. He examined the corpse and supervised its removal. Following a *post mortem*, Jerreat decided that the cause of death was intracranial haemorrhage and fractured skull, the injuries being consistent with more than one blow. He stated that the sexual mutilation had been inflicted after death.

An inquest was opened by the Essex coroner, Dr Charles Clark, and adjourned pending Evans' trial. He was formally charged with murder on May 11 1984. He made no reply. During a subsequent interview with Little, he admitted committing the offences on May 6. 'I put it to him that, had he been successful in abducting any one of the children that Sunday morning, they would have befallen the same fate as Marie Payne,' Little reported. 'He answered "… I thank God that nothing came of my activities … I dread to think what may have happened." '

Little's report also revealed that Evans had asked him whether he would accept a plea of guilty to manslaughter. 'I told him that this was absolutely out of the question. Every effort must be made to see that this man is never again released from custody because I am convinced he will kill again if given the opportunity,' he wrote.

In September 1984, while Evans was awaiting trial, there

was a further development. It appeared that the occupier of a flat where Evans had formerly lived, in Western Elms Avenue, Reading, had lifted a carpet and discovered hidden beneath it the negatives of a number of indecent photographs of children. Among them were those of the pictures taken of Marie's body in the forest, which Evans had told Little he had destroyed on a bonfire. For reasons best known to himself, the finder chose to supply the negatives to the *Sun* newspaper, through which they were handed to the police.

Evans' 35mm single lens reflex Zenith camera, a 58mm lens and a flash gun had been found under the front passenger seat of his car and were sent to the Metropolitan Police Forensic Science Laboratory for examination. In the hope of gaining positive proof that the damning photographs had been taken by Evans, Little also forwarded the negatives to the laboratory for fingerprint tests and for comparison with the camera. The latter was a task of a kind that had been undertaken many times before by the laboratory's chief photographer, 47-year-old Kenneth Creer, during his 16 years of service there.

'If you look at the masking frame inside a camera, its edges appear to be absolutely straight and level,' Creer told me during an explanation of his scrutiny. 'But when you put it under a microscope, you see that that is not so at all. During the paint spraying of these parts, tiny specks of dust adhere to the metal, including the extreme edges of the frame. Despite their smallness, these irregularities are registered on the negatives when films are exposed. Thus, with the exception of Polaroids and instamatics, every conventional camera can be said to leave its microscopical "fingerprint" on the films that are shot in it.'

He had carried out examinations of that type in many investigations of pornographic photography, in some cases of stolen cameras and in a few instances of suspected espionage, he said. In respect of the camera found in Evans' car and the negatives found in Western Elms Avenue, there had been a perfect match. Coupled with the other evidence, this made the case against Colin James Evans incontrovertible.

The forensic work was necessary because, as the reader will

have observed from earlier chapters, a suspect's confession during interrogation by the police by no means guarantees that a plea of guilty will be offered in court. For that reason, appropriate proof of culpability has to be obtained and held in readiness. But, in this instance, Creer was not required to prepare formal documentation on his findings. Faced with the apodictic evidence that had been assembled against him, Evans, advised by his legal representatives, admitted that he had murdered Marie Payne. Tried at the Old Bailey, he was sentenced to imprisonment for life, with a recommendation that he should serve a minimum term of 30 years.

Only isolated confinement would protect him from the covert beatings that child molesters usually receive at the hands of other prisoners, I was told. Removed even from the society of fellow-criminals, Evans faces a solitary existence.

The cost of the police inquiries that finally brought him to justice amounted to many hundreds of thousands of pounds, Little told me. 'We found that he had taken hundreds of indecent and pornographic photographs of little girls and boys,' he added. 'The Reading police were able to trace many of the children. The amazing thing was that, for quite a while, he had been employed as a part-time baby-sitter. He had assaulted children in Reading right, left and centre. It was the Evans case which made Parliament direct that the police could, in future, give information about any criminal convictions of people entrusted with children. Until then, there was no way in which, legally, the police were allowed to tell local authorities about such peoples' backgrounds.'

CHAPTER 27

'Railway' rapist-murderer

'THREE MILLION POUNDS WOULDN'T BE unrealistic,' 44-year-old Detective Chief Superintendent Vincent Mc-Fadden, head of Surrey Constabulary's Criminal Investigation Department, told me as we sat in his office at the pleasant Mount Browne, Guildford, headquarters of that organization in September 1988.

He was answering a question I had asked as to the cost of the police work that had been done to bring 29-year-old multiple rapist-murderer John Francis Duffy to justice at the beginning of that year. As co-ordinator of 'combined operations' involving four police forces in inquiries following the murders of three young women and a long series of rapes, McFadden had, at one stage, directed the endeavours of more than 500 police officers engaged on the assignment. The outcome was achieved in consequence of the co-operation engendered between detectives of the Metropolitan, Hertfordshire, Surrey and British Rail forces, of information collated through a special databank of criminal statistics begun by the Metropolitan Police at West Hampstead and later transferred to Hendon, of assistance provided by a professor of applied psychology, of efforts made at the Home Office laboratory at Aldermaston and of blood group testing, contact tracing, and sexual assault index searches at the Metropolitan Police Forensic Science Laboratory. It was all encapsulated in a *Times* headline: 'Killer captured by intuition, science and sheer hard work'.

No flicker of emotion crossed Duffy's face when, on

February 26 1988, he was found guilty of five rapes and two murders. Nor did he appear disturbed when Mr Justice Farquharson sentenced him to 30 years' imprisonment for his crimes. Only his parents reacted, his tearful mother declaring that she still considered her son innocent of the charges and his father describing him as 'a God-fearing man'.

Just five feet four inches tall, weedy, acne-ridden and taking size four shoes, ginger-haired Duffy rebelled against his lack of physical comeliness. A workshy carpenter, he was for a time employed by British Rail. His marriage, at 21, to an 18-year-old girl who was impressed by his boasts and promises, turned out to be turbulent and violent. It failed to produce the child he wanted. He liked to tie his wife up before having sexual intercourse with her. On one occasion he told her it was her fault he had raped a girl. He informed a friend that rape was 'a natural thing for a man to do'. The marriage foundered but there was an attempt at reconciliation, and further efforts to produce a child, in 1983. Both ventures failed and the couple parted. In 1985 he raped her and she reported the assault to the police. During the evidence she gave at his trial in 1988 she said that 'the nice man I married' had turned into 'a raving madman with scary eyes'.

Duffy's sexual attacks on women are believed to have begun in June 1982, when he and an associate (who has not yet been apprehended) took to dressing up as joggers and, in the north London area of Hampstead, some two miles from Duffy's home in Kentish Town, seizing and dragging their victims to pre-selected lonely places. Many of the attacks took place near railway lines. But in 1983, the year of the reconciliation, there was none.

In July 1985 there were three assaults on women on the same night, all later believed to have been carried out by Duffy. In August that year, after being remanded in custody by Hendon magistrates in connection with his estranged wife's accusations against him, he was released on bail at Acton Crown Court by Peter Archer QC, a former Solicitor General. But, fortunately, his name had by then been routinely entered in Scotland Yard's computer record of sexual offenders and individuals given to violence against women, a system which

had been started by Detective Superintendent Ian Harley and
was codenamed Operation HART – the initials standing for
'Harley's Area Rape Team'.

Three months after his release (which was achieved despite
an objection by the police) Duffy attacked a 20-year-old
female in Copthall Park, north London. A detective assigned
to the case was already investigating Duffy and thought he
might match the girl's description. But Duffy's luck had not
yet run out. Suffering from rape trauma syndrome, a
condition in which victims obliterate details of their ordeals
from their minds, she failed to identify him. But sometimes
the memories return. A year later she was able to recognize
Duffy as her assailant.

Until that time Duffy had allowed his victims to escape with
their lives, but on December 29 1985 the insignificant-looking
little man who loved sex but loathed women added a more
terrible action to his savagery. Having followed 19-year-old
secretary Alison Day from a train at Hackney Wick, east
London, he forced her to accompany him to a rat-infested
garage block, tied her hands behind her and subjected her to
bestial violation. He then cut a strip from her red tartan shirt,
tied it round her neck and used a short stick of wood to twist it
tight, throttling her to death. Next he threw her body into the
nearby River Lea. It was recovered 17 days later. Two hundred
yards away a frogman under training found her sheepskin coat
on the river bed. There were heavy stones in the pockets.
Taken to the Metropolitan Police Forensic Science Laboratory, the garment was carefully dried out. Despite its immersion, fibres which might have come from the clothing of the
attacker were found on the coat. Other 'foreign' fibres were
lifted from Alison's shirt and jeans, which were still on her
body, although her knickers and brassiere were missing.

Pathologist Peter Vanesis reported that the tightening of the
ligature knot at the front of Alison's neck had affected the
voice box. This was taken as indicating that her killer was
acquainted with the martial arts or had been in the forces. As
well as strangulation, the girl had suffered several heavy blows
to the head. She was her parents' only child.

Grey-haired, bespectacled Detective Superintendent Charles

Farquhar took charge of the investigation. At his instigation, his team of detectives consulted the HART unit but, although the killing had occurred near a railway line, no firm connection with the earlier rapes could be ascertained.

Four months passed. Then, in April 1986, 15-year-old Maartje Tamboezer, a Dutch schoolgirl whose father was employed in England by an oil company, was reported missing from the family home in East Horsley, Surrey. Last seen alive when setting off on her bicycle to buy sweets, her body was found deep in woodland bordered by a footpath near East Horsley railway station. She had been savagely raped. Like Alison Day, her hands had been tied behind her. Also like Alison, Maartje had been garrotted with a stick-tightened tourniquet and had suffered severe head injuries.

The links with the earlier murder were obvious. 'It was probably the worst killing I had ever seen in my career,' the police officer who led inquiries in the case, youthful-looking Detective Chief Superintendent John Hurst, said later. 'There had been a clear attempt to destroy forensic evidence.'

Parts of Maartje's body had been burnt. Tissue paper and matches were found at the scene. It was apparent that the rapist/murderer was a man who knew what his pursuers would be looking for by way of clues. As Hurst put it 'We realized that we were hunting for someone experienced in crime.'

News of the murder appeared in the press and on radio and television. A number of people provided information to the police. The sighting of a man dashing across the footbridge at East Horsley station, colliding with other travellers in his haste to catch a train standing at a platform, led to exhaustive but unproductive inquiries that included the checking of two million used tickets. More helpfully, a man told of finding a strong nylon line of the type used in gardeners' strimmers tied across the footpath not far from the places where Maartje's bicycle and body had been discovered. It appeared to be the means by which her shopping journey had been halted.

More constructively still, articles of her clothing were examined by forensic scientist David Northcott at the Home Office laboratory at Aldermaston, Berkshire, and were found to carry semen stains which revealed that her attacker was a

'Group A' secretor. 'This simply meant that there were some blood group substances in his semen and other body fluids,' Anne Davies, of the Metropolitan Police laboratory, explained later. 'One person in three has an A secretor blood group. But another, more discriminating, test narrows the search still further. By measuring an enzyme in the blood, called PGM, scientists can divide people into ten distinct categories. We could tell that Maartje Tamboezer's killer was either group PGM 1+, group PGM 2+ 1+ or PGM 1+ 1−. This meant that, taken together, the police could elminate four out of five potential suspects by the blood grouping alone.'

Biologist Davies was experienced in matters of rape. During her 20 years at the laboratory, she had been involved in the investigation of nearly 1,000 cases. She and her colleagues had examined evidence from the series of north London rapes that had begun in 1982, she told me during a conversation at the laboratory in May 1988. The tests had shown that there had been at least two assailants, and that a pair had sometimes attacked together. The findings were checked against the index of sexual assaults that is maintained at the laboratory. The information it yielded suggested strongly that the series of rapes were linked. 'We quite often find that people involved in sexual assaults are into body building or martial arts,' Anne commented. Duffy and a known associate were both found to be members of a martial arts club.

Checking on the origin of the string used to pinion Maartje, the investigators learned that it was made of paper and was called Somyarn. It was manufactured at a factory in Preston, Lancashire. When the makers examined the piece from the crime, they were able to say that the type of paper of which it was composed had not been used since 1982.

With Operation HART, which had then been placed under the leadership of Detective Superintendent Kenneth Worker, and officers from the Surrey force working at top pressure to track down Maartje's killer, a third female went missing. She was 29-year-old Mrs Anne Lock, who vanished during a journey to her Brookmans Park, Hertfordshire, home from her place of employment at London Weekend Television on May 18 1986. Hertfordshire police set up an incident room at

Welwyn Garden City. When Mrs Lock's bicycle, which she used for part of her daily home-work-home travel, was found near a footpath beside the railway line a short distance from Brookmans Park station, squads of policemen searched the lush undergrowth that covered the area. But it was not until July that her body was found, just a few yards beyond the point at which the searchers had halted. Although badly decomposed, the remains yielded clues indicating that the murder had been committed by the same attacker who had killed Alison and Maartje. Like Alison and Maartje, she had been bound and then strangled with a ligature. Like Maartje, one of her socks had been rammed down her throat. Like Maartje, the clothing on the upper part of her body had been burnt. Like Maartje, keys and money had been taken from her handbag.

The Hertfordshire incident room was transferred from Welwyn Garden City to merge with the HART unit at Hendon and Worker took charge of inquiries in the Brookmans Park case. By a Home Office edict, McFadden was appointed co-ordinator of the efforts that were now being made by three police forces and investigators employed by British Rail.

Another link came with a rape near West Hampstead railway station. Although the victim survived, her hands were tied and clothing cut as in the murder cases. The laboratory produced the same blood group findings as those discovered with Maartje.

With his name already in the HART system because of his estranged wife's complaint against him, Duffy was interviewed by detectives on three occasions, one just six days before the finding of Anne Lock's body. Still on a list of suspects that the HART officers had whittled down to 1,486 from a starting total of 4,874, he gave an alibi that he hoped would eliminate him from the inquiries about Alison. Although unconvinced, his interrogators could not be certain that he was the man they were seeking. But Duffy sensed that the police net was closing around him. He refused to give a sample of his blood. After paying a friend to slash his chest with a knife, he claimed that he had been mugged and assaulted and had, in consequence, lost his memory. By this means he was admitted to Friern Hospital, Barnet, north London, an establishment previously known as Colney Hatch lunatic asylum. Although nominally occupying a bed there, he was allowed free movement in and out of the hospital.

On October 21 1986 he struck again, blindfolding and attacking a 14-year-old girl at Watford, Hertfordshire. When the blindfold slipped and the terrified child caught sight of her assailant she realized that her life hung in the balance. For some reason unknown, she was allowed to live.

But the police trawl was steadily narrowing. In September 1986, having examined a computer printout showing patterns of rape across London and other information gathered by the investigators, Hurst saw that details of the Copthall Park assault in November 1985 closely resembled methods used in the attack on Maartje. A squad of officers was assigned to the task of keeping surveillance on Duffy.

His name also came to the top of the list of suspects in a computerized technique devised by Professor David Canter, a psychologist and expert in behavioural science, based at Surrey University. Called Psychological Offender Profiling, it collated 'personality sketch' material with statistical analyses of witnesses' statements and details of the attacks. The findings that pointed to Duffy were later found to be correct in 13 out of 17 points.

Duffy was arrested when he headed back to Copthall Park, apparently planning another attack. Under the Police and Criminal Evidence Act, his captors were empowered to detain him for only 36 hours before producing evidence to justify his continued detention. That was done. His home and that of his parents were thoroughly searched. In the latter, officers found a quantity of the unusual Somyarn that had been used to tie Maartje. The Metropolitan Police laboratory received some 70 items of Duffy's clothing for examination. Bearded biologist Dr Geoffrey Roe and his colleagues found that over half were made of fabrics that did not readily shed fibres. The scientists were, however, able to take samples from about 30 garments for comparison with the fibres discovered on Alison's clothing – some 2,000 individual fibres in all. The results, achieved a few weeks before Duffy was due for trial, showed that, after eliminating some that might have originated from elsewhere, there were 13 separate identifications of fibres which had been deposited from Duffy's clothing onto that of his victim. 'It was virtually a fingerprint,' said a delighted Farquhar. Roe told me that his work on Anne Lock's garments, through which her body had decomposed during the weeks before it was found, had been 'much more difficult'. When a sample of Duffy's blood was tested, it was found to tally with the forensic findings from the Tamboezer killing.

After the news of Duffy's detention became public, the friend who had been persuaded to knife-slash him contacted the police and disclosed how the rapist-murderer had cajoled him into the action. When the deed was done Duffy had told him that, unless he remained silent about it, he could be charged with aiding and abetting and might be imprisoned for life.

Duffy's disillusioned wife also volunteered information. During their time together she had found that the more she had tried to repel his sexual advances the more he had enjoyed it. 'If I didn't resist he seemed to lose interest,' she said.

The facts gathered by the police and their scientist colleagues indicated that, since 1982, Duffy had carried out 27 rapes. Victims' accounts showed that, on some occasions, he had had a male accomplice who had taken part in the assaults. At other times he had attacked alone.

During the process of preparing the case for the prosecution, it was found that some of the women who had been assaulted had left Britain and others were unwilling to revive memories of their ordeals. Finally, however, five of those who had suffered at Duffy's hands picked him out at separate identity parades. 'At no time did he admit or deny any of the rapes or murders,' McFadden told me. 'His answer to nearly all of our questions was "I can't remember".'

Duffy was charged with five rapes and the three murders, but the judge accepted a defence argument that there was insufficient evidence in the case of Anne Lock. The jury was ordered to return a verdict of not guilty in respect of that killing. 'As far as his reaction to the sentence was concerned, the judge might just as well have said "You are fined £25",' McFadden recalled.

The crimes ultimately traced to Duffy had, of course, received massive coverage by the news media. Predictably, with the advantage of hindsight that became available after his conviction, sundry critics accused the police of various failings. Instead of becoming bogged down in a mass of computer checks, the officers should have been out interviewing suspects, said one. Another alleged that messages provided by a woman who had been followed by Duffy on a train had not been dealt with properly. A third claimed that, although a butterfly knife had been used in some of the rapes and victims had been offered paper tissues to clean away evidence, no attempt had been made to have his bail rescinded when, after being stopped and searched in May 1986, Duffy was found to be carrying a butterfly knife and tissues. A fourth argued that the finding of Anne Lock's body had been needlessly delayed in consequence of Hertfordshire police mistakenly halting their search 400 yards short of their boundary with Metropolitan territory.

The six-feet-three tall, quiet and cautious McFadden was not amused by the gibes. 'A very professional job was done,' the *Times* quoted him as saying. 'The right man was put into the system. It was picked through and shaken until he came out. I would attack anyone who said there was a little bright reflective arrow pointing in his direction.'

CHAPTER 28

Internal evidence

THE MEN WHO TORTURED, BEAT and finally stabbed to death a 20-year-old 'loner' pushed his body into a layby ditch near Crawley, Sussex, after removing everything that might provide a clue to his identity. They drove away in the minicar that had been the final transport of his life, confident that their victim would be one of the unknowns who go to their graves via the ministrations of baffled officialdom.

It was 1974. Inquiries began when the corpse was found. The stomach contents were sent to the Metropolitan Police Forensic Science Laboratory, where they were received by biologist Geoffrey Willott. He was asked to determine what had been the dead man's last meal, in the hope that this information might be of some help towards discovering who he was.

During his examination, Willott came upon what appeared to be tiny pieces of screwed-up paper. Spending most of a day at the task, he gradually teased the sodden fragments apart. When flattened out it became clear that the majority of the pieces were parts of a single sheet. With these scraps fitted together, Willott saw that it was a printed message opening with the words 'Dear customer' and appealing for care in the treatment of fashion shoes. But scribbled on the reverse side of the sheet was something much more telling – a London telephone number.

This discovery opened the way to further investigation, conducted by Detective Sergeant Brian Tilt, of Sussex police. It revealed that the dead man was William McPhee, a Scot who had travelled south in search of excitement. Known as 'Billy Twotone' because of his dyed hair, he had been in some trouble as a lawbreaker. Fingerprints in police records removed all doubt about his identity.

Patient probing unveiled the end of his story. McPhee had obtained accommodation in a hostel, an establishment run by a fanciful man who called himself a bishop. It appeared that McPhee had expressed unhappiness about what he claimed to be unfair exploitation of the social security benefits that were paid for him and other inmates at the hostel. Receiving no satisfaction, he had announced an intention to carry his complaints to the authorities. The threat had led to his murder. Willott found bloodstains of the same group as McPhee's in rooms in the hostel and on the minicar in which he had been driven on his last journey.

Charges of murder and causing grievous bodily harm were brought against 27-year-old Philip Holland, 36-year-old Michael Woodland and 20-year-old David Johnson. The 'bishop', aged 43, faced two accusations of causing actual bodily harm and two charges of buggery. Three other men were accused of causing actual bodily harm and one of them, a 19-year-old, with taking a motor vehicle without the owner's consent.

All were found guilty. Holland, Woodland and Johnson were each sentenced to life imprisonment for murder. On the charges of GBH, Holland and Woodland were sentenced to three years' and Johnson to 12 months' imprisonment, those terms to run concurrently with the life sentences.

The 'bishop' was sentenced to 18 months' imprisonment, to run consecutively, on each of the charges of buggery and six months', consecutively, on each of the accusations of causing actual bodily harm. The latter sentences were ordered to be served consecutively with the former. The 19-year-old was sentenced to six months' imprisonment for the ABH and one day on the vehicle charge. The others each received sentences of 10 months' for the ABH. Having been in custody for that period, they were then released.

CHAPTER 29

Headless, handless ...

THE OLD ADAGE PROCLAIMING THE existence of honour among thieves makes no mention of the punishment that may be meted out for any breach of the code. Such penalties can be fearsome, extending even to murder. As was the case with a suspected 'grass' (police informer), 21-year-old Stephen Gaspard.

On April 14 1983, the headless, handless and partially burnt corpse of a young, coloured male was found on waste ground off Heckford Street, to the south of Cable Street, in London's multi-racial East End. Wrapped around the body were a strip of black plastic, which had seemingly been cut from a refuse bag, and a semi-burnt blanket. Swift police work, directed by Detective Chief Superintendent Michael John, located a witness who described seeing a 'a great big ball of flame' at the spot in the early hours. Knowledge of the area and its inhabitants, coupled with careful house-to-house inquiries and road blocks, led the investigators to a hostel in White Horse Road, Stepney, that was known to its inmates as 'Kippers'. From there the search fanned out, resulting in a series of arrests – of 22-year-old David Amani, 22-year-old Andrew Esterphane, Esterphane's younger brother, David, 23-year-old Jaspal Rathur, 18-year-old Matthew Paul and 20-year-old Gabriel N'jie. Amani had recently been released from prison. All were detained on suspicion of involvement in the murder but all, at first, denied having any knowledge of the Cable Street corpse.

One of John's major concerns was, of course, to discover the victim's name. The local news media were, therefore, informed of the find and anyone anxious about an absent male relative was asked to contact the police. A surprising number of people did so. Among them were the parents of Stephen Gaspard. His mother, living apart from her husband, had, in fact, reported him as missing on April 14, the day the body was found. But the remains from the fire, which had been fuelled with diesel oil, provided nothing that would serve as a means of identifying the dead man. A meticulous examination by pathologist Peter Jerreat enabled him to give an estimation of the victim's age, height, weight and overall physical characteristics.

Slowly, progress was made. After repeated interviews with the suspects, police confidence in the rightness of their actions began to be confirmed. Although Amani remained 'a hard case', some of the others began to weaken. Gradually, it became clear that, while they were not prepared to admit to having any part in the killing, some of them knew about the disposal of the body.

As a result of information received, a police underwater search unit succeeded in recovering an axe and a saw from the River Roding.

On May 6, just five days before his 19th birthday and a week before the tools were taken from the water, Paul was found dead in his cell at Leman Street police station. Using an article of clothing, he had hanged himself from a projection on the inside of his cell door. Anxious to avoid any repetition, the police required their prisoners to surrender clothing which could be put to such use. The turban worn by Rathur was clearly a danger in this context, but he refused, on religious grounds, to remove it.

Further information was obtained. The dead man's head had, it was learned, been thrown into the Thames at a certain point. Again an underwater search team went into action and was successful. Wrapped in two black plastic bags weighted with concrete, the relic was recovered on May 16, a month after discovery of the torso. There was some discussion as to who should open the bags, a duty that was finally undertaken by John. Although the wrappings had preserved the skull from the most destructive deterioration, its disclosure was 'quite gruesome', he told me during a discussion of the case in November 1988.

Amani's reaction to questions remained a repetitive vocabulary of oaths. Described by John as 'an outrageous, dangerous, violent hooligan,' it was apparent that he had held his associates in a state of fear.

The detectives went to the home of one of his friends in an East End street of small, terraced houses. The officers had information to the effect that the victim had been lured to the house and murdered there, but a painstaking search of the premises on May 7 revealed no evidence of the killing. A dark red stain seen on a linoleum-covered floor turned out to have been made by spilled blackcurrant juice. The investigators removed parts of the plumbing, four black plastic bags and other articles for more detailed scrutiny.

When they were examined by 35-year-old David Castle, a chemist with nine years' experience at the Metropolitan Police Forensic Science Laboratory, the bags were found to carry a dot-impressed notation: 'BD9'. When they were held in front of bright lights, it was seen that the surfaces of the bags bore fine striations which had been formed during the extrusion process of manufacture. There was a good match of these striations between all four bags. Checking on their origins, Castle learned that the 'BD' coding signified that they had come from the London borough of Barking and Dagenham and the '9' that they had been supplied in November 1981 or November 1982. He also ascertained that they had been made by a company named ICI Visqueen at Stockton-on-Tees. The markings on the bags taken from the house matched exactly with those on the bags that had been used to wrap the head and with the strip found around the body, establishing a clear connection between all three sources.

Accompanied by one of the investigating officers, Castle visited the ICI Visqueen factory in September 1983 to check on the method used for production of the bags, so that the evidential value of the information he had gathered thus far could be established. There, he was shown four lines of machines, each producing some 35,000 bags per day. After taking samples of the output during a two-day stay, he realized that the surface striations varied according to the amount of detritus that built up around the extrusion mandrels. Whenever production was stopped and the mandrels cleaned, the striations changed. Thus, it became clear that the matching bags found at the house, those wrapping the head and the piece from the corpse had all come from a batch manufactured at the same time, for the Barking and Dagenham refuse clearance department.

Back in London, Castle turned his attention to other items from the crime. He examined neck vertebrae and thyroid cartilage from the head, neck vertebrae from the torso, bones from both wrists, other bones that had been found on the partly-burnt blanket near the body, impressions and photographs of the left foot from the body, two left shoes that had belonged to Stephen Gaspard, the saw and axe which had been recovered from the river and another axe and partly-used bottles of household cleaning products. His written statement as an expert witness recorded his findings that (a) the exposed neck vertebra from the body had been cut, from front to back, with a coarse-toothed saw; (b) the left wrist had been similarly severed, marks within the cut showing that a saw with 6½ teeth per inch had been used; (c) the right wrist had been partially severed with a blow from a blade, such as an axe; (d) the exposed vertebra and thyroid cartilage from the head had both been cut with a coarse saw, marks on the vertebra indicating that the tool used had 6½ teeth per inch; (e) the direction and angle of cut on the vertebra from the head corresponded with those on the body vertebra; (f) comparison of the shoes with the photographs and impressions of the left foot from the body showed good correspondence of size, width, toe positions and areas of pressure; (g) the saw recovered from the river, a curved type normally used for pruning trees, had 6½ teeth per inch.

Listing his conclusions, Castle gave the opinions:

'1. The left foot of the body from Heckford Street almost certainly wore the left shoes from Stephen Gaspard.

'2. The head from the River Thames and the body from Heckford Street were originally joined and had been severed by a coarse saw such as the pruning saw.

'3. The left wrist bones and bones from the blanket had also been cut with a saw such as the pruning saw.
'4. The right wrist bones could have been severed with either of the axes.'

Recovery of the head made it possible to confirm that the victim was Stephen Gaspard. His hands, thought to have been thrown onto a rubbish tip, were never found. Piecing the story together, John deduced that, inflamed by the belief that Gaspard had given information to the police about his involvement in a robbery, Amani had lured his associate to a rendezvous where he had been stabbed some 30 times and finally garotted with an electrical cable. After initial concealment of the body in a suitcase, the head and hands had been removed. The police reached the opinion that, to avoid leaving traces of blood in the house, the murder and *post mortem* mutilation had been carried out in a room protected by a tarpaulin which had later had all evidence of the crime washed from it by the use of a common domestic cleanser. The investigators found a tarpaulin stored under the stairs. It was extraordinarily clean. As an added precaution, to frustrate any efforts that might be made by police 'sniffer' dogs, chili powder had been scattered on the floor.

Amani, the Esterphanes and Rathur were sent for trial at London's Old Bailey in October 1983. Amani was charged with murder, the Esterphanes with manslaughter, conspiracy to assault and conspiracy to pervert the course of justice and Rathur with conspiracy to pervert the course of justice. They all pleaded not guilty.

The jury's verdicts were announced on November 10. Amani was found guilty as charged and was sentenced to life imprisonment. The Esterphanes were convicted of manslaughter. Andrew was sentenced to six years' imprisonment and David to nine years' youth custody. Rathur was acquitted. Charged with assisting in the disposal of the body, N'jie was tried separately. He was acquitted.

CHAPTER 30

Stockwell strangler

THERE CAN BE LITTLE DOUBT that a burning hatred of people who are seen as being more comfortably situated than themselves is one of the motivations that prompt the criminally-minded to inflict suffering and degradation on their victims. Such was evidently the case with the killer who, in 1986, became known as 'the Stockwell strangler'. Short, thin and no match for anyone of normal physique, he chose the elderly and infirm, of either sex, living alone or in old peoples' homes, as the recipients of his savagery. Four of the seven, aged from 67 to 94, who died at his hands were subjected to buggery immediately before or after he choked them to death. The resistance put up by a 73-year-old man, who survived, contributed significantly towards his capture, conviction and punishment.

All the killings occurred late at night or in the early hours, most of them in the south-west area of London. First to die, on April 9, was 78-year-old Miss Eileen Emms, a retired schoolteacher, of West Hill Road, Wandsworth. Three more murders of the same type were committed in June, the victims being 67-year-old Mrs Janet Cockett, of Warwick House, Overton Road, Stockwell, and 84-year-old Valentine Gleim and 94-year-old Zbigniew Stabrawa, both of Somerville Hastings House, Stockwell Park Crescent, Stockwell. In July, three more old people died in similar fashion: 82-year-old William Carmen, of Sybil Thorndike House, Marquess Estate, Islington; 74-year-old William Downes, of Holles House, Overton Road Estate, Stockwell, and 80-year-old Mrs

Florence Tisdall, of Ranelagh Gardens, Fulham.

In none of the cases was there any sign of forced entry or violent struggle. The intruder had evidently gained access through unsecured windows. Some of the dead were also robbed. In two cases photographs of friends and relatives of the victims were seen to have been covered, placed face downwards or turned to the wall. Two of the corpses were so tidily tucked up in their beds that it was not, at first, realized that anything was amiss.

But the killer did not always succeed. In the early hours of June 27, 73-year-old Frederick Prentice was awakened by sounds in his bedroom at Bradmead, a local authority owned home for the elderly, in Cedars Road, Mortlake, Surrey. Switching on the light, he saw a slim young man approaching him. When told to get out of the room, the intruder put a finger to his lips as a gesture for silence. He then leapt onto Prentice, putting a knee on each of the old man's hands and seizing him round the neck. Uttering only the word 'Kill', the assailant began to exert a pumping action with his thumbs on Prentice's windpipe. Prentice managed a muffled shout and contrived to free one hand to reach the alarm buzzer beside his bed. At this the attacker fled.

Although the nature and circumstances of the crimes implied that they were linked, it was necessary to establish that this was so. Pathologist Iain West reported that the pattern of injuries indicated the same assailant or assailants, who appeared to have killed by holding a left hand over the victims' mouths while effecting a choke grip high on the front of the neck with the right. In such elderly people, unconsciousness could have been caused in under 30 seconds and death within two to three minutes, he added. In five of the cases he had found injuries to the naturally brittle rib cages which suggested that the attacker had either knelt or pressed on their chests. Downes, Emms and Gleim had suffered facial injuries from 'blows of no more than moderate force' while Carmen's neck and facial injuries appeared to have been inflicted with more violence. Carmen and Tisdall had received fractures to the cervical spine, but their necks were extremely arthritic and 'could be broken by manual pressure with relative ease'. Emms, Gleim, Carmen and Downes had suffered anal injuries from perverted sexual assault.

Detective Chief Superintendent Kenneth Thompson co-ordinated the police inquiries and Dr Sheila Keating, a biologist at the Metropolitan Police Forensic Science Laboratory, took charge of the scientific work. On a bedsheet at the scene of the Emms killing she found a single hair of negroid or Afro-Caribbean origin. One of her colleagues, Janet Gilburt, discovered matching shoe marks at the scenes of the attacks on Gleim, Stabrawa and Prentice. Another scientist at the laboratory, Anne Davies, examined the scene of the attack on Downes and later tested swabs, contact trace tapings, clothing, bed clothes and other items from the case. She found that internal and external anal swabs were heavily stained with semen but this gave reactions for the same blood groups as Downes himself, probably due to the presence of anal material. With the exception of four small seminal stains on a sheet taken from under Downes' body, which gave reactions for group GLO 1 – different from that of the dead man – no other biological traces which could have come from a human intruder were discovered. Urine-soaked tracksuit trousers belonging to Downes – who was said by his son Alan, a chauffeur, to be a recluse who never went out – and a piece of towelling were found to be covered with black, curly, canine hairs. Their presence was never explained. Similar checks were made in each of the other cases but nothing of significance was gained.

Senior fingerprint officer David Llewellyn fitted crucial pieces into the puzzle with the finding of fingerprints on a displaced plant pot at the scene of the Cockett killing and a palm print on a wall in Downes' kitchen. When checked they were found to match the prints of 24-year-old Kenneth Erskine, whose criminal record showed that he had been imprisoned for burglary. But his whereabouts were unknown to the police. More specific inquiries were initiated by Detective Superintendent Brian Jackson, in consequence of which it was learned that social security payments were being made to Erskine. Watch was kept and he was arrested when calling to collect money.

During questioning he admitted that he had been stealing from flats – 'to survive' – but denied killing anyone. When it was pointed out that bodies were found in places he was said to have burgled, he replied 'I don't remember. I could have done it without knowing. I am not sure if I did.'

He was asked how he had left Mrs Cockett's home after his robbery there. He answered that he had jumped from a window onto an old mattress laying outside. The mattress had long since been removed with other rubbish, but when the detectives checked police photographs taken immediately after discovery of the murder, the mattress was seen to have been there, on the ground.

At an identity parade, Prentice unhesitatingly recognized Erskine as the assailant who had tried to throttle him.

Further inquiries disclosed that Erskine had opened a number of building society savings accounts. During the three months of the murders he had paid in credits totalling some £3,000. The morning after the Carmen murder he paid in £350. Carmen was known to have kept about £400 in cash in his bedroom. It was never found.

A hairdresser told of Erskine visiting her shop and asking her to bleach his head and pubic hair. She had agreed to do the former but not the latter. She said that, as he sat waiting for the process to take effect on his head hair, he had picked up a bowl containing the bleach and applied it to his pubic region. Next he had rubbed it into his eyebrows and eyelashes, getting some of the chemical into his eyes. In agony, he had needed help to wash the stuff away.

Items taken from Erskine were examined at the laboratory. Samples of his head and pubic hair were found to have been bleached and the head hair subsequently dyed. The inside front of his blue underpants was discoloured, thought to be due in part to the action of the bleach. A cardigan he had been wearing was found to be buttoned on the left front, indicating that it was a female's garment. Trying to explain this, he said that he bought most of his clothing secondhand. Despite checking at some 300 'squats' where Erskine was believed to have stayed in south-west London, the police found no shoes which matched the marks discovered at three of the murder sites.

The Home Office Central Research and Support Establishment at Aldermaston was then beginning to apply the new DNA technique – colloquially christened 'genetic fingerprinting' – to forensic work. Dr David Werrett, head of the biology division at CRSE, was asked to process an anal swab and blood sample from Downes and blood samples from his son and from Erskine. He reported that distinguishing profiles had been obtained from the blood, with similarities, to be expected from a family relationship, between those of Downes and his son. The partial profile obtained from the swab had demonstrated that the spermatozoa absorbed onto it could not have originated from either of the Downes but could have come from Erskine. Werrett added that a theoretical calculation had shown that the frequency of occurrence by chance of the five bands obtained from the swab and the corresponding five bands from Erskine's blood would be of the order of one in 2,000.

Erskine's trial opened in courtroom two at London's Old Bailey on January 12 1988, coinciding (to the irritation of the news media) with the proceedings against John Francis Duffy – the 'railway' rapist/murderer – that were heard in court one. Charged with seven counts of murder and one of attempted murder, Erskine pleaded not guilty to all. Prosecuting, James Crespi QC told the court that the 'appallingly wanton' killings were marked by such striking similarities that they could only have been the work of the same man. They had been committed by 'a killer who likes killing' and that man was Kenneth Erskine, he asserted. The defence was conducted by Roy Amlot QC.

When the jury returned a verdict of guilty on all counts, the judge, Mr Justice Rose, said that, before passing sentence, he wished to have a statement from the police as to whether there had been any further murders of the same type in south-west London since Erskine's arrest. Told that there had not, he sentenced Erskine to imprisonment for life on each of the murder charges and 12 years for the attempted murder, those terms to run concurrently. He added a recommendation that a minimum of 40 years should be served – the longest period of detention ever recommended to the Home Secretary.

In 1986 Brian Jackson was promoted to the rank of detective chief superintendent and transferred to duties dealing with police discipline and complaints against members of the force. In July 1988 he became a lecturer at the Police Staff College at Bramshill House, near Basingstoke, Hampshire. Now a commander, he supervises the input on crime and addresses senior officers on a range of techniques, including communications systems for dealing with linked offences. With understandable pride he told me that, in the modern police force where many officers hold university degrees, he found pleasure in looking back on his days as a grammar schoolboy, on becoming a police cadet at 16, on spending two years 'on the beat' and on serving as a detective for 28.

Talking of the Erskine case, he said that high priority had been given to apprehension of the killer because the murders were increasing in frequency. Based on the legal tenet of 'strikingly similar facts', the police had argued, successfully, for all the charges to be tried together. The many similarities in the killings had shown beyond all doubt that they were of the same origin. It was, in fact, believed that Erskine was responsible for at least one other murder, of an old man found dead in his bath in Clapham, south-west London, but the body had not been found for some time and its deterioration had obliterated most of the forensic evidence. Semen had, however, been found on an anal swab.

Erskine had kept a hand inside his trousers and apparently masturbated during police questioning and during the proceedings in court, Jackson told me. 'In number two court the dock is raised and on the same level as the judge,' he said. 'This means that the lower halves of defendants' bodies are not visible to people in the well of the court, but they can be seen from the public gallery. There were complaints from the public about the way Erskine behaved in the dock.'

Forensic scientists usually have no recollection of noticing the appearance of defendants during trials, but Anne Davies remembered that Erskine looked 'weird; he kept grinning at women in the court'.

CHAPTER 31

Underground holocaust

THE FIRESTORM THAT RAGED UP a 50-year-old escalator and into the ticket hall at King's Cross underground station just after 7.30 pm on November 18 1987 took the lives of 31 passengers and that of a London fireman who braved flames, smoke and toxic fumes in a vain attempt to extricate those trapped by the blaze.

'If those 31 had only gone downwards instead of upwards in their efforts to escape, they would almost certainly have survived,' 33-year-old chemist David Halliday told me during an explanation of his work in the case. We talked at the Metropolitan Police Forensic Science Laboratory where, for eight and a half years, Halliday had been a member of the Fire Investigation Unit, one of the specialist teams that form part of the scientific staff. The inquest into the fatalities had closed the previous day, returning a verdict of accidental death on each of the victims. The evidence provided by Halliday was crucial to that conclusion.

For two days after the fire, Halliday and four of his colleagues clambered among the charred debris beneath the escalator in their search for the cause of the tragedy. I was shown a series of coloured slides of photographs that had been taken to record the investigation.

Summarizing the events that preceded the outbreak, Halliday said that, at about 7.35 pm, five passengers told station staff they had seen smoke coming from escalator number four. Witnesses who came forward after the fire said that they had noticed 'sparks' under the footway. Also at about 7.35, a

British Transport police officer saw a passenger operate the 'emergency stop' device on escalator four. The officer made a radio call to British Transport police headquarters and the Fire Brigade was summoned. Their appliances were dispatched at 7.36 but were faced with the difficulties of dense traffic in the area. At 7.41 the flames on the escalator were reported to be two feet high and smoke was thickening. Three minutes later the Piccadilly Line side of the escalator shaft was virtually obscured by smoke.

At 7.42 Victoria Line trains were ordered to pass non-stop through King's Cross station. A Piccadilly Line train having stopped and discharged passengers at 7.43, that line then received the non-stop order. The other lines interconnecting at King's Cross, the Northern and Metropolitan/Circle, were not affected.

Halliday's remark about the wisdom of escape downwards was based on the fact that the lower section of the stopped stairway suffered no damage from the fire. The photographs showed a remarkably sharp cut-off point, the lowest step involved in the fire being deeply charred but the next downwards and those lower still being untouched by the flames. With the normal draughts flowing through the tunnels, the fire, coupled with the natural convection of heat, had moved swiftly higher into the ticket hall, which became a furnace fuelled by combustible materials.

The main items that took fire on the escalator were the wooden treads and risers of the staircase, Halliday said. Decorative plywood facings on the escalator sides had also burnt fiercely. Seventeen layers of old paint were found on parts of the walls and ceiling of the affected area.

The colour pictures focused attention on the findings from which Halliday deduced the cause of the conflagration. The wheels carrying the staircase were surrounded by heavy deposits of lubricating grease. This had, in places, in the course of time, become coated with fluff, derived from dust, fragments of fibres abraded from wooden parts of the escalator and from passengers' clothing and even scales of human skin ('People shed more skin than they realize,' Halliday remarked). Many matchsticks and even some pencils were also found stuck into the grease. The whole comprised an ignitable mixture needing only a smoker's dropped match to set it alight. That, in Halliday's view, had been the cause of the fire. During his team's work at King's Cross they had identified no less than 18 places in the grease beneath the escalator where there was evidence of charring following tiny fires which, fortunately, had not spread. 'One might term November 18 1987 as "the day the luck ran out on the underground",' Halliday observed. 'Conditions have to be just right for fire to build up and those were the circumstances that prevailed.' His understanding was that the periodical cleaning that was carried out beneath the escalators had become less frequent because of difficulties with staffing.

There is now a total ban on smoking throughout the London underground system. At the time of writing, almost a year after the King's Cross calamity, one of its victims, a male, remains unidentified.

CHAPTER 32
Hit-and-run death

THE FUNCTIONS OF THE METROPOLITAN Police Forensic
Science Laboratory include a significant volume of cases
arising from the use (or misuse) of motor vehicles. Some of
this activity forms part of investigations concerning drivers
suspected of having been under the influence of drink or
drugs, but an appreciable amount of work is also done in
connection with traffic accidents and tests for mechanical
faults.

Most of the endeavours that are made under these headings
are of a routine nature, too mundane to merit calling to the
reader's attention, but there are occasional exceptions to this
rule. The efforts that followed the death of Denise Rumney
provide an example.

It was just after three am on Sunday February 22 1987 when
17-year-old Denise and her young male companion left a
minicab office in Seven Sisters Road, Tottenham, north
London, to take a taxi to her parents' home about a mile away.
They were crossing the well-lit, 10 metres wide road to reach
a cab awaiting them on the other side of the otherwise
apparently empty thoroughfare when a small, swiftly-moving
car appeared. It struck Denise, throwing her into the air, then
into its windscreen and finally onto the ground. The vehicle
was later said to halt momentarily, reverse for a short distance
and then, swerving to the right to avoid Denise's inert body
and passing a small traffic island on the wrong side, speed
away.

Hearing the noise of the impact, people ran from the

minicab office and from their homes above shops. The police and an ambulance were called, but Denise was beyond help.

The area of the accident was marked off with police tapes and inquiries began. They were directed by Inspector Derek Talbot, who was later assisted by Sergeant Julian Headon. Summoned from his home in Brentwood, Essex, 25-year-old Constable Stuart Anderson, a trained accident investigator, arrived at the scene just before five am. Painstakingly, he searched the tarmac surface of the road. There were no skid marks, but he found and collected fragments of glass, part of a broken black plastic moulding thought to have come from a foglamp and a 4cm × 6mm (1¾″ × ¼″) sliver of paint with a pale green metallic topcoat.

Statements were taken from nine eye-witnesses and a number of others. Denise's companion, badly shocked, said that he and the girl had been to a nearby public house called the *Flowerpot*. Descriptions of the car varied widely. Two people said they thought it was a white Volkswagen Golf. Someone else said it was a Ford Fiesta. No one had noticed the registration number. It seemed that the hit-and-run driver had escaped.

Together with heavily bloodstained articles of Denise's clothing, the items collected by Anderson were delivered to the Metropolitan Police laboratory early the following day. They received the immediate attention of 40-year-old Dr Brian Gibbins, a chemist engaged in the Criminalistics Division.

He began by reassembling, as far as possible, the pieces of glass. They formed part of a headlamp lens. Fortunately, there were sufficient fragments to enable the manufacturer's coded markings to be read. By interrogating a computer through which such details are recorded, Gibbins learned that the unit had been made by a company named Carello and that such components had been fitted to Fiat Uno cars sold in the UK from 1983 onwards.

The broken black plastic moulding was found to bear the letters 'oni', seemingly the end of an Italian name.

'Having got this information, we compared the flake of paint with the range of Fiat car colours that were available,'

Gibbins told me during a conversation at the laboratory in June 1988. 'The flake had a topcoat colour which corresponded very closely with a colour that Fiat called aquamarine, a pale metallic green. So, at the end of day one of our examination, we were able to tell PC Anderson by telephone that they were looking for a pale green Fiat Uno registered since 1983.'

More work was done at the laboratory on day two, including a scrutiny of the undercoat sequence on the fragment of paint, but this did not narrow the search any further. Nevertheless, because of the pristine condition of the surface finish, Gibbins was able to tell Anderson that he believed the vehicle concerned was of fairly recent origin – a 'C' rather than an 'A' or 'B' registration.

Examination of the victim's leather jacket and blue denim jeans revealed the presence of numerous glass particles on both items. All but one of the fragments in a sample taken from those found on the jacket were seen to contain a green tint. Some had a flat surface, indicating that they had come from window glass. A sample of the fragments found on the jeans corresponded in refractive index to the glass from the damaged headlamp lens. It appeared, therefore, that, as might be expected, Denise had first been struck by the front of the car below waist level and then hit on the head or body by the windscreen.

Consulting a Fiat garage in Camden Town, north London, Anderson was told that the broken black plastic moulding was part of the housing of a door-mounted mirror made by a firm called Vitaloni. Such mirrors were a standard fitting on Fiat Uno cars.

Bearing in mind that a favourite ploy of 'hit-and-run' drivers is to abandon their vehicles and report that they were stolen at some time prior to the incidents, Anderson consulted the police national computer at Hendon. 'At that time we didn't know whether this car would be classified under blue or green, because the computer lists only the basic colours, not names like azure or pink. So we ended up by pulling out every stolen Fiat Uno. The computer also produced every stolen vehicle that hadn't got a model name on it. But we finished up with about 250, a very manageable number,' the fast-talking young officer told me during a conversation in September 1988. 'I went through it all, crossing out everything that wasn't a Fiat Uno or the ones that were red and so on, leaving us with only the blue and green ones. Then I telephoned Fiats, who were very helpful. We verified that these aquamarine ones would definitely be classified as green. Out of the whole batch, we were left with one stolen Fiat Uno and that was way up north and most unlikely to be our car. So at that stage we could say that the one we were looking for hadn't been reported stolen.'

With the help of the Fiat company's computer, the investigators were able to eliminate cars finished in other shades of green in the Fiat colour range. When Talbot and Anderson departed on previously arranged holidays, Headon took up the trail, working against time in the knowledge that the driver they were seeking would be eager to remove the traces of damage from his vehicle. Narrowing the search to north-east London and parts of Essex and Hertfordshire, Headon compiled a list of the names and addresses of some 95 owners of aquamarine-painted Fiat Unos registered since 1983. Officers stationed at police stations near those addresses were then asked to make investigatory visits.

One such call was made to the home of 33-year-old Robert Henry Dale, the registered owner of Fiat Uno C706 EMP. Having explained his purpose to a woman who opened the door, the officer was told that Dale was out. When a return visit was made shortly afterwards, the house was found to be deserted, but inquiries revealed that the family had gone to stay at the nearby home of a relative. Finally confronted, Dale, who was said to be unemployed, admitted that his car was being repaired at a garage. There, it was found that £550 worth of work had been completed from total repairs estimated to cost some £800. The vehicle was taken to the Metropolitan Police laboratory, where Gibbins examined it on March 6 – just 12 days after Denise Rumney was killed.

Gibbins listed nine findings:

1. The original topcoat colour corresponded closely with that of the paint flake found at the scene of the accident.
2. The nearside headlamp unit was new.

3. The windscreen, which appeared to have a green tint, was new.
4. The nearside door mirror was missing.
5. A quantity of 'window type' glass fragments was scattered about inside and outside the vehicle. Most of the pieces in the bonnet recess were tinted green.
6. A new front nearside door mirror was found in a Fiat/Lancia parts box on the front passenger seat.
7. A box on the rear seat contained a severely damaged headlamp unit, fittings for a door mirror and a damaged radiator grill.
8. Seven pieces of the headlamp glass recovered from the scene of the accident fitted perfectly into the damaged headlamp unit.
9. The damaged body of the door mirror found at the scene was entirely consistent with the replacement found in the car.

When he was questioned, Dale said that, in the early hours of February 22, he had been driving around 'choked up' and with tears in his eyes because he had had a row with his wife. The girl had suddenly appeared in front of him, giving him no time to brake. He had not stopped at the scene because of fear that 'people there would get hold of me. I couldn't stand any more problems.' He added that he thought the car had been damaged by a bollard on the traffic island, but a police photograph taken immediately after the accident showed that the bollard at that end of the island had been removed some time previously.

In the absence of evidence of excessive speed or dangerous or careless driving, Dale was charged with two offences – failing to stop after an accident and failing to report an accident. He was fined £225 and disqualified from driving for 12 months.

On July 16, after recording a verdict of accidental death at the conclusion of the inquest concerning Denise, the coroner, Bernard Pearl, paid tribute to the police work carried out by Headon and Anderson. Both officers also received an official police commendation. In a note to Gibbins on the subject, Anderson observed 'I hope you feel this reflects on the work of you and your colleagues even though the appreciation has not been explicit.'

CHAPTER 33

'Autocide' that killed another

ALTHOUGH IT WAS DARK AT six pm on Monday January 5 1981, the weather was clear and the B1007 road that links Billericay with Great Baddow, in Essex, was quiet. Nevertheless, it was there and then that 42-year-old Anthony Victor Gladen met his death, at the wheel of a white Ford Escort van, registration number EKE 948K. The van, the property of a Romford firm making plaster castings, was struck, head-on, by a white Ford Cortina car, index number WJN 545J, driven by 23-year-old David Philip Jobling. Although the vehicles met at a combined impact speed estimated as 95mph, crushing the fronts of both into a tangled mass of metal, Jobling escaped with injuries to a foot, an elbow and his ribs.

Seeking an explanation, the investigating officers called upon the services of the Metropolitan Police Forensic Science Laboratory, which was then dealing with the provision of forensic evidence to the Essex police. Thirty-year-old Douglas Stoten, a physicist and material scientist with six years' experience at the laboratory, went to the scene and examined the evidence. He noted that the collision had occurred on the wrong side of the road for Jobling's vehicle.

While driving back to London he remembered reading a scientific paper on the subject of suicide by the use of motor vehicles which had been published in the USA. 'The term used for such cases in that country is 'autocide'. Acting on this prompting, Stoten telephoned the police at Chelmsford and asked them to send to the laboratory the shoes Jobling had been wearing at the time of the collision and the brake and accelerator pedals from his car.

These items duly arrived and were dealt with by 33-year-old chemist David Castle. The shoes, he found, were of a well-known make, called Hush Puppies. The brake pedal was capped with the usual rubber cover, bearing an all-over pattern of small squares. The accelerator pedal carried a totally different design, of horizontal bars. The sole of the shoe from Jobling's right foot bore a clear impression of the pattern from the accelerator, imprinted by the enormous deceleration ('of the order of 20 times the force of gravity', said Stoten) when the two vehicles met. It showed, beyond dispute, that Jobling had been urging his car forward right up to the moment of impact.

When questioned by the police, Jobling claimed that drugs had been put into sugar at his home. A bag of sugar and a partly-filled sugar bowl were collected from the house and sent to the laboratory, where they were examined by Dr John Hughes. He found that the contents were, in each case, merely sucrose, entirely free of drugs.

Further investigation disclosed that Jobling appeared to have made a previous attempt at suicide, by forcing the point of a compass into the electric cable of a hair dryer. This had melted the insulation and burnt a hole in the carpet, but left him unharmed.

Charged with manslaughter, he appeared before Chief Justice Park at Chelmsford Crown Court on October 5 1981. Found guilty, he was sentenced to 12 months' detention under Section 60 of the Mental Health Act, 1959.

When I commented that choosing a head-on crash with another vehicle, probably taking the life of another driver, seemed a singularly selfish route to self-destruction, Stoten answered that, if it remained undetected, the method had the advantage of appearing to have been an accident, thereby softening the shock to relatives and not invalidating any relevant insurance cover.

Castle added that the case was by no means the only one of its kind that the laboratory had been asked to deal with. 'Similar things crop up at least once a year,' he said.

CHAPTER 34

Truth told by tachograph

TWENTY-FOUR-YEAR-OLD MARK MELLOR was indulging in the favourite sport of reckless lorry drivers, hurling a laden, 32-ton, articulated Leyland along just a few feet from the rear of the car in front of him. The scene was the busy suburban area of Harlington, near Isleworth, west London, and it was just after 8.30 on the dry, bright morning of October 31 1985.

Appropriately marked, the car was being driven by a learner-driver, 22-year-old Mrs Gillian Bennett, who, seeing the closely-approaching, massive machine in her rear view mirror, accelerated to avoid what appeared to be a coming collision. But Mellor accelerated too, the powerful, diesel-engined truck being capable of overtaking the smaller vehicle with ease. His speed reached 51 miles an hour – 21 above the legal limit there.

Hurtling into a lefthand bend at such velocity, the huge lorry was unbalanced. It toppled over, crashing down on its right side. Mellor climbed, uninjured, from the cab. But 38-year-old cyclist Christopher John Stafford lay crushed to death beneath the fallen juggernaut.

Under European Economic Community regulations, all goods vehicles with a gross weight in excess of three and a half metric tons and all passenger vehicles carrying 15 or more people have to be fitted with a tachograph – the 'black box' of road transport. These devices record, on circular charts covering each period of 24 hours, the distances covered and varying speeds of the conveyances to which they are attached.

By law, the drivers of such vehicles are required to change the charts daily and to produce them, when required, as evidence of their movements.

Reading the charts for forensic purposes is, however, something of a skilled operation. Thirty-nine-year-old Dr Richard Lambourn, a physicist with 12 years' experience at the Metropolitan Police Forensic Science Laboratory, had spent time learning the techniques at the Black Forest, West Germany, factory of Kienzle, the European market leaders in tachograph manufacture. The police asked him to examine the chart from the vehicle, registration number B414 MLY, driven by Mellor.

Lambourn noted Mellor's written statement that his day's journeying had begun in Acton, west London. He followed the tachograph's revelations that there had been two periods of driving. The first, from 05.50 until 06.25, had included several stops and had covered a total distance of 13½ kilometres (8½ miles). The second period, from 08.06 to 08.32, covered 12 kilometres (7½ miles) and ended with what Lambourn described as 'a disturbance of the recording trace, indicative of a violent impact to the vehicle'.

In his written analysis of the accident, Lambourn stated that, two minutes before it crashed, the lorry had been stationary, when it had stopped at a road junction on Mellor's declared route. It had then moved off and reached 26 mph before dipping to a low speed near another junction, where there was a controlled pedestrian crossing. After that there had again been a return to 26 mph, which was maintained as the lorry entered Harlington High Street. The speed had increased to 41 mph as the vehicle approached the foot of a motorway bridge and that rate of progress had been maintained round a righthand bend. Another 10 mph had been added before the lorry entered the lefthand bend where it overturned.

'From the maps I have measured the radius of curvature of the bend on which the lorry rolled over to be about 130 metres,' Lambourn's expert witness statement concluded. 'A vehicle attempting to negotiate such a bend at 51 mph would experience a sideways acceleration of 0.41g. Subjectively this would be very uncomfortable in a car, while in a lorry the discomfort and the risk of a loss of control would be even greater. In my opinion it is very clear that this lorry rolled over because of its excessive speed.'

The evidence gathered by the police included a statement by Mrs Bennett, telling of the way Mellor had 'pressurized' her with the lorry.

Charged with causing death by reckless driving, Mellor was tried at Isleworth Crown Court in January 1987. He pleaded guilty and was sentenced to two months' imprisonment and disqualified from driving for five years.

CHAPTER 35

Lying lorrymen

IT WAS SOON AFTER 10.15 pm on Friday August 28 1981 that a shattered British Leyland minivan, index number UMA 673J, was seen on a bend near a junction with the A260 road in the village of Denton, Kent. Its driver, 26-year-old Paul David Ray, had been killed. A shocked and dazed passenger, 21-year-old Trevor Paul Rootes, told of the van being crushed under a wheel of the first of a pair of giant articulated lorries which had been travelling, northbound, in the opposite direction. Among the debris found nearby were chips of paint of a colour different from that on the van and pieces of rubber that had evidently come from a large tyre. It seemed inconceivable that the driver of the vanished vehicle could have failed to notice the impact that had done such damage.

Denton is only a few miles from the port of Folkestone. Inquiries were therefore made at the docks, where records were examined for details of lorries which had departed on August 28 bound for London or other northerly destinations. An entry was found for a pair of vehicles which were believed to have been destined for the premises of P & O Roadways in Brentwood Road, Orsett, Essex. Police officers went there and located a 40 feet long Craven Tasker trailer which showed signs of damage to its offside rear. Pieces of rubber were seen to be missing from the sidewall of a tyre. The chunks of rubber found at the scene of the collision and the tyre were sent to the Metropolitan Police Forensic Science Laboratory (which was then dealing with the forensic requirements of the Kent police) where chemist Dr John Brennan established that the items fitted together. Examiners also found that the rear axle of the trailer had been thrown out of alignment.

Given this evidence, the police interviewed the driver who had been in charge of the trailer on August 28, 38-year-old Roy Ernest Cavalier, a part-time employee of F P Smith, haulage contractors, of Great Worley, near Brentwood. At first he claimed that he had not been in Denton on that date and therefore had no knowledge of the accident, but later changed his statement to an admission that he had driven the unit through the village that night. He added that, as the vehicle was articulated and only the rear of the trailer had been involved in the collision, it was not surprising that he had been unaware of any mishap.

This comment was made known to Douglas Stoten, a physicist at the laboratory. 'I felt that it wouldn't have been the case, for three reasons,' he told me during a description of the affair in November 1988. 'First, he was an experienced lorry driver and would have been negotiating a righthand bend, so that the rear of his trailer would have been visible in his offside driving mirror. Second, quite a bit of noise would have been involved. The mechanics of the collision seemed to suggest that the lorry wheel had ridden over the van so that, apart from the impact, there would have been the noise of the wheel crashing back down to the ground. The noise brought people out of neighbouring houses to the accident scene. Thirdly, I felt that he should have been able to feel the impact as well.'

Stoten said that he had then examined the tell-tale tachograph charts covering the movements of a Daf 2800 turbo tractor unit, index number DVX 7T – the vehicle Cavalier had driven on August 28 – and those of the other tractor – index number OUD 143P – that had accompanied him on the fatal journey. Also a part-time worker for the haulage contractors F P Smith, the second driver was 37-year-old Anthony Leonard Doble. Stoten noted that the readings on the two charts tallied very closely, but was puzzled by the fact that one was 30 minutes out of phase with the other. This mystery was cleared up when inquiries disclosed that one of the vehicles had suffered a discharged battery earlier in the week and the clock mechanism driving the tachograph had not been powered for the half hour when the battery was being recharged.

Cavalier and Doble – both married, with children – were accused of conspiring to pervert the course of justice. Pleading not guilty, they appeared at Canterbury Crown Court. At the outset both denied having any knowledge of the accident, claiming that, after collecting the trailers from Folkestone docks, they had stopped at a fish and chip shop in the town. Doble said he had overtaken Cavalier on a hill out of Folkestone and both asserted that they had driven without stopping until they had halted at a café near the M2 motorway, north-west of Canterbury.

This claim was contradicted by Stoten who, testifying on the first day of the trial, Monday April 11 1983, said that his expert analysis of the tachograph charts had shown, firstly, that there was evidence that the vehicle driven by Cavalier had suffered an impact when it was travelling at 28 mph in Denton at about 10.15 and, secondly, that both lorries had stopped for just under a minute when they had been some 850 metres past the scene of the accident – the only point on that section of the A260 where there was a lay-by which would have made it possible for vehicles of such size to pull off the road.

Doble then changed his plea to guilty, admitting that he had been lying. He said that, while following Cavalier through Denton, he had seen the crushed van and flashed his lights to attract Cavalier's attention. When they stopped along the road he had asked Cavalier about the van, but he had said he knew nothing about it and they had driven off.

When questioned further, Cavalier also admitted being in front of Doble and agreed that they had stopped after Doble had flashed him. But he still insisted that he had not known his trailer had struck the van. 'I didn't see or hear anything. I stopped because I thought Tony was in trouble,' he declared.

Both men said that they had made false statements because Doble had had his son with him in his cab, which was contrary to company policy, and he was worried that he 'might get the sack and have to go back on the dole'. The court was told that, following the accident, Doble had burnt his licence and taken employment as a plasterboard tacker.

After a four-day hearing, both were found guilty. Each was sentenced to three months' imprisonment, suspended for two years, fined £500 and ordered to pay £500 costs.

CHAPTER 36

Drug pit

FROM OUTSIDE THERE SEEMED TO be nothing unusual about the industrial building that nestled in a former gravel pit at Grays, Essex. Known as Titan Works, it was divided into small units that were rented by a number of tenants who were engaged in sundry forms of apparently legitimate enterprise. In police parlance, 43-year-old Detective Sergeant Barry Strong and his colleagues in Scotland Yard's Drugs Squad had gone there 'as a result of information received'. That intelligence, vouchsafed by a contact in the underworld, had at first persuaded them to set up covert observation on a semi-detached house a few miles from Grays, in Collier Row, Essex. It was the trailed movements of vehicles from that place, the home of a criminal then serving a term of imprisonment, that led the investigators to the factory complex.

On May 16 1984, concealed atop a 60 feet high embankment, the detectives stayed in place as, one by one, the lights were extinguished at the end of the working day and people drove away. Finally, only two sections remained illuminated. The doors were opened from time to time as individuals passed in and out. As they did so, the police officers noticed 'a very sweet smell' that was unmistakable in their experienced nostrils. It was the odour created by the manufacture of the chemical compound amphetamine, a stimulant drug widely used by addicts.

A full-scale surveillance operation was mounted the following day. In the morning a Dodge motor van was seen to leave the Collier Row house. Shortly afterwards it arrived at Titan Works, where two men alighted and entered the 'suspect' section. A Ford Cortina car that had also been seen at the Collier Row dwelling then arrived at the factory. Its driver, the only occupant, also went into the units that were being watched. Some black plastic sacks were loaded into the van, which was driven away by the man who had arrived in the car.

Strong sent a radio message to colleagues asking that the van be stopped at a point well away from the factory. The vehicle was followed to a rubbish dump, where the plastic bags were found to contain amphetamine and items which had been used in its production. The driver, 35-year-old Jose Luis Larios, was detained and the officers still keeping watch on the factory were informed by radio of what had been discovered. Descending from their hiding place, they hammered at the door of the premises. It was opened by 44-year-old George William Strange. Inside, the policemen found what appeared to be innocent premises used for the making of picture frames, adjoined by a simple kitchen. But, on forcing a tiny, locked door, they saw, mounted on workbenches, a range of chemical equipment that was being used to produce the drug. The apparatus was set out in a skilful way, with curtains that could be used to conceal it in an instant. Hiding under a bench behind some of the curtaining was 32-year-old Philip Ralph Nicholas.

It was the first time that Strong and his fellow officers had seen illicit drug production equipment in actual operation. It was 'bubbling away before our eyes', he told me during a conversation in September 1988. A message was sent to the Metropolitan Police Forensic Science Laboratory and 41-year-old chemist Dr John Metcalfe hastened to the factory to examine the setup, make it safe and arrange for identification and storage of the material until the legal processes had been completed.

'It was sophisticated equipment, being used by a person with a good knowledge of chemical procedures,' Metcalfe recalled when we talked together at the laboratory in June 1988. Explaining that amphetamine is rated as a class B controlled drug (heroin and cocaine are class A – the most dangerous) he said that it was the product most commonly made in clandestine laboratories. Its street value was between £1,500 and £2,000 a kilogram, while that of heroin was between £25,000 and £30,000. The equipment found at Grays would have cost between £2,000 and £3,000 and was capable of producing at least £10,000 worth of amphetamine a day, he added. Four kilograms of the substance were taken from the Ford Cortina car.

Nicholas was the 'chemical brain' of the partnership and the others were his 'minders', Strong said. All three had previous convictions for criminal offences, Nicholas for illegal possession of amphetamine in 1982, Strange for stealing woollen goods in 1966 and Larios for possession of cannabis in 1982.

After preliminary appearances before Grays magistrates, the men were committed for trial at Snaresbrook Crown Court. Charged with producing a controlled drug in contravention of section four of the Misuse of Drugs Act, 1971, Nicholas pleaded guilty and was sentenced to eight years' imprisonment. Strange and Larios pleaded not guilty to charges of conspiracy to manufacture the drug. Both were convicted and sentenced to three and a half years' imprisonment.

When I asked whether it had been possible to trace any of the customers who had been buying the amphetamine, Strong answered that the police had had no success in that direction. He said that Strange, the leader of the trio, had been asked to look after the Collier Row house on behalf of its imprisoned criminal owner and all three men had, at times, used the place for overnight accommodation. The case had not been unique, because habitual criminals sometimes used people with chemical knowledge to produce drugs, Strong commented. It was, he thought, unlikely that Nicholas would have known where the amphetamine was being sold; his task was simply its production.

Metcalfe made the point that the uncovering of such activity was important because it was mainly class B drugs like amphetamine that were being manufactured illegally in the UK. The smuggling in of heroin and cocaine raised other problems, he remarked.

CHAPTER 37
Death of a 'mule'

IT WAS 45-YEAR-OLD Dr Brian Connett, a chemist and toxicologist at the Metropolitan Police Forensic Science Laboratory, who was called upon to advise in a case of illegal heroin importation that killed the smuggler. His findings led the Battersea, south London, coroner, Dr Paul Knapman, to issue a grim warning to anyone thinking of emulating the folly of 22-year-old Ian Fuller. Those foolish enough to attempt to beat the law in the manner tried by Fuller could expect to be searched by a pathologist in a mortuary, Knapman declared.

Fuller's mentality had not matured in step with his six-feet-seven physical stature. A fitness fanatic who ate health foods and went jogging, he had romantic notions of travel and adventure. He and a close friend, Garry Foster, left their family homes in Birchington, on the Kent coast, and took up another style of life, working as part-time barmen in London and staying in a flat in St Helier Avenue, Morden, Surrey.

According to Foster's account of the events that led to his associate's tragic end, Fuller had been approached by an Asian 'businessman' in a public house. A smooth talker, this new acquaintance had, allegedly, told Fuller that he was just the sort of young fellow who was needed to take two video recorders and some cassettes to Delhi. Would he be willing to do it in exchange for a fortnight's all-expenses-paid luxury holiday for two in India? He did not need to worry about the heavy import tax on the goods, his tempter was said to have added, because a corrupt customs officer would contact him at Delhi airport and see him, his companion and the property through all the formalities.

'He was over the moon,' Foster recalled. 'He said India was a country he had dreamed of visiting – a place he never expected to get to because of the cost.'

However, it seemed there had been no sign of any crooked customs man when Fuller and his 29-year-old girlfriend, Jane Stuart, arrived in Delhi on August 27 1983. Instead, he was told that he would have to pay the duty due on the equipment – over 300 per cent – or have it impounded until he returned to Britain. He left it with the officials.

It appeared that, as had presumably been prearranged by his London persuader, Fuller was met as he left the airport. There had been no recriminations about the video items and he and Jane were, she said later, treated with extensive generosity. After a stay at a luxury hotel they were invited to a home in the country. The two-week holiday extended to a month, by which time Fuller had begun to realize that he was considerably in debt to his hosts. Back at the hotel, Jane had noticed that he had become quiet and withdrawn. She also became aware that he waited for her to leave the room before having earnest conversations with the people who were paying their bills.

Foster was at the Morden flat when the couple returned home on September 30. They told him they were feeling tired, which they attributed to jet-lag, and went to bed early. Foster was awakened by Jane's screams. Dashing into their room, he found Fuller in the extremity of a seizure, his body jerking wildly and blood oozing from his bitten tongue. Taking his friend in his arms, Foster tried to quieten him while Jane telephoned for help, but Fuller died before the ambulance arrived.

A *post mortem* examination was carried out by pathologist Rufus Crompton on October 3. Fuller's stomach and intestines were found to be full of what appeared to be medicinal capsules enclosed in double wrappings of latex rubber that had evidently originally formed the tips of condoms or the fingers of surgical gloves. Each rubber container was crudely knotted to hold its burden within. Injection sites were located inside Fuller's left elbow and on the back of his right hand. The stomach and intestines, together with samples of blood, urine and liver, were sent to the laboratory, where they were attended to by Connett.

On dissecting the organs, he extracted 367 capsules and a number of capsule fragments, the latter being equivalent to about eight whole capsules. Each capsule was of a size designed to accommodate one gram of medication. But each held pale brown powder weighing some 1.1 grams – a 10 per cent overload. The powder was found to contain diamorphine of approximately 60 per cent purity. Fuller's blood contained morphine at a total level of two micrograms per millilitre. Low levels of cocaine and a body breakdown product of cocaine were also detected. The urine contained morphine and codeine in quantities which Connett said were consistent with the previous ingestion of impure diamorphine. He also found traces of cocaine, pheniramine (an antihistamine), chloroquine (an anti-malarial) and nicotine. Morphine and codeine were present in the liver. In a written statement, Connett concluded 'The level of morphine [in the blood] is greatly in excess of that at which fatalities have been reported. Fatalities have also been reported from codeine at the level detected in this item.' Giving evidence at the inquest, he said that the dose Fuller had received from the eight broken capsules was the highest his department had seen.

Scotland Yard Drugs Squad detectives took up the task of trying to trace the traffickers by whom Fuller was said to have been induced to act as a living container. The police made it known that the technique had often been used before. The usual arrangement, they said, was that the 'courier' would take a compound which provided a lining to the stomach and then swallow a calculated number of plastic or rubber-protected capsules containing the drugs. After the carrier had succeeded with the importation, the capsules would be recovered with the aid of a laxative. But it seemed that, for some reason, Fuller had been persuaded to swallow a much greater quantity than was usual. This led to the conjecture that, in addition to the amount assigned to him, he had agreed to ingest those that his pay-masters had demanded Jane should swallow. His wish to protect her was substantiated when friends revealed that he had told them he hoped she was pregnant.

Detective Chief Inspector John Grieve, the officer in charge of the case, said that the street value of the quantity (nearly half a kilogram) and quality of the drug found in Fuller's internal organs was about £48,000. The couple's trip to India, including the purchase of the video equipment, had entailed an outlay of about £2,500.

I talked with Connett and Grieve at the laboratory in November 1988. Aided by documents, they both recalled the case with clarity. Forty-two-year-old Grieve said that, although there had been no success in tracking down the people who had reportedly led Fuller to undertake the fatal mission, he was inclined to accept that version of events in preference to believing that the young man had embarked upon the affair of his own volition. There was, however, he pointed out, no firm evidence either way. Sadly, he added, such enterprises were all too common among vulnerable young people – known to police and traffickers as 'mules' and categorized as 'swallowers' or 'stuffers' according to the route chosen to insert the contraband into their bodies. If traffickers had persuaded Fuller to do what he had done, they, like all others of their kind, were 'bad, wicked people', the vigorously-forceful officer (who had received promotion to the rank of detective superintendent) declared. 'They weren't satisfied with getting hold of the boy – their greed was such that they had to overfill the capsules as well, so that, for every 10 he swallowed, they were getting him to carry an extra one.'

Connett said that, after the two halves of each of the overloaded capsules had been brought together, they had been sealed with wax. But the knots in the rubber wrappings had created rough surfaces which had caused them to be 'churned around' by the normal activity of the stomach, until some of the rubber envelopes had ruptured. The released capsules, being designed to dissolve when taken internally, had thereupon discharged their contents into Fuller's system. These processes would have been hastened by the overfilling. Fuller would have suffered intense pain before becoming unconscious.

In Connett's opinion, Fuller must have ingested the capsules shortly before leaving Delhi on the long flight to London. Swallowing them would, he thought, have been a fairly lengthy business – 'something like gulping down 375 small, whole grapes'.

Both of my informants mentioned the consequences of the recently-introduced Police and Criminal Evidence Act in such cases. Empowered to hold suspects in custody for only 36 hours before producing evidence to justify longer detention and limited by restrictions on the taking of 'intimate' body samples, the police are also faced with the difficulty that some 'mules' do not excrete their 'cargoes' until after much longer periods. Connett said he was aware of an instance in which excretion had taken place 11 days after ingestion.

CHAPTER 38

Gunfire in the gallery

MERCIFULLY, GUNFIRE IS NOT A frequent occurrence in Britain's National Gallery, in London's Trafalgar Square, but twice within the space of a few months its elegant chambers echoed to the roar of a twelve-bore shotgun. Happily, on neither occasion was there a living target, but both events concerned an attack on one of the world's greatest artistic masterpieces.

The first time was at six pm on Friday July 17 1987, when 37-year-old unemployed ex-soldier and social misfit Robert Arthur Cambridge waited for room seven to empty of visitors and then, taking a sawn-off shotgun from its hiding place beneath his clothing, blasted the sole exhibit in that section of the gallery – Leonardo da Vinci's charcoal-and-chalk cartoon called *The Virgin and Child with Saint Anne*. The concentrated shot, fired from a distance of only a few feet, struck the protective glass in front of the cartoon, causing the laminate to punch a large depression into the fragile canvas behind and shredding a six-inch diameter area of the paper on which the artist had portrayed his main subject's breast. Described by Harold Macmillan, when prime minister, as 'One of the most beautiful things in the world', the work had a value conservatively estimated as £20 million.

Cambridge did not resist arrest and 'obligingly' indicated the exact position from which he had fired. Divorced and living with his mother, his declarations indicated that his action was meant as a protest about the current political situation. Charged with causing criminal damage, he was duly tried at the Old Bailey and sentenced to be detained during Her Majesty's pleasure in Broadmoor Hospital for the criminally insane.

After the shooting, the National Gallery's chief restorer, Martin Wyld, was confronted with the daunting question of how to set about repairing the damage. Bits of paper were hanging from the cartoon and tiny pieces were scattered on the floor. On his hands and knees with a magnifying glass, he gathered some 70 fragments from the carpet. Eric Harding, a British Museum expert on paper, was asked to assist with the solution of one of the most intricate and valuable jigsaw puzzles of all time.

Also called in, to replicate the shooting, was the Metropolitan Police Forensic Science Laboratory. The job was assigned to Brian Arnold, head of the Firearms Section.

What was needed was a reproduction, on similar material, of the post-shooting condition of the cartoon, to enable restorative tests to be made on the specimen before work on the original was attempted, Wyld explained to me in August 1988. 'Leonardo produced the cartoon somewhere in the 1490s, on sheets measuring about 20 inches by 15. We made a mock-up from 18th-century canvas and aged it artificially under ultra-violet light for a few weeks on a stretcher. We used the same bullet-proof, three-layer laminate glass that was damaged and put it on the wall in the same place that the cartoon had been.'

Arnold's colleagues Peter Brookes and Jonathan Steel then took over. Early one morning, before the gallery opened to the public and after suitable precautions had been taken against the possibility of ricocheting pellets (using a policeman's riot shield) a shotgun of the same type and calibre as that used by Cambridge was fired at the test piece. This shooting was photographed and videotaped by the National Gallery.

In a letter written to the director of the laboratory, Dr Brian Sheard, on June 8 1988, Wyld expressed thanks for the help that had been given. 'The experiment was a complete success in that the glass was damaged in exactly the same way and produced a perfect dent in the mock-up,' he commented. 'After practising on the mock-up we were able to shrink back the canvas of the cartoon itself, which was the most dangerous stage of the repair. We can now continue the job of piecing together the paper fragments and hope the restoration will be finished by the end of this year.'

As Arnold put it, 'It was an interesting and gratifying little exercise.'

CHAPTER 39

Murder or ...?

IT IS PERHAPS FITTING THAT a presentation of case histories such as this should close with a mystery that will almost certainly never be solved. It concerns the deaths of two women – an octogenarian and a nonagenarian – in surroundings and circumstances that might have served as the setting for an Agatha Christie 'thriller'.

It began on Wednesday August 14 1985 at West Park Hospital, Epsom, Surrey, a long-stay psychiatric establishment on a large campus. Soon after the evening meal – of chicken soup and cottage pie – had been eaten, many of the 24 female psychogeriatric patients who were accommodated in Exford ward experienced bouts of coughing and heavy salivation. Five of them were seriously affected, having difficulty in breathing. Two regained normality but the condition of the other three deteriorated and they were taken to Epsom District Hospital after receiving treatment with oxygen. One of the trio, 85-year-old Nelly Armitage, improved after two days and was returned to West Park. But 82-year-old Nora Swift, a widow, did not recover and died on August 19 and 99-year-old widow Florence Reeves also declined and died on August 22.

'Hospital bug death alert' and 'Two die in bug scare' were among the headlines that appeared in the local press. The District Medical Officer, Dr Harvey Gordon, was quoted as saying that the patients' symptoms had been consistent with DDT, paraquat or muscarine (mushroom) poisoning. Epsom's Environmental Health Officer, Mrs Carol Gilbert,

was said to have given the opinion that the food could have
been poisoned 'either accidentally or deliberately'. The police
officer who took charge of inquiries, Detective Superintendent
Wallace McLarty, was reported to have said that foul play
could not be ruled out.

Epsom being within the territory of the Metropolitan
Police, the laboratory was called upon to assist. Thirty-two-
year-old toxicologist Raymond Fysh attended the *post mortem*
examinations, which were carried out by Australian-born
pathologist Stephen Cordner. They revealed that both deaths
had been due to broncopneumonia, brought on or intensified
by some cause that was still to be discovered.

Fysh was given blood and urine samples which had been
taken from the victims soon after their admission to the
district hospital. Nothing remained of the soup consumed
during the suspect meal and all the crockery had been washed
up immediately after it, but scraps of the cottage pie were
found and handed to Fysh in a plastic bucket. No mushrooms
had been served. Each of the specimens was analysed for the
presence of drugs and pesticides. Nothing was found in the
food or the blood, but pilocarpine (a drug used to produce
parasympathetic nerve stimulation in the management of
glaucoma) and atropine (an anticholinergic agent used,
among other purposes, to reduce salivary and bronchial
secretions) were detected in the urine. Atropine had been
administered during the emergency treatment of the women,
but pilocarpine is normally used only externally, as drops
applied to the eyes.

With 14 years' experience at the laboratory, Fysh was able
to report that the medical and scientific literature was devoid
of references not only to the disposition and excretion of
pilocarpine following ingestion or external application but also
to its detection in biological specimens. He had, therefore, to
devise a method of detecting the compound at low levels in
urine. He found it impossible to detect pilocarpine in blood,
even after its deliberate addition. To test his method and to
show whether the compound was excreted following external
application, he asked for 'control' samples of urine from
patients who were receiving treatment with pilocarpine eye

drops. Samples were taken from three such patients on September 11. Fysh detected the drug in each of them. But neither of the dead women had suffered from glaucoma and were not receiving such treatment.

In his statement as an expert witness, Fysh commented 'The oral ingestion of small amounts of pilocarpine (approximately three to five drops of a four per cent solution) can give rise to effects such as pin-point pupils, increased production of saliva, sweat and tears, bronchial congestion with difficulty in breathing and wheezing. These effects are reversed if atropine is then given.'

Fysh gave his evidence at the opening of the inquest at Epsom Coroner's Court, when it was formally established that the cause of the deaths had been pilocarpine poisoning. But the question of how, and by whom, the substance had been administered remained unanswered. The Surrey coroner, Lieutenant Colonel George McEwan, adjourned the proceedings to enable the police to complete their inquiries.

Those inquiries were far from simple, I was assured by Inspector (formerly Detective Inspector) Norman Till, McLarty's deputy in the case, when we discussed the details at the laboratory in November 1988. After explaining that, because of domestic circumstances, he had chosen to leave the CID and resume uniformed duty, he summarized the difficulties by pointing out that the locale was a hospital for people suffering from mental disorders; that, of the 24 patients in Exford ward, only two were sensibly articulate and the rest, stricken by varying degrees of senile dementia, rambling and disorientated; that such patients, some incontinent, some aggressive and others little more than shambling shells of people, can be extremely stressful and provocative to those who have to deal with their most intimate care; that the average age of the inmates in the ward was 88; that one old lady among them was known to have been greatly put out when two others deprived her of her customary place at the dining table; that there had been certain disturbances among the staff which were known to have left one discharged employee with a grudge and that the poisoning appeared to have been inflicted randomly, affecting, to some extent, most of the women in the ward. 'The problem was', Till said, 'that one had to keep one's mind open to all the possibilities, eliminating them one by one, but there were some possibilities that we were never able to eliminate entirely.'

As to the availability of the pilocarpine, this had been kept, with other drugs, in a lockable sideroom which was, in fact, rarely secured. The drug itself, produced by the well-known manufacturers Smith and Nephew Pharmaceuticals Ltd at Romford, Essex, was packaged in plastic minim sachets, each holding approximately 0.5 millilitre – about 14 drops – of clear, colourless fluid. The sachets were supplied in transparent plastic and paper enclosures carrying several items of coded information and marked, in small type, 'For external use only. Sterile if unopened. Use once and discard.' This latter injunction was the basis for the clinical practice of squeezing two drops only into patients' eyes and, since the remainder would not be sterile if retained, abandoning it. Thus, with several glaucoma sufferers in the ward, there would soon be a build-up of discarded pilocarpine. This waste material had, it was found, been put into a sack on the bottom tray of a dispensing trolley. Fysh estimated that about four drops of the substance would produce adverse effects if swallowed by elderly, frail people and that about 60 milligrams (approximately four sachets) would be a fatal dose for a healthy adult.

As Till pointed out, suspicion is only one aspect of an investigation and the gaining of proof entirely another. The poisonings in Exford ward displayed no discernible pattern showing, for example, that women sitting at any particular table had been affected more gravely than those seated at others; the basic symptoms had been spread throughout the room. With great patience, the officers contrived to conduct interviews with women who had lucid moments. It became clear that it was the soup that had carried the pilocarpine. Patients who said that they had left it because it tasted bitter had not experienced any upset. Moreover, although the soup had been distributed throughout the hospital for the evening meal on August 14, only the inmates of Exford ward had suffered ill effects. This, the detectives concluded, showed beyond doubt that the food had been contaminated after its arrival in the ward. Interviews with nursing and other staff were more easily accomplished but produced no leads towards a solution of the puzzle.

An interesting fact that emerged during the investigation followed a check of the quantities of drugs held on the ward. It was found that, not only was no pilocarpine missing, but, overall, the stock of medications there exceeded the amounts shown on the records.

Till said that he and his colleagues had departed from the hospital with no firm conclusion other than that the pilocarpine could not have found its way into the soup by accident. They did, however, evolve a theory which he still regarded as valid. This was that, after the clean soup mugs had been placed on their trays in the ward kitchen awaiting the arrival of the meal, someone, knowingly or unknowingly, had sprinkled them with the discarded pilocarpine. This would, he pointed out, account for the random occurrence of the poisoning and, since some of the mugs would obviously have received more of the scattered drops than others, also explained why some women had suffered more serious effects than their companions.

'Killer stays on loose in poison hunt' said a *Daily Express* headline on October 23 1985. Reporting the open verdict reached at the resumed inquest the previous day, the paper quoted McLarty as saying that all the staff concerned with the preparation and serving of food had been interviewed. 'The mystery killer ... could still be working there,' it added.

New arrangements to improve the security of food at the hospital entailed capital expenditure totalling £43,000 and added £3,000 a year to working costs.

PART FOUR
The Future

CHAPTER 40

What is to come?

What shall be tomorrow, think not of asking.
Each day that Fortune gives you, be it what it may,
Set down for gain.

– Horace. (65 BC)

You can never plan the future by the past.
– Edmund Burke. (1729-97)

DESPITE THE ADVICE OF THE ancient Horace and the assertion of the otherwise perspicacious Burke, a situation of escalating crime and degenerating morals indicates a need to legislate for tomorrow from the lessons of today.

In considering such issues it is necessary to take account of the prevailing trends of society. Dealing first with childhood, the continuing diminution of discipline in places of education and the home offers little hope of reversing the misbehaviour of the unruly young. It is the successful, or lightly punished, offence of youth that often paves the way to more ambitious wrongdoing in maturity.

Moreover, the children of today are the parents of tomorrow, passing on their concepts of acceptable deportment. Each generation grants some further leniency to its offspring, 'to give them a better time than I had when I was a child'. So the deterioration snowballs. Teachers with 'old fashioned' ideas about the management of juveniles are often menaced by their pupils, sometimes battered by parents and occasionally, hounded by the brash and brainless who have clambered into positions of power, forced out of their posts.

With so large a proportion of current crime being committed by minors, coupled with distressing levels of illiteracy, the cynic might be forgiven for reflecting that the original meaning of 'the three r's' – reading, 'riting, and 'rithmetic – seems to be changing to rape, rob and run.

Trite historians maintain that the savagery which has now become commonplace in Britain is no worse than that which took place in the murkier times of the 18th and 19th centuries. Such argument is not easy of acceptance by those, like the writer, whose upbringing was received in the 1930s and early 40s. In those days, 'mugging' was virtually unknown. Women could walk alone or travel unaccompanied on public transport without fear of molestation and comforted by the knowledge that they would receive swift aid in any emergency. Anyone who attacked the old or handicapped was regarded as irredeemably contemptible. Police officers, schoolteachers and clergymen were figures of benign authority, evoking respect. Sports events were not followed by drunken (or sober) bloodbaths.

It has been said that the demeanour of its road-users exemplifies the behavioural standards of a nation. In my early years of motoring a form of camaraderie prevailed among those making use of the internal combustion engine. Anyone suffering a breakdown or punctured tyre would soon be offered help by other drivers. Nowadays anyone attempting to change an offside wheel puts his life at risk. Speed-crazed knaves turn the overcrowded streets into battlefields. The prevalence of company-owned cars, which can be damaged at no cost to their users, has contributed to the mayhem. Lorry drivers, in the past the courteous 'knights of the highway', now hurtle gigantic juggernauts at 70 and more miles an hour a menacing few feet from the rear of any car daring to precede them.

It must, of course, be acknowledged that it is the publicized misdeeds of the few that taint the reputations of all, but there are signs that such minorities are burgeoning. Collectively, the unavoidable truth appears to be that the economic betterment of ordinary people is breeding greed and selfishness instead of the happiness and contentment that were intended by those who strove to improve their lot. We live in an environment permeated by televised rubbish glorifying belligerence and the lunatic misuse of motor vehicles. The man (and woman) in the street is encouraged to adopt a 'me first, get out of my way' philosophy. The consequences are exacerbated by pathetic, usually politically-motivated, meddlers who search out excuses for any criminal act, portraying the perpetrators as persons of such under-privilege and deprivation as to make their conduct wholly the fault of the uncaring community.

Although I hold no strong theological beliefs, I am saddened by the declining influence of religion. I recall interviewing, for a newspaper article, the Right Reverend Mervyn Stockwood, Bishop of Southwark, shortly before his retirement in 1980. Having talked with him for a similar purpose once before, 18 years previously, I asked him what had been the greatest alteration he had seen in that period. Without hesitation he answered that, in the conditions existing at the time of our earlier meeting, it had been possible to leave every church in the diocese open for visits by those who wished to pray, to meditate quietly or simply to look around. 'Now,' he told me, 'if any church were left unlocked for a few hours, it would be robbed, desecrated or burnt.' People had, he said, become so immersed in avarice that the only course was to wait for them to 'become sickened and vomit'.

There is no need here to dilate on the acts of monstrous cruelty, to helpless people and to animals, that are described daily in our newspapers. Cowards acting for perverted 'causes' plant bombs that kill or maim anyone unfortunate enough to be nearby. Sexual offences and abuses of children occur everywhere. Losses by theft and burglary are run-of-the-mill. Vandalism and the defacement of public property with hideous graffiti are 'normal'. Football hooligans foul the name of Britain. Knife-brandishing gangs plunder shops and rob travellers on underground trains.

Some events of recent years deserve individual mention as apparent pointers to current trends. A policeman trying to help control a riot in a London suburb was hacked to death by a ravening mob. Refusing to blame the rioters, a Guyanan-born leader of neighbourhood opinion declared that the police had received 'a bloody good hiding'. The popularity of his views in the locality was shown when, a short time later, he was elected to parliament. In central London a woman police constable was shot to death by a foreign 'diplomat' who, protected by the privileges he had profaned, walked freely away from his dastardly crime. In the southern outskirts of the capital a police officer performing special surveillance duties suffered a frenzied attack and ten stab wounds to his chest and back, two of them fatal, inflicted by a multi-millionaire property owner. The assailant was found not guilty of murder after claiming 'I thought I was fighting for my life.'

Overflowing prisons testify to the ineffectiveness of present deterrents and the repeated outbursts staged by convicts tell of the difficulties endured by their custodians. To appreciate something of the problems confronting those engaged in the prison service, the reader need only imagine himself faced with the duty of controlling, day and night, the ruthless killers whose actions have been described in this book.

In considering punishments, it is worthy of note that sentences of 'imprisonment for life' rarely incur actual incarceration for more than 15 years. Lesser penalties are generally similarly shortened. Teenage delinquents deride the imposition of 'short, sharp shocks' and become heroes in the eyes of their uncaught associates.

A tide of responsible public opinion is rising against a system that bestows an undue imbalance of sympathy in favour of the transgressor. Sooner or later, legislators will be compelled to rethink their failing policies. For example, it has long been plain that the majority of the population (including the prime minister) is in favour of the resumption of capital punishment, especially for the more heinous taking of life. Yet, after debates that have almost become annual events, the representatives who were elected to give effect to the public will, properly expressed, refuse to comply. There can be little doubt that many people accept their contention that hanging is mediaeval, barbarous and may brutalize those called upon to carry it out. Nor can it be denied that legal processes are not infallible and that persons executed cannot be resuscitated should they later be found to have been innocent.

But there are, of course, counter-arguments. First, men of suitable (i.e., military) training have made it known that they would be willing to serve in effecting the ultimate penalty. Second, more humane methods are available – e.g., a painless lethal injection administered simultaneously with two or three harmless parenteral infusions, none of the panel of 'executioners,' screened from the prisoner, knowing which of them causes death. Third, the dramatic progress made in the techniques of forensic investigation minimizes the possibility of erroneous conviction. The fundamental questions appear to be (a) whether the death penalty is morally permissible and (b) whether it is more sensible to face the relatively remote risk of an error or to allow every murderer, however vicious, to escape the fate they inflict on their victims.

There is also the view, taken by a number of people qualified to hold such opinions, that imprisonment for a lengthy span of years inflicts greater suffering than does the swift termination of existence. I know that, for myself, I should much prefer the latter to the former. And having, as a journalist, covered murder trials when the death sentence was available, I find it difficult to believe that the dread of hearing a judge pronounce those fateful words did not (and would not) help to curb the urge to kill.

These, then, are the developing conditions under which the forensic scientists of tomorrow appear likely to have to operate. They will need profound tenacity of purpose and every form of assistance with which they can be provided.

Science itself is innovative and ingenious if not always imaginative. Some of its most historical achievements have been reached by happenstance rather than design, as exampled by Alexander Fleming's finding of penicillin. The sphere of forensic science is not outwith such possibilities; there may well come a time when infinitely less tangible contact traces than those at present required for the production of admissible evidence will become detectable, recordable and legally allowable. The galloping realms of electronics and microcircuitry may spawn further advances to add significantly to the armoury of detection.

Sensational strides have been made in the field of genetics, following discoveries pioneered by Leicester University's Professor Alec Jeffreys with his study of chromosomes, the thread-like carriers of instructions which govern the building and characteristics of human (and other) bodies.

Chromosomes consist of a chemical called deoxyribonucleic acid – DNA. The transferrable material of life, DNA is also found in viruses and bacteria. Its molecule is able to duplicate itself to give two similar daughter molecules. This ability is the basis for the formation of hereditary substances for the next generation. Two sets of chromosomes occur in the normal body cell, one set derived from each parent. The number of chromosomes in each set – called the haploid number – is usually constant for any one species. With few exceptions, notably the red blood cell, every living cell in the physical makeup contains the complete genetic code, which is incorporated as a separate package within the cell called the nucleus. A pattern of chemical sequences has been discovered in the DNA molecule which, with a specific exclusion, is as unique to each individual as their actual fingerprints – hence the term 'genetic fingerprinting'. The pattern is read by a laboratory process and is presented as a series of bands on an x-ray film, in somewhat similar, albeit more sophisticated, fashion to the bar coding used on a variety of consumer goods.

The exclusion from the rule of uniqueness occurs with human identical twins, whose physical construction is derived from a single, divided egg fertilized by one sperm – i.e., offspring with a shared DNA coding. Because almost all multiple human births in excess of twins arise from the separate fertilization of more than one egg, the possession of matching DNA profiles seldom extends to simultaneous conception/parturition beyond an identical pair.

One obvious application of DNA profiling is the establishment of parentage when progeniture is disputed. But its greatest value, by far, lies in enhancing the ability of forensic scientists to determine, from comparisons with body fluids found at or connected with the scenes of crime, whether suspects are guilty or innocent of association with the offences under investigation. Intensive research is in progress to bring the technique into use as a common tool for this purpose. It has been hailed as the greatest breakthrough in forensic science this century. But, as was the case with the discovery of penicillin, this utilization was not the original aim of the research which made it possible.

What other aids may emerge to advance the work of detecting the deeds of law-breakers can only be subjects of conjecture, which are not matters for discussion here. The law-respecting reader may, however, rest assured that the pre-war attitude to the laboratory is long gone from Scotland Yard; closed minds have no place now among those responsible for combating crime in the capital.

This is not to say that forensic scientists are now free of criticism. At a meeting of the House of Commons Select Committee on Home Affairs shortly before this book went to press, I heard a former chairman of the Criminal Bar Association, Michael Hill QC, claim that the close relationship between forensic scientists and the police causes many members of the legal profession to doubt assertions that such scientists are providing a wholly impartial service.

His argument was presented in a 15-page memorandum described as 'the work of one member of the [Criminal Bar] Association whose views, however, are not noticeably distinct from those of the broad majority of the independent practising criminal Bar in England and Wales'. The document alleged, *inter alia*, that:

> The Home Office and the police have imposed a functional objective on the Forensic Science Service which is ultimately inimical to proper scientific standards.
>
> Although, in theory, the FSS caters impartially for whoever approaches it, in practice the police alone make use of it.
>
> The only true independence the FSS has from the police is the independence of establishment.
>
> One of the unforeseen consequences of the Criminal Justice Act of 1967, allowing evidence to be received by statement rather than oral testimony, has been that forensic scientists have become unused to giving evidence in person and explaining and justifying their conclusions.
>
> The forensic scientist examines what he is asked to examine for the purpose for which the examination is requested. If he

discovers something for which the examination was not requested, he may ignore it.

The work of forensic laboratories is directed towards assisting the police. Judgment as to the effectiveness of the FSS relates entirely to the incidence of requests from and the quality of assistance given to the police.

Even in London, where respect for forensic scientists working in the Metropolitan Police laboratory is 'at least as high, if not higher' than elsewhere, such scientists 'tend to be regarded as (police) detectives with special skills'.

Doubts about impartiality are not assisted by the performance of some forensic scientists when under cross examination, 'as they seek to sustain the insupportable'.

The danger of incorrect conclusions from the evidence given by forensic scientists lies 'not so much in the reporting of findings as in the expression of opinion'.

As defence experts can be accused of 'partisanship or worse' when scientific evidence for the prosecution is disputed ('He would say that, wouldn't he?') the fact that the FSS is a government establishment whose function is to assist the police renders it liable to similar accusations of bias. 'What is sauce for the goose …'.

The FSS, the administration of justice and the public whom both exist to serve, suffer because the forensic scientist is not accepted from the outset as an independent expert who is not identified with any party to the proceedings.

Forensic scientists' reports are sometimes written in 'insiders' shorthand', employing terminology which makes it 'not always possible, let alone easy' to know what they mean. Scientists' responses to this criticism are sometimes based on the question 'Why don't you ask us?' This situation, and other considerations, argue strongly for the arrangement of pre-trial conferences between lawyers and scientific experts for the prosecution and defence.

The CBA document included the comment 'Readers of this memorandum should not be led, by its critical structure and tone, into the mistaken belief that, as a group or as individuals, the criminal Bar is universally condemnatory of the work of the [Forensic Science] Service and of its members. Quite the contrary is the case. It is to us a remarkable tribute to the integrity of the individual scientists involved that the occasional "mistakes" (to choose a neutral and all-embracing noun) are so significant.'

The administrative 'case for the defence' was put to the Select Committee in a memorandum prepared, with the assistance of staff at the Metropolitan Police laboratory, by the secretariat of the Specialist Operations Department at New Scotland Yard.

Arguing for the *status quo* by maintaining the position of the MPFSL in its relationship with the Metropolitan Police, the authors declared that the unique character of the laboratory produces distinct advantages. The following points were among those presented:

The volume of work and geography of London, involving advantageous response times and shortened lines of continuity, militate in favour of a single laboratory and single customer.

There would be no advantage in the MPFSL becoming a seventh laboratory in the Home Office Forensic Science Service, because it would threaten the excellent user/provider relationship which currently exists, without producing any compensatory benefit.

The MPFSL is, and has to be, in a position to innovate in response to developments in crime and criminal methods, a factor that is particularly important as so much organized and terrorist crime occurs in London.

Although the quest for cost-effectiveness and useful performance indicators has been fully embraced by both the MPFSL and the Metropolitan Police, any move towards 'agency status' or charging for services on a 'piece work' rather than *per capita* basis would be undesirable. The danger of 'influencing the operational decisions of investigating officers or the scientific decisions of laboratory staff in a manner which militates against the proper exploitation of available or potential evidence' must be avoided.

False economies could lead to scientists or police officers being questioned about tests which had not been carried out, the implication being that a fuller analysis might have cleared the defendant.

Economic benefits can often be gained by the early involvement of scientists in investigations. Scientific expertise and access to the specialized indices maintained by the MPFSL can effect considerable savings in police time.

In respect of work done by scientific support staff and court-going scientists at the laboratory, all findings are carefully scrutinized for accuracy and clarity by line supervising officers with great experience.

The MPFSL participates in the programme of trials prepared by the Home Office Central Research and Support Establishment at Aldermaston. These programmes are augmented by internal trials at the Lambeth laboratory.

Facilities are available for independent scientists briefed by defendants or potential defendants to examine forensic exhibits at the MPFSL or to carry out their own tests where physically possible.

There is little questioning or concern as to the scientific integrity of the MPFSL or the factual accuracy of its findings. Any disputes tend to lie in the interpretation of data.

Forensic science is a specialized discipline in which the MPFSL and the Home Office Forensic Science Service are, in England and Wales, virtually the sole employers; there is no readily available reservoir of expert talent upon which to draw for useful and perceptive outside views.

The close liaison between the MPFSL and its main customer has facilitated the development of a number of courses designed to heighten the awareness of police officers to the nature and potential of forensic evidence. MPFSL staff lecture at the police training centre at Hendon and police officers visit the laboratory. Short courses have been arranged for people engaged in the new Crown Prosecution Service. Special forensic training is, of course, given to scenes of crime officers, who deal with the majority of scenes in the absence of scientists.

Answering questions from the Select Committee chairman, John Wheeler MP, Deputy Assistant Commissioner James

Huins explained the plans for enlargement of the MPFSL but added 'It cannot be done overnight.' Pointing out that the present limited accommodation restricted the number of new appointments which could be made, he said that permission had been given for the recruitment of 12 additional members of laboratory staff during the past 12 months. 'A lot of thought' had been devoted to the problem of measuring the service provided by the laboratory, he declared.

Nearing the end of his first year as director of the laboratory, Dr Brian Sheard said that he was aware of the argument alleging a lack of impartiality on the part of scientists employed at the MPFSL but did not believe that it carried any real weight. 'Since I came into forensic science the thing that has surprised me is that there is a complete absence of any question about the quality of the work being done,' he went on. 'I think it is a tribute to all concerned that we get thanks from judges and counsel.'

On taking up his post at the Lambeth laboratory, he had learned that backlogs of between 20 and 26 weeks existed in respect of forensic work on certain cases, he said. He had decided to 'have a blitz' to get rid of the worst of the delays and some good results had been achieved. But such emergency measures could not continue indefinitely and it would soon be necessary to return to a more normal situation, whatever the backlog might be.

Answering a question regarding the condition of staff morale at the MPFSL compared with that in the Home Office Forensic Science Service, he said 'I think the Met lab started out with a high spirit and it has, therefore, taken longer for its scientists to become dispirited.' As to the causes of declining morale, he did not believe that rates of pay were the biggest consideration. The things that preserved the right spirit were good research and development and a good atmosphere in the workplace. Attending at scenes of crime and being in London 'at the sharp end' were also helpful elements. That being said, there was, unavoidably, the point that when people with good scientific qualifications realized the disparity between what is paid to them and what is paid to others, they were sometimes persuaded to leave. 'It is very much a question of having somewhere to move on to.' As had been the case with a number of experienced scientific staff in the fire investigation unit, 'when something comes along, they take it.'

'The Old Bailey regularly sees some of the most skilful barristers in Britain putting Metropolitan Police forensic scientists under pressure, often in a manner designed to ridicule their interpretations and make them appear incompetent, and even dishonest, in open court,' he concluded. 'The compensations are poor. Scientists know that police officers, pathologists and lawyers earn far more for equivalent training and experience.'

The Select Committee's report, published in March 1989, declared that the government's Forensic Science Service, 'once the envy of the world', was underfunded, overworked and suffering from low morale. The conservative majority on the committee recommended that the service should be funded so that police forces paid for it according to its use and that it should be expanded and ultimately given executive agency status, with the ability to sell its services to other public bodies and to defendants.

The report disclosed that, between 1982 and 1988, expenditure on the service had increased by just nine per cent in real terms despite the soaring crime rate and greater demand for its services. Its annual budget of just over £13 million was said to represent a mere 0.3 per cent of police expenditure. One result had been that the service had had to turn away the less serious cases referred to it, leaving the police 'increasingly dissatisfied'.

In a unanimous recommendation, the members of the committee called for legislation to permit the 'genetic fingerprinting' of convicted criminals. Computerized DNA profiles would improve detection rates, it was said.

In April 1989 an advertisement in the *Pharmaceutical Journal* revealed that the Horserace Betting Levy Board (a statutory body providing funds and services to horseracing) was offering a salary of 'circa £37,500' for a successor to the soon-to-retire director of its horseracing forensic laboratory in Newmarket. Operating in part on a commercial, fee-earning basis, the testing carried out by this establishment was described as 'increasingly automated'. The number of staff reporting to the director was given as 55.

Thus, the leadership of a team of 55 dealing with drug screening and the detection of prohibited substances in racehorses was valued at nearly £6,500 a year more than the maximum reward envisaged for the direction of a laboratory employing 250 people and dedicated to the unmasking of crime in the nation's capital. This comparison is drawn from the MPFSL director's salary scale of £25,756–£29,344 as listed in *Whitaker's Almanack* for 1989, plus the current London weighting of £1,750 a year. It should, moreover, be borne in mind that the top level of such scales is normally reached only after the completion of several years of satisfactory service.

The question as to whether the London laboratory should remain linked with the Metropolitan Police, become an autonomous organization in its own right or be included within the Home Office Forensic Science Service leaves unchanged the fact that the chief rein on future progress in establishing the guilt of malefactors (and the blamelessness of the innocent) by means of forensic science is likely to be the measure of pecuniary support that guardians of public purses see fit to have apportioned to that aid to justice. In coming days and circumstances such financial judgment will be crucial to the task of demonstrating, by the scientific detection of malfeasance, that crime does not pay.

Bibliography

Milestones in Forensic Science, FREDERICK THOMAS, American Society for Testing and Materials 1974

The Marks of Cain, JURGEN THORWALD, Thames and Hudson 1965

Science against Crime, Editor: YVONNE DEUTCH, Marshall Cavendish 1982

Science & the Detection of Crime, C R M CUTHBERT, Hutchinson & Co Ltd 1958

Mac, I've Got a Murder, JOHN McCAFFERTY, Arthur Barker Ltd 1975

Crime and Science, JURGEN THORWALD, Harcourt, Brace & World Inc 1966

Expert Witness, Dr H J WALLS, John Long 1972

The Crime Busters, ANGUS HALL, Verdict Press 1976

Proof of Poison, JURGEN THORWALD, Pan Books 1969

Legal Medicine, SIR SYDNEY SMITH (R B H GRADWOHL), The C V Mosby Company 1954

Forensic Science, Dr H J WALLS, Sweet & Maxwell Ltd 1968

Obsessive Poisoner, WINIFRED YOUNG, Robert Hale & Company 1973

The St Albans Poisoner, ANTHONY HOLDEN, Hodder & Stoughton 1974

The Detection of Secret Homicide, Dr J D J HAVARD, Macmillan & Co Ltd 1960

The Criminal Courts, Criminal Law and Evidence – An Introduction for Forensic Scientists, ANN PRISTON, Metropolitan Police Forensic Science Laboratory 1981

Index

351